PRODUCTIVITY BY OBJECTIVES

PRODUCTIVITY BY OBJECTIVES

James L. Riggs

Director, Oregon Productivity Center
Head, Industrial Engineering Department
Oregon State University

Glenn H. Felix

Deputy Director
Oregon Productivity Center

PRENTICE-HALL, INC.
Englewood Cliffs, New Jersey 07632

Library of Congress Cataloging in Publication Data

RIGGS, JAMES L.
Productivity by objectives.

    Includes bibliographical references and index.
    1. Industrial productivity. 2. Management by
objectives. I. Felix, Glenn H. II. Title.
HD56.R54 1983   658.3'14   82-23186
ISBN 0-13-725374-5

Editorial/production supervision and interior design: **Joan Foley**
Cover designer: **Jeannette Jacobs**
Manufacturing buyer: **Ed O'Dougherty**

Printed in the United States of America

10 9 8 7 6 5 4 3 2 1

ISBN 0-13-725374-5

Prentice-Hall International, Inc., *London*
Prentice-Hall of Australia Pty. Limited, *Sydney*
Editora Prentice-Hall do Brasil, Ltda., *Rio de Janeiro*
Prentice-Hall Canada Inc., *Toronto*
Prentice-Hall of India Private Limited, *New Delhi*
Prentice-Hall of Japan, Inc., *Tokyo*
Prentice-Hall of Southeast Asia Pte. Ltd., *Singapore*
Whitehall Books Limited, *Wellington, New Zealand*

CONTENTS

PREFACE

Productivity is a mission of every responsible organization. The intent of this book is to suggest ways to accomplish that mission by identifying and achieving objectives. If productivity ideas are weapons to overcome productivity problems, this book is your arsenal.

Productivity is like physical fitness: Nearly everybody wants to be fit, but not everyone knows what to do or is willing to make the necessary commitment. The early chapters present an overview of the productivity puzzle, showing how troubles developed, why they need attention, and what can be done on a national scale to alleviate them. Awareness is the first step.

Productivity is next proposed as a measure of an organizations's fitness. After a discussion of conventional techniques for measuring productivity, a simple but effective method is introduced—the Objectives Matrix—which serves both manufacturing and service operations. Matrix scores are progress benchmarks that motivate better performance by recognizing the contribution of individual units in the organization. Measurement leads to improvement.

Productivity then gets more personal with chapters on management practices, technological challenges, and the ever-present quest for quality. A productivity perspective provides fresh insights into traditional managerial lore, ranging from strategic planning to executive pay, from innovative processes to sharing programs. Attention is further directed to robot-driven processes, quality-conscious teams, and computer-aided everything. Opportunities for improvement are boundless!

Productivity as a total improvement process that features employee involvement is presented in the concluding chapters. Productivity by Objectives (PBO), as the process is called, stresses training, measurement, and communications. From a business standpoint, it encourages employees to seek workplace innovations that reduce costs and enhance quality. From an individual viewpoint, PBO supports a cooperative environment where productive work is psychologically and physically rewarding. The proverbial "win/win" situation is created.

Enthusiasm to write this book was generated by our activities with the Oregon Productivity Center. We have worked with several organizations and observed a growing commitment by managers and workers alike to push productivity. The suggested paths to improvement are based on this collective wisdom and practical experience. In particular, we are indebted to Dave Klick (Northwest Food Processors Association), Pete Gartshore and Jim Ward (Mail Well Envelope Company), and Wally Masters (Electro Scientific Industries).

The final step toward productivity is continuing commitment at all levels of an organization. We have observed what ingenuity, participation, and action can do. Attaining productivity objectives can indeed make tomorrow better than today.

Dr. Jim Riggs

Glenn H. Felix

PRODUCTIVITY BY OBJECTIVES

THE PRODUCTIVITY PUZZLE

1

Productivity *is* puzzling. It is a huge subject, encompassing the entire economy and affecting everyone, yet each person can draw a meaning to fit his or her own situation.

To generalists—legislators, educators, corporate moguls—productivity is a web of interacting influences radiating from their favored nexus. Its strands are taxes, government policies, capital, access to resources, adequacy of labor and management, competitors, and the flow of goods and services.

Special-interest groups have their own perspectives. Union and industry leaders often position themselves on opposite sides of a productivity issue. Conservationists and consumerists will direct attention to other facets of the same issue. Parties and issues can be further fractured by divergent views from regional or political factions. Possible permutations are endless.

Many of these entanglements are excluded when productivity is viewed from the reference point of a single organization, be it a factory, government agency, or service unit. Cause-and-effect relationships are more visible, and more urgent. Managers coordinate input with output to meet schedules. They buy technology within budgetary limits. They search for efficiencies. They perceive productivity improvement as a duty of their office, but less imperative than the drive for profitability. The perception is devastatingly short-sighted.

Individual workers, concerned with their immediate occupations, have a still narrower view. To them, productivity means sharp tools, materials being available, knowing what to expect and what is expected of them, and a supportive environment. These anticipations apply to workers at all levels, but fulfillment depends on individual situations. A desk jockey and a janitor may share equal motivation yet suggest entirely different paths toward productivity improvement.

Varying views should be expected and cultivated. They make the pursuit of productivity always challenging—and frequently frustrating. Chances of winning expand by conceding, without being intimidated by the resulting complexity, that there is never a one-shot solution. There is no all-purpose productivity elixir, no guru to point out the proven way. There is, however, a wealth of productive practices that can be screened to reveal those that conform to each perspective. Awareness is the first step toward productivity.

EXHIBIT 1   *PRODUCTIVE SLOGANS*

As individuals, we know when we are being productive. We also have our personal interpretation of that state. Beyond the trite statement of "working smarter, not harder," the following slogans have been suggested by participants in productivity awareness programs (fitting sources are gratuitously suggested):

Engineer—doing more with less
Scholar—working wisely
Manager—getting it all together
Philosopher—knowing you've done your best
Psychologist—striving, yet at ease
Pragmatist—performing effectively
Optimist—making tomorrow better than today

AWARENESS BEGINS
WITH DEFINING

The dictionary says that *productivity* is "the quality or state of being productive." Furthermore, *productive*, in an economics sense, means "the creation of goods and services." This accounts for the output but only implies the existence of inputs. The epithets in Exhibit 1 focus more on the act of producing. Exhibit 2 continues this emphasis.

In Exhibit 2 the three circles together represent an organization, small or large. The organization produces a *product* or a *service*. In so doing, it consumes *resources* under the direction of *people*. Resources include machines, capital, land, raw materials, and energy. People consist

EXHIBIT 2   *FACTORS THAT AFFECT PRODUCTIVITY*

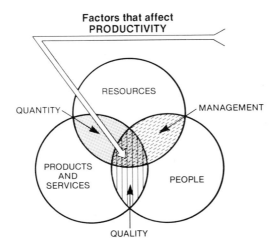

of supervisors, operators, professionals, clerks, and so forth. *Management* guides human talent to utilize physical resources to produce the timely and correct *quantity* of products at a designated level of *quality*. These factors collectively represent *productivity*.

It looks so simple.

What the gross factors fail to reveal is the complex interaction that takes place where people interface with resources and products. Nonetheless, the overlapping areas of the circles symbolize two tenets of productivity:

- Quantity is irrevocably linked to quality.
- Management actuates and controls the conversion of inputs to outputs.

These relationships are premises for the time-honored equation for conversion efficiency:

$$\text{Productivity} = \frac{\text{OUTPUT}}{\text{INPUT}}$$

This equation too is an oversimplification. It leads to a single number like a reading from a thermometer. A temperature reading lacks meaning until it is associated with reference points such as freezing and boiling points. Similarly, output/input is a meaningless figure until it is related to performance expectations. Then it becomes a powerful statement.

> *PRODUCTIVITY IS THE MEASURE OF HOW SPECIFIED RESOURCES ARE MANAGED TO ACCOMPLISH TIMELY OBJECTIVES STATED IN TERMS OF QUANTITY AND QUALITY.*

AWARENESS GROWS
WITH UNDERSTANDING

Sometimes it is easier to understand something by realizing what it is not. Productivity is usually categorized with patriotism and motherhood as being obviously worthy. It is, but there are skeptics. Both boosters and detractors tend to magnify its virtues and its faults. Some of the more flagrant claims are discussed below from the standpoint that

PRODUCTIVITY GAINS DO NOT NECESSARILY . . .

. . . **INCREASE PROFITS.** A product or service can be produced with less input and still be a money loser if no one wants to purchase it. Equivalently, little is accomplished by boosting the productivity of one segment of a process when the gain cannot be passed along because the next segment is not prepared for it—the old bottleneck constraint. Unplanned productivity growth can be unproductive.

...**RESULT FROM INCREASING OUTPUT.** When a higher level of output is achieved by disproportionately increasing the input, productivity actually declines. Producing more products with the same input is a gain only when the quality level is maintained. Sacrificing quality is an easy way to boost the quantity of output, but it seldom increases the *value* of the output. Productivity is a measure of value.

...**DECREASE THE NUMBER OF JOBS.** The relationship between productivity and employment is sticky. On one side it is evident that a job is forfeited whenever a labor-saving change eliminates a position. On the other side is evidence that more productive industries have higher employment growth than less productive industries. It is also evident that reducing a company's labor force by 10 percent may save the jobs of the other 90 percent. However, such rationalization is absurd to those dropped from the payroll. It is both humane and economically defensible for managers to avoid productivity-induced layoffs through retraining, relocation, or retention until natural attrition provides an opening. A pledge of job security is the conscience of the productivity movement.

...**RESULT FROM A FASTER WORK PACE.** Raising the tempo of work will probably reduce the value of output from a combination of lower quality and increased costs that are caused by accidents, turnover, and general turmoil. In cases where the work pace has gradually deteriorated from lack of attention, or performance expectations have never been set, establishing a realistic pace is only logical as long as it is justified to the workers. Improving the work methods usually does far more for job performance than a pepped-up pace.

...**REQUIRE WORK RULE CHANGES.** There are assumed work rules and real work rules. Production efficiencies can be instituted within the latter and atop the former. Knowing which to respect and which to demote is a stiff test of managerial capability.

Make-work positions are the antitheses of productivity. They deserve abolishment because they serve a privileged clique at the expense of everyone else. But flagrant featherbedding is relatively rare. Restrictive work rules designed for craft protection are less rare and less inhibiting, yet they too can drag down productivity. Negotiations should yield compromises, especially for archaic rules out of tune with today's needs and expectations.

More serious are the informal work limitations that have evolved from habit. These are not actual rules, just unwritten codes that limit the scope of performance: traditionally having work done by a certain person or department, doing a job "the way it's always been done," aiming for quality that is "good enough to pass," and suppressing output to a contrived quota. Quick productivity gains accrue from detecting and correcting time-wasting customs that would otherwise continue as testimony to lazy management.

... **FOLLOW A PRODUCTIVITY-IMPROVEMENT PROGRAM.** There are assumed productivity-improvement programs and real productivity-improvement programs. The difference is easily distinguished by measuring results. An assumed improvement is a blip on the record, while a real one yields a long-term upward trend.

There is nothing wrong with a flag-waving, chest-thumping campaign if there is something to it besides emotional appeal. Too often, there is a rah-rah kickoff and no game plan. The reverse is more likely to succeed. A modest beginning followed by carefully orchestrated activities builds confidence for lasting effect. Each phase of the program should be narrowly directed toward defined and measurable objectives. If an improvement can't be proved, it wasn't.

... **REQUIRE MAJOR INVESTMENT.** Robots are expensive. So is a new plant. Even a word processor can be a major investment for a struggling firm or a tax-chastened government office. Big-ticket items are splendid productivity boosters when expenditures can be justified by market conditions and the new technology can be introduced without serious work flow disruptions.

Comparable advances can sometimes be accomplished through in-house innovations. Gradual improvement is not as dramatic as the acquisition of a packaged breakthrough, but it is more affordable and builds we-did-it pride. Ongoing workplace innovation is characteristic of a productive work force. A collection of minor changes in work methods can accumulate savings equivalent to those promised by a shiny new machine.

... **ACCRUE FROM PRACTICES THAT WORKED ELSEWHERE.** There is no shortage of advice about how to become more productive. Some of it is imported. Japan has replaced Germany and Sweden as the prototype. Some of it is hype. Old routines are repackaged and stamped with a productivity slogan. Yet most of it is worth considering. Exposure to new ideas, coupled with caution to screen out the inappropriate ones, is both instructive and constructive.

The current theme for productivity improvement is not as comforting as the approaches proposed a few years ago. Those human resource promotions were nonthreatening, leaving a warm, fuzzy feeling with everyone involved. Now the emphasis is on hardware and employee-involvement plans that promise measurable returns. This means that a decision about adopting a new practice is tougher to make because a stronger commitment is required when a positive productivity flux is the final yardstick.

... **NEED TOTAL-FIRM COMMITMENT.** Nearly every organization gives lip service to productivity. The more progressive or more desperate ones back their words with resources dedicated to the productivity movement. Where money is scarce, the backing can take the form of sharing authority, encouraging innovative actions. Strong leadership from the top down creates a fertile seedbed from which improvements can flower with minimal financial nourishment.

While there is no true substitute for vigorous support from above, creative leadership can build pinnacles of productivity growth anywhere. We have seen worker-involvement teams evolve and thrive in single departments, their contribution to productivity seemingly unnoticed by other departments in the plant. A gutsy leader can stir a crew toward spectacular performance in contrast to all around them. Though it is harder to do without topside backing, this should only increase the satisfaction of accomplishment. After all, at whatever level one is, there is always someone above to convince.

... **GUARANTEE A LOWER INFLATION RATE.** Credit for a productivity gain is owed to many sources. The people who fostered the gain and the capital that nourished it deserve a share. Customers who purchased the products or services have a claim. Prudent management suggests that those directly responsible for the gain be rewarded first to promote continuing improvement. Then the consumers should receive a share via price reductions. This is not an altruistic gesture. According to the law of supply and demand, lower prices increase demand in a competitive market. A company can then supply more goods to the market if it offers a lower price. The additional goods are supplied by the same work force through its higher productivity. Thus employment is stable or rising, and the consumers enjoy stable or declining prices.

This price-sales-productivity spiral is confirmed by the data in Exhibit 3. Prices for products from the more productive industries held steady or changed slightly over the twenty-year period. Sharply inflated prices are associated with less productivity growth. The same pattern emerges in every country where data have been plotted.

Many factors besides productivity affect the general inflation rate, unfortunately. Fiscal policy is a major influence. Political decisions at home and abroad, resource shortages, cartels, and consumers' spending philosophy also contribute to price escalations. However, the rate of productivity growth is the underlying governor. Whenever wage increases exceed gains in production efficiencies, the goods produced from labor and capital have become more expensive. Competitiveness is lost in the world marketplace. A dollar buys less at home.

The long-term effect of declining productivity is even more disturbing than immediate inflation. A drop in productivity means that more resources are consumed to produce the same output. Less output is avail-

EXHIBIT 3   *PRICE ESCALATION VS. PRODUCTIVITY GROWTH*

Output per employee hour and prices,
selected industries, 1960-79

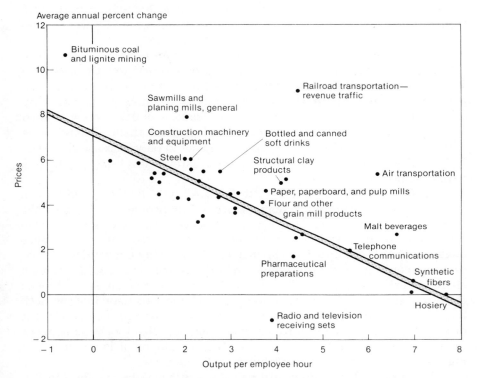

Average annual percent change

Bituminous coal and lignite mining

Railroad transportation— revenue traffic

Sawmills and planing mills, general

Construction machinery and equipment   *Bottled and canned soft drinks*

Steel

Structural clay products   *Air transportation*

Paper, paperboard, and pulp mills

Flour and other grain mill products

Malt beverages

Telephone communications

Pharmaceutical preparations

Synthetic fibers

Hosiery

Radio and television receiving sets

Prices

Output per employee hour

U.S. Department of Labor, Bureau of Labor Statistics, *Annual Report to the President and Congress* (National Center for Productivity and Quality of Working Life, 1976), p. 21.

able per person. The scramble to maintain the share we have grown accustomed to becomes hectic; the battle required to improve our status becomes fierce. Expectations dim, and we realize that today's children may be much less prosperous than their parents. It is this sobering assessment of the future that fuels current concern about productivity.

EXHIBIT 4   *OPINIONS ABOUT PLUNGING PRODUCTIVITY*

Americans are the most surveyed people in the world. Pollsters probe sex lives, political leanings, kinky habits, and even opinions about productivity. Two extensive surveys suggest that people are well aware of the productivity problem and have strong feelings about how to cope with it.

A 1981 Harris survey found a majority of respondents agreeing that a decline in productivity leads to a lower standard of living, fewer jobs, and less influence in world affairs. They direct much of the blame toward government, especially the federal regulatory agencies. Only 29 percent felt that more intervention by government could turn things around.

Public expectancy for improvement rests with management and workers. Strategies deemed important for managers were to devote less attention to short-term profit and more to R&D, new production facilities, and international sales. It was generally agreed that workers would be more productive if they received a direct share of gains earned, had more say in decisions, and were treated with more respect.

A Gallup poll of U.S. workers reveals similar beliefs.[1] An overwhelming majority agreed that they would work harder and do a better job if they were allowed to take part in the decision process that affected their work. They believe that hard work makes a big difference in the success of their organization and that they deserve monetary rewards and personal recognition for extra effort.

The attitudes and abilities of both management and workers were selected as changes that would yield the largest improvement in performance and productivity. Eight out of ten workers believe that improving productivity will reduce inflation. A majority are convinced that quality is a major concern of employees, management, and consumers.

Yes, Virginia, there is a productivity problem. There are ways to solve it, too.

UNDERSTANDING LEADS
TO OBJECTIVES

Rubik's cube could be a model for productivity. Assume that the six sides of the cube represent the most significant factors affecting the productivity of an organization:

Side 1: Workers—attitudes and abilities
Side 2: Management—planning and competence
Side 3: Facilities—plant and equipment
Side 4: Technology—processes and products
Side 5: Government—regulations and support
Side 6: Environment—materials and energy

When each face of Rubik's cube shows a solid color it is in harmony, as is an organization when it is everywhere productive. There is an orderliness to a congruous cube, as there is in an organization when the factors of production mesh smoothly.

Orderliness is fragile. The harmony of the cube disintegrates with a few quick twists. Equivalently, the productivity of an organization—section, firm, or nation—is rapidly disrupted by imbalances among its constituent factors—labor unrest, equipment breakdowns, waste, revised regulations, hasty reorganization. It is far more difficult to array than disarray Rubik's cube. Reassembling the factors of productivity is correspondingly difficult.

The disruption of productivity growth in the United States did not happen overnight. It has been unmistakable since 1977. Nor will it be corrected overnight.

Quality of Work Life (QWL) is a multipronged approach to correct productivity ills. It dates back to the early 1970s, although it is based on participative management theories proposed much earlier. QWL is a good example of the interplay of factors affecting productivity and the patience needed to put them in harmony.

As the name suggests, the intent of a Quality of Work Life program is to improve the total job experience. A natural outgrowth of a successful QWL program is productivity improvement, but program development is not contingent on measured productivity gains. It is a good-faith endeavor. And it has enhanced productivity in the plants of several major corporations, most notably General Motors, where QWL is an exemplary joint effort between the GM management and the United Auto Workers.

When management and union representatives get together, as they did at the Chevrolet Gear and Axle plant, to discuss what should transpire to maintain a healthy company and work force, a consensus usually emerges.[2] Both sides made a list of objectives at the GM meeting. The lists matched almost point for point when compared. It was not too surprising that both parties wanted satisfying jobs, quality products, stable employment, and a profitable company. The predictable difficulty was how to move toward the objectives.

Presuming that workers' opinions expressed in surveys represent the attributes of high work-life quality—shared gains, respect, and participation in work decisions—many elements need to be brought together to attain genuine satisfaction. Capital is needed to secure comfortable, efficient, and safe working conditions. Profitability that affords monetary rewards relies on capable leadership. A dramatic turnabout in supervisory practices may be required before workers are regularly included in the decision network.

Every element in the process is demanding. Yet the elements cannot be addressed one at a time because their effects mingle. Consequently, like the solution to Rubik's cube, an overall plan is necessary. Each twist has direction. Actions are mutually supportive. Maneuvers are guided by goals. The objective is productivity.

EXHIBIT 5   *PRODUCTIVE WORK-LIFE QUALITY CURVE*

QWL programs take many forms, ranging from full employee participation in planning, designing, and scheduling their jobs to the more structured quality-circle movement borrowed from Japan. Their common goal is to bridge the gap of distrust between those who work and those who manage work. Greater productivity is expected to flower in a climate of labor-management trust and a healthy work environment.

The theoretical framework for QWL has formed over the past four decades in accordance with the writings of Mayo, Maslow, McGregor, and other behavioral theorists. In essence, they postulate that workers need more than just wages to motivate performance. Mayo suggests stable work groups. Maslow advocates means to meet workers' personal-fulfillment needs. McGregor advises management to trust and cooperate with employees.

Now the pressing question is whether job satisfaction obtained through QWL and related practices translates into greater productivity.

A suggested relationship between work-life quality and productivity is displayed in the accompanying diagram. Productivity doubtlessly benefits from satisfying the basic security needs of workers, as indicated in the survival sector. Steep incremental gains continue from providing increasingly better working conditions and benefits; employees deserve to be comfortable. Then the marginal rate of productivity gain levels off as it becomes in-

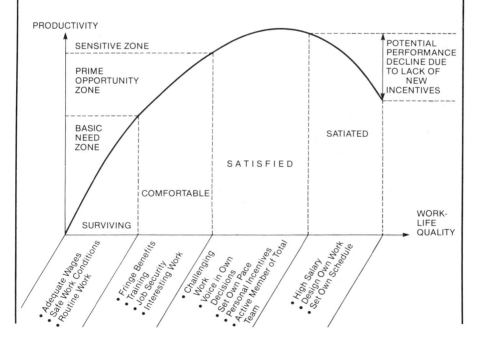

creasingly difficult to amplify worker satisfaction. Finally, a drop in productivity could occur if dedication to work is lost in the luxury of a utopian
work life, the satiation sector.

The proposed relationship might best be called a "supply-side productivity curve." It is intuitively logical up to the satiation sector. Since workers in most QWL programs are already supplied with the job characteristics of the comfort sector, the next source of productivity gain lies in the
sensitivity zone where there is very little recorded experience to guide development. Which provisions should be supplied first? To whom? In what
form? Will the increased supply indeed raise productivity? The jury is still
out. Some companies report greatly improved worker relations and some
improvement in productivity. Others have been disappointed. A few have
retreated to more conventional tactics. The successful ones have attempted to fulfill almost all of the job characteristics of the sensitivity
zone, *gradually*. Such changes take much time and total commitment. But
the effort is worthwhile if it yields that extra edge in productivity.

The productivity dip in the satiation zone is hypothetical, but reasonable. Instances have been reported in high-tech spark shops and cutthroat
professional ranks which suggest that intense motivation breeds remarkable accomplishments when employees act as their own boss. There are accompanying dangers of early burnout and misdirected energy that do
more damage than good. The sad fact is that drooping productivity may be
concealed by commotion masquerading as progress.

The twin missives of the productive work-life quality curve are caution
and opportunity.

CONVERTING OBJECTIVES
TO ACHIEVEMENT

The flow of subjects in the preceding sections—awareness to understanding to objectives—is replicated in the rest of this book. It is also the conventional sequence for any attempted improvement—discover an opportunity, find the facts, and lay out plans. Then do it! "Doing it," too, is
this book's mission.

Two initial chapters set the stage for a productivity push. The next
six describe the strategic options available: collective action, performance measurement, shrewder management, technologically advanced facilities, more productive work processes, and extensive employee involvement. The remaining chapters advocate a specific action plan
we call *Productivity By Objectives (PBO)*.

As evident from the myriad factors affecting the productivity puzzle, there is a bewildering variety of pros and cons to consider. Certain
factors are more relevant to manufacturing than service industries. Some
are more pertinent to government agencies. Others impact everywhere.

Such complexity underlines the necessity for clear objectives, goals specifically addressed to counter defined obstacles.

Two organizations impacted by identical external difficulties will nevertheless concentrate on different objectives. The reason is, of course, that their internal strengths and weaknesses differ. This is the same reason why a productivity plan that works for one organization often fails in others. Consequently, productivity planning must be customized.

Possible internal obstacles worth watching are described in the scenarios below. What follows in this book should be placed in perspective against these proprietary attitudes. Know first thyself.

✓ Pressure for a Quick Fix

A directive from above is distributed to all departments: Raise your productivity now! Its threat sends managers scrambling, all seeking schemes to produce immediate results. With time being of the essence, budget balances are checked to see what price can be paid. Consultants offer a host of programs. There is new technology on the shelf. The human resource department may have a promotion ready. A choice is made, wheels spin, and smoke is blown in many directions.

We-want-it-yesterday edicts are not all bad, especially when accompanied by a blank check. Throwing fast money at a problem at least gives it recognition and may even help solve it. But the chances of lasting gains are slim. An oblique advance may be the answer, especially when the checkbook is limited. Buy a productivity awareness promotion from inside or outside. That gets people thinking about the subject. It will also uncover a few quick gains. Then use the aroused interest to determine where new technology, processes, and involvement programs really fit.

✓ If It Ain't Broke, Don't Fix It

Like a cuckold, a company may not realize that it has been left behind. Competitiveness can erode even while profits climb. When the day of reckoning arrives, more than a tuneup will be needed.

A modest productivity program is an antidote to complacency. It is likely to first call attention to overstaffing, an ulcer of prosperity. When things are going well, it is easy to gloss over situations in which the amount of work to be accomplished is less than the amount of labor assigned to it:

- Labor levels are established to meet service demands for peak periods, leaving idleness between peaks.
- Extra people employed to introduce new technology stay on after installation is complete.
- Schedule slippage or a rising defect rate is countered by adding expeditors and inspectors. They become permanent personnel.

- Low productivity in one operation of a fixed sequence reduces the flow to undermine the productivity of other operations in the chain.
- Method changes that decrease the amount of production labor needed are not reflected by a corresponding adjustment in staffing.

Just as preventive maintenance is the accepted way to keep a good machine going, productivity maintenance can keep a good system productive.

⌙ Our Cake Needs No Frosting

Most executives have been impressed sometime in their career by the realization that too much of a good thing causes a decline in its value. It shows up in productivity effort as reluctance to go beyond a convenient level of participation. It is supported by confidence in the existing system and judgment that diminishing returns will be delivered from additional expenditures. If the confidence is deserved, the executives should be content with their piece of cake.

In the flush of productivity concern a few years ago, many companies created an internal productivity-oriented empire. Often it was too much of a good thing. Sometimes the backlash was excessive; a piece of the cake was lost under the frosting.

Any temptation to addiction is avoided by appreciating that productivity has always been and will continue to be a natural concern of every well-run organization. A thriving operation already has productivity mechanisms in place. These can be put in higher gear without upsetting existing relationships. Good can be made better without forfeiting value.

⌙ Since We Didn't Invent It, . . .

Pride of authorship is commendable when it is not blinding. No one has ever acquired a monopoly on improvement, yet the reluctance of some organizations to adopt new ways leaves that impression. It is usually more apparent at the department or section level than at higher levels. Not only can misguided pride block the transfer of technology from outside, and even between departments, but it intimidates people who are not in the traditional idea-generating cliques. Witness the reluctance of domestic companies to adopt local conventions in their overseas operations, the slow reaction to innovations by competitors, and a general insensibility to productivity suggestions when they fall outside the party line.

⌙ Blame Anyone but Me

Blame bouncing is a popular pastime with productivity novices. Complaints by the players are hard to distinguish from alibis. Censures quite likely deter solutions. When businesses slander trade unions with accusations of poor productivity, and vice versa, neither gains. Nor is finger pointing at the government rewarding.

Bumper stickers that proclaim "UNEMPLOYMENT . . . made in Japan" do nothing to correct the situation. When the CEO of American Motors starts a speech with "Welcome to Detroit, the Pearl Harbor of the American auto industry,"[3] you get the idea that a counterattack is forthcoming. Pogo said it all: "We have seen the enemy and they is us."

✓ Mistrust of Measurement

Numbers are a powerful language. They add authenticity to reports of monitored events. Their use has assuredly been abused at times, or we would never have had books like *How to Lie with Statistics*.[4] On the other hand, what would be on the bottom line of a profit-and-loss statement if *all* numbers were suspect? *A, B, C, D,* or *F*?

Mistrust of numbers in productivity measurement probably stems from unfamiliarity. There is cause for caution here because the numbers are subject to misinterpretation. More fundamental to the issue is recognition that most people simply do not like to have their performance measured, and performance improvement is the gist of productivity. The usual excuse is that no measurement units are applicable. How can the value of a nurse's "tender, loving care" be measured? What are the units for business sense, dedication, and loyalty? There are none. But the end effects from applying business sense, being dedicated, and showing loyalty are measurable from the results of the operation in which they are employed.

The whole concept of setting objectives is thwarted by divorcing it from measurement. There would be no way to tell if or when the objectives were achieved.

Productivity without measurement is akin to a theatrical production without an audience.

FROM BLOOM TO GLOOM: Causes and Effects

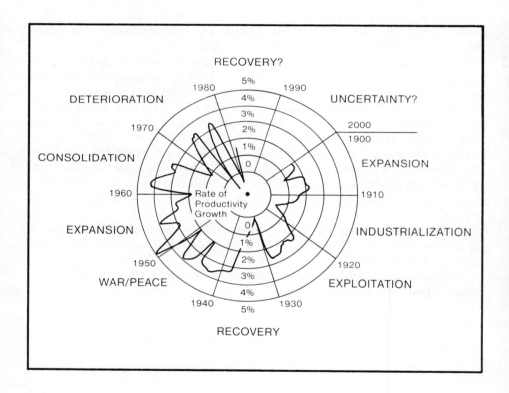

2

The annual percentage gain (or loss) in U.S. labor productivity is shown by the wandering line in the facing productivity clock. It is a pattern to be proud of, one that has produced a standard of living renowned throughout the world. But recent data have put continued growth of that standard in jeopardy. A quick tour through the decades reveals how far we have come, and why. Following the tour are discussions of causes and effects, heavy with data and ponderous with implications. This chapter gives an eye-opening overview of factors that led to the present situation.

Working conditions during the first two decades of this century were deplorable by today's yardstick. Hours were long, workplaces were insulting and unsafe, and workers' rights were but a dream of reformers. Nonetheless, annual productivity growth averaged almost 2 percent, due largely to the substitution of machine-power for muscle-power.

The 1920–47 period continued the productivity surge, reaching about a 2.2 percent increase per year. A nationwide distribution system supported industrial vitality spawned during World War I. Consumption soared during the freewheeling twenties. Consumption soured during the depressed thirties. Fires from Europe rekindled industrial activity in the United States in preparation for World War II. Attempts to do everything at once, and to do it faster, created a fertile hotbed for productivity practices. Statistical quality control came of age. Women workers won acclaim. New training techniques and mechanized processes were perfected. Above all, new technologies were born or bred. Their effects would be felt for years: jet aircraft, rockets, atomic power, new drugs and plastics, and computers.

Following World War II, the stage was set for twenty years of bountiful productivity. It grew at the splendid annual rate of 3.2 percent from 1948 through 1968 in response to the enormous amount of technology and management skill acquired during the forties. The nation's pent-up demand for peacetime consumer goods fueled a barrage of new products. Industries in most of the developed world were in shambles, creating a hungry market for exports in both war-devastated and developing nations. Predictions for everlasting production and productivity growth were irresistible.

Caught up in the euphoria of prosperity, anything seemed possible. It was the go-go age. The heavens could be explored and the earth's environment purified at the same time. Wars could be waged simultaneously on poverty and in Asia. Workplaces could be made safer and cleaner by edict. Accomplishments were incredible, but flaws were accumulating insidiously.

During the five years from 1969 through 1973, productivity growth dropped a full percentage point to 2.2 percent. Capital needed to upgrade plants and equipment was siphoned off for other purposes. Spending for research and development declined. Inflation accelerated. The first of almost continuous trade deficits occurred in 1971. Prospects for perpetual abundance were being questioned, but few corrective actions were initiated.

Alarms started ringing during the remaining years of the decade. The bottom fell out of productivity in the deep recession of 1974, to an ominous level of −3.1 percent. This was a precursor of what was yet to come. Productivity decayed to minus marks again in 1978, 1979, and 1980, the only time this has happened since data collection began in 1909, and caused a dismal average growth rate from 1974 through 1980 of 0.6 percent.

EXHIBIT 6   *PRODUCTIVITY GROWTH: 1948-80*

SECTOR OF U.S. ECONOMY	ANNUAL PERCENTAGE CHANGE IN PERIOD		
	1948–58	1959–69	1970–80
Private business	3.3	2.9	1.4
Farm	6.8	4.5	3.0
Nonfarm business	2.5	2.6	1.2
Manufacturing	2.7	3.0	2.3
Nonfarm, nonmanufacturing business	2.4	2.3	0.7

U.S. Bureau of Labor Statistics.

All the major sectors of the economy shared the productivity decline. It even affected the farm sector, a consistent leader in productivity growth. Performance among sectors is compared according to time periods in Exhibit 6.

EXHIBIT 7   *STARS IN THE GLOOM*

Many industries escaped the productivity plunge, and some performed handsomely. Both the synthetic fibers and telephone communications industries had annual gains over 7 percent during 1974–79. Interestingly, a top performer from 1974 to 1978 was wet corn milling at +9.0 percent, and near the bottom was blended and prepared flour at −6.4 percent.[1] Still wider divergencies occurred among individual companies.

Zippo Manufacturing Company demonstrates how a relatively small company (six hundred employees) can maintain prosperity. It produces the snap-top cigarette lighter made famous during World War II. "Our only bad year was in 1964, the year the surgeon general's warning came out," says Bob Galey, president of Zippo. "We've grown ever since."

In the 1950s Zippo was threatened by cheaper Japanese copies. Its quality and unconditional guarantee repulsed the invasion. Every lighter is guaranteed to work forever, regardless of age or condition, or it will be fixed or replaced at no cost. A real Zippo became a status symbol in Japan and is marketed widely in the Far East.

An original Zippo sold for $2.00 when it was first introduced in 1932. By

1981 the price had gone up to $5.95, an increase remarkably below that of the Consumer Price Index.

A CLOSER LOOK AT EFFECTS

Productivity is an index of economic welfare. More goods and services per worker-hour are produced when productivity increases. More output per input means more product value can be purchased from the same paycheck. This translates into a rising standard of living.

Real hourly earnings represent the buying power of people and substantially indicate the people's standard of living. Productivity has a close statistical relationship with real hourly earnings. In Exhibit 8, where the scale on the left is weekly spendable income, what is left after deducting Social Security and federal income tax is given in constant dollars—equivalent purchasing power after compensating for inflation. The right-hand scale is productivity calculated from a base of 100 for the 1967 year. Real wages of an average married worker with three dependents dropped 7 percent between 1979 and 1980, back to the level earned in *1961*. This epitomizes the gloom settling over the American dream. That greater productivity is needed to buttress the dream is visually apparent in the graph; earnings and productivity climb and dip in concert.

One of the effects of declining real wages is the recent flood of new workers, especially women, into the labor force. From 1965 to 1979, the percentage of the total population employed in the United States rose from 38 to 44.9 percent.[2] Family budgets have been insulated to some extent by the resulting increase in disposable income per capita. This cushion is weakening, however, as the reserve of potential wage earners dissipates. Any future erosion in real earnings will consequently hit households harder.

Good jobs may also become more difficult to find if the export of manufactured goods continues to decline. In the early 1970s, U.S. leadership in exports was lost to Germany, a country with one-fourth as many people. Now Japan is about to surpass us too. Long-running decreases in domestic employment opportunities have plagued our mature industries, such as steel, consumer electronics, and automobiles, as a consequence of adverse import/export conditions. Price competitiveness in these industries and others has deteriorated with respect to other trading nations. The resulting unfavorable balance of international trade contributes to inflation, in addition to unemployment.

Another indicator of a nation's prosperity is its Gross Domestic Product. GDP is a measure of the overall flow of goods and services

EXHIBIT 8   *RELATIONSHIP OF REAL SPENDABLE WAGES TO PRODUCTIVITY*

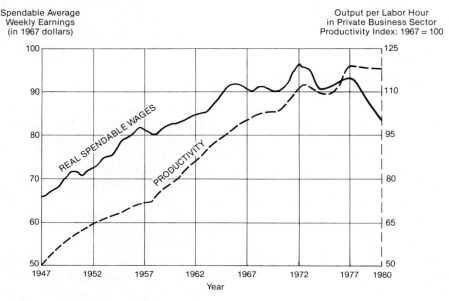

Adapted from U.S. Bureau of Labor Statistics data.

within the geographic borders of a country. Between 1970 and 1980, the GDP of the United States showed an average annual growth of 2.7 percent in constant dollars. This rate compares with 3.1 percent in the preceding decade. While the absolute value of America's GDP is substantially higher than that of its trading partners, its rate of increase is less. Only Great Britain's GDP had slower growth in either the 1960s or the 1970s.

Since GDP is the sum of output from the total population, it can be increased by improving the efficiency of individual workers and by increasing the percentage of workers from the population. That is, GDP gains can be achieved by higher productive efficiencies or working more hours. Recent gains have mostly been drawn from more hours due to more workers.

Charts, graphs, and statements of percentages just confirm what people already suspect from comparing price tags in stores with pay from their work. They are less likely to associate these statistics with workaday activities, not realizing that what they do at work—how well they operate and manage the levers of production—has a real influence on the quality of their leisure and working life. This awareness is needed to maintain the life style to which everyone has grown accustomed.

EXHIBIT 9   *A PORTRAIT OF PRODUCTIVITY PROBLEMS*

Cause-and-effect (C&E) diagrams are an import from Japan. They were originated in 1953 by Kaoru Ishikawa of Tokyo University for quality control studies and have since gained considerable fame as one of the analysis tools associated with the Japanese QC (Quality Control) Circle movement. A modified version is shown as it could be applied to define causes and effects of the national productivity problem.

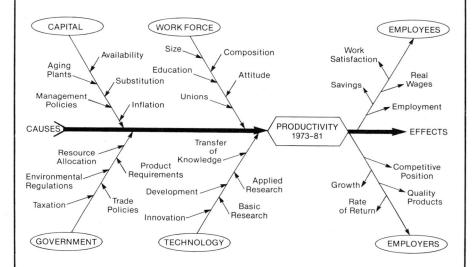

A C&E diagram, nicknamed "fishbone," is drawn to explore a situation. The visual impact tends to strengthen an investigation by suggesting additional considerations associated with the factors already recorded. There are no rigid rules for construction. The first step is to develop a pithy statement of the problem, situation, or objective. It is entered in the center box. Then the main ribs are drawn and labeled with the primary causes and effects, the former on the left, and the latter on the right of the statement box. The dominant factors are usually circled for emphasis. Finally, smaller arrows identifying subfactors run to or from appropriate ribs, and, if needed, sub-subfactor arrows can be inserted to provide greater detail.[3]

The portrait of the 1973–81 productivity situation in the C&E diagram spotlights the four most discussed causes of the period's productivity distress on the left ribs. Specific issues associated with each rib are noted by arrows. Effects are treated similarly. Numerous other entries are possible, depending on the focus desired. And further refinements could be inserted. For instance, the *Composition* arrow on the WORK FORCE rib could be supplemented by subarrows for *Age, Sex, Status, Skills,* and *Location.*

> The four prime causes are examined in the following sections. Their
> seemingly independent positions from the C&E diagram are blurred by the
> way subfactors influence each other.

CAPITAL: FOUNT
OF PRODUCTIVE ASSETS

"The name of the game is business, and the score is kept with money" is
a catchy old saying. A revised version attuned to today's concerns is
*"The name of the game is prosperity, and the score is kept by produc-
tivity."* Or the two could be combined: *"The name of prosperity is productivity, and you score with capital."*

Newer factories and equipment take advantage of the latest technology to produce more with less input.[4] They conserve energy and often
yield higher-quality goods. Their products cater to current needs. They
are the instruments of productivity, and ours are old compared with
those of our major manufacturing competitors. West Germany and
Japan enjoyed well over twice the rate of our productivity gain during
the past decade. The average age of plant and equipment is sixteen to
seventeen years in the United States, while in West Germany it is twelve
years, and in Japan ten. Part of the difference can be attributed to postwar replacement, but that excuse is becoming flimsy with time. Their
current progress is more indicative. During the 1970s Japan and West
Germany invested an average of 17.0 and 12.6 percent, respectively, of
their Gross National Product (GNP) in plant and equipment. The U.S.
average investment was only 10.2 percent.

The knee-jerk solution is to invest more. Aside from the question of
where the money should be directed, an equally intricate question is
where it will come from. A larger chunk of the GNP devoted to investment shrinks the share for individual consumption and government programs. If consumers increased their savings to propel capital formation,
there would be less money to spend on discretionary goods. Similarly,
federal budgets would be squeezed by any tax rebates granted to companies to increase cash accumulation, causing fewer dollars for social programs unless taxes were raised elsewhere. Every pro has a con.

Inflation further confounds the problem. Without measures instituted to restrain other claims on GNP, capital poured into the production
base would boost inflation by increasing the demand for goods and
services before supply increases. That is, a surge of spending for construction materials, new equipment, and skilled labor to build the production base necessarily precedes any marketable output, thereby overheat-
ing demand. Resulting price escalations then tend to boost interest rates,

which in turn tends to discourage long-term investment. Since inflation and business uncertainty march in tandem, escalations make short-term, safer investments look more attractive. Accordingly, money to modernize is shunted to the acquisition of existing assets and revamping of current product lines.

A climb in the personal savings rate offers an exit from the enigma. Accumulated savings would allow additional business borrowing without straining the financial markets. Government spending then suffers only to the extent that savings were encouraged by tax incentives, and the savings, extracted from spendable income, reduce personal consumption to help balance a rise in demand owed to outlays for capital stock. Ergo, no inflationary pressure. Now, how do you increase the personal savings rate?

Americans have never been enthusiastic savers. Since 1948 the average household has put away only about 6 percent of its annual disposable income, and the 1981 rate was under 5 percent. Meanwhile the personal savings rate in West European countries is close to 14 percent, with Italy leading the way at 24.5 percent. In Japan it hovers around 20 percent.

There are many explanations for savings rate disparities, and very little agreement on the causes. Government-run Social Security systems range from generous in European countries to skimpy in Japan, compared with the U.S. system. Economists argue over the effect of Social Security, some saying that it encourages earlier retirement, pushing up the overall costs and hence the need to save, and others saying that it discourages private pension building. More agreement exists on the influence of age and economic conditions. Savings rates are low for young people, picking up with middle age and continuing until retirement. The relative youthfulness of today's population thus inhibits savings. Higher inflation also retards the inclination to save by impelling an urge to buy before prices go up again, and by eroding real income which leaves less money to save.

The composition of savings is as important as the rate. Money invested in gold and rare stamps does nothing for productivity. Expenditures for education and health are a form of saving that permits a higher level of consumption in the future, contributing indirectly to productivity. By contrast, the pool of capital available for economic growth is fed directly by money put in stocks and bank accounts. Less than 4 percent of current after-tax private income finds its way to investment in nonresidential structures and equipment.[5]

Since household savings typically provide about a third of the total capital investment, persistently low savings rates retard the rate of capital formulation needed to promote productivity. Several tax policies forwarded by the Reagan administration were aimed at correcting this situation. Lower personal income tax rates and reduction in capital gains taxation are strong incentives to saving. Limitations on federal spending and controls on the money supply are designed to curb inflation, bettering the investment climate.

Changing the composition of savings has a much quicker effect on business investment than changes in the savings rate. Tinkering with tax laws to alter composition could take many forms, all expensive to the federal tax take and none proven. A shift appears most likely from increasing the rate of return awarded by business investment.[6]

More accelerated depreciation allowed by the new 10-5-3 schedule is intended to increase corporate investment. Since companies reinvest about forty-five cents of each dollar of income, more liberal depreciation allowances boost the nation's savings rate and companies get relief from expensive credit.

Finally, after all the ifs and hows of capital formulation have been plumbed, the actuality is that investment funds are scarce and will remain so until legislated or market stimulants take effect. It could be a long wait. During the interim, high-yield industries will attract the bulk of what is available, redistributing capital to the most deserving. More than ever before, management must wisely allocate its available capital, putting it to work domestically into productive assets, to increase efficiency rather than expanding capacity.

GOVERNMENT:
CULPRIT AND SAVIOR

Ask who is to blame for the nation's productivity ills, and government is on everyone's list. Then ask for the cure, and you get government again. Any action the government takes is at once acclaimed and criticized, depending on whose pocket is fingered.

We mentioned earlier that the taxation arm of government affects capital formulation. That same muscle subsidizes certain industries at the expense of others, distorting the marketplace. Trade agreements, tariffs, and informal import limits similarly provide an umbrella from competition that dissuades pursuit of productivity by the protected industries. These parochial political tactics will probably always exist, occasionally serving public interests, more often just delaying the day of reckoning for the sheltered.

Energy disturbances of the past decade illustrate the dependence of industrial productivity on broad government policies. Ignoring the role of statesmanship in the birth of the energy blowup, federal containment policies shook the roots of the production base. The focus of investment and innovation shifted away from labor efficiency toward energy efficiency. Labor was substituted for more expensive energy, often to the detriment of productivity. Money spent for energy conservation was money unavailable for productivity improvement in labor and materials categories.

Circumstantial evidence, drawn from the inverse relationship between price jumps in energy and productivity growth, suggests that productivity was hurt in all industrial countries by the oil-fired energy problems of the seventies. Policy makers now face the difficult choice between conserving energy at the expense of higher productivity and increasing the supply of energy at some cost to the environment and real wages. Stop-and-go actions have thwarted productivity planning. A consistent energy policy is needed before long-range capital commitments can be made with confidence.

Government regulations to protect the environment, workers, and consumers are at least as controversial as energy policies. These regulations, introduced mostly since the mid-1960s, are aimed primarily at social objectives. Instead of bad-mouthing government, industrial leaders should first question why intervention was ever needed to save the environment, provide healthful working conditions, and ensure safe products. Roger Smith, then executive vice-president of General Motors, noted that the regulations burdening the automobile business would not be on the books now "if business had earlier done what we are doing today . . . one antecedent of regulation lies in our own shortcomings in satisfying our customers."

Much of the consternation concerning regulations focuses on instances of excessive zeal in exercising them. Frightful tales abound. At times enforcement has indeed been abusive, causing resentment and outrage. Current reports indicate that nitpicking and uneven administration are being curtailed. Just as the regulated must acknowledge that their own interests are being served by higher standards of health and safety,[7] the regulators must take a balanced view of industry, including broader economic considerations.

Two kinds of government regulations more directly impinge on productivity. *Economic* regulations, covering matters such as price setting and entry into an industry, have been around a long time. Business has learned to live with them. However, recent deregulation of transportation and major antitrust suits have strong productivity implications. Where inefficiencies have hidden behind the shield of limited access, allowing the franchise holders to escape competition, deregulation will contribute to productivity growth. Breaking up vertically merged companies has debatable effects on pricing and productivity because most observers believe the United States needs a cadre of strong, research-talented giants to compete with other giants overseas. Big is not necessarily bad.

The other kind of government regulation pertains to public issues. Intense proliferation of *social* regulations occurred in the 1969–72 period. The industries most affected—mining, paper, chemicals, refining, and primary metals—have suffered sharp decelerations in productivity growth since 1973.[8] Estimates of the private business cost of implementing pollution abatement in 1977 alone totaled $22 billion, which is roughly 5 percent of all capital outlays for that year.

Money allocated to satisfy regulations, and thus not available for productivity investments, is only one regulatory effect. Regulations also slow innovation and diminish business incentives to invest in new projects. For instance, more stringent requirements are set on new, as opposed to existing, facilities and products, which discourages investment. Witness the drug industry, which waits years for approval of new products. Small businesses especially suffer from the financial burden of compliance; they lack the resources to wade through the paperwork required to get started or keep going. When it is realized that 66 percent of all new jobs are created by firms with twenty or fewer employees, and that innovations often flow profusely from small concerns, the negative impact of government regulations on productivity is foreboding.

Business is often mistakenly characterized by the public as being categorically opposed to regulations. Nothing could be further from the truth. Companies positioned in a profitable refuge behind regulatory boundaries fight to retain their position. Most executives who speak up admit that regulations usually align with their conscience. What they want is even-handed treatment in which the combined effects of regulations are represented.

Government regulators have an image problem too. They sometimes come across as incompetently and blindly pursuing a mandate whether it is feasible or not. Agencies' responses to this perception have led to streamlined procedures and better coordination. As Thorne G. Auchter, assistant labor secretary who heads OSHA, observes, "We see it [OSHA] as a partner lending assistance to those demonstrating a desire to improve workplace conditions."[9]

Public opinion resides uneasily between wanting the security that regulations promise and fearing excesses from Big Brother interference. Both reservations are heard. With respect to Auchter's directive that only firms with below-average safety records and more than ten employees will be targeted for regular OSHA visits, Ray Denison, the chief AFL–CIO lobbyist, says, "This exception scheme makes second-class citizens of millions of workers and removes one of the most effective compliance tools available to OSHA—the threat of a general-schedule inspection."[10] Equivalently, consumers are reminded regularly of the extra costs and product delays attributable to government regulations (see Exhibit 10).

Productivity measurement could be the intermediary instrument for evaluating opposing postures. Compliance inputs would be compared with output benefits. Unequivocal data are difficult to muster in complex cases, but at a minimum the resulting balance sheet of numbers would forestall the more exaggerated claims of either side. It would force policy makers to weigh alternative regulatory objectives, applying budget discipline to regulations, and industry managers to weigh their perceived costs against long-run benefits bestowed by regulations.

EXHIBIT 10   *FARCE, FABLE, OR FORETOKEN?*

The following message was entered in the Congressional Record on January 31, 1980 (p. E296) by the Honorable J. William Stanton, representative from Ohio:

This is the story of the U.S. pencil industry. Remember, we are looking back from our vantage point of 1990. It's strange to think that, back in 1979, just anyone could use a pencil any way they wanted to.

You see, it all started when the Occupational Safety and Health Act carcinogen policy went into effect. The graphite in the pencil lead always contained a residue of crystalline silica. And there was at least one animal test and one in-vitro test indicating that crystalline silica produced tumors, so the material became regulated as carcinogen. There was no alternative for pencils, so exposure had to come down almost to zero.

The Environmental Protection Agency, acting under the Clean Air and Clean Water Acts, required drastic reductions in emissions and effluents. The control technology was quite expensive, and only the largest manufacturers could afford it. This caused a flurry of anti-trust suits in the early '80s when there were only three pencil makers left in the country. One of the three was split into smaller companies, but they soon went out of business since they were unable to afford increasingly stringent workplace and pollution control requirements. Then foreign pencil manufacturers began to threaten to dominate the pencil market, and our government, in an abrupt about-face, allowed a merger of the two remaining companies.

The Consumer Product Safety Commission then became concerned with what the newspaper headlines were calling the "pencil problem." Rubber erasers could be chewed off and choke small children. The sharp points of pencils could also be dangerous. There were residual solvents in the paint used on pencils, and pencil-chewing seemed to be a more widespread habit than anyone had realized. Printing a legend on each pencil that said: "This Pencil Could Be Hazardous to Your Health" did not seem to affect consumer pencil habits, a Harvard study indicated. In fact, the study found additional potentially harmful uses, such as stirring coffee. This led FDA to declare that harmful substances could be dissolved out of the pencil into the coffee, and thus pencils violated food additive laws.

Trying to salvage its business, the pencil company began making pencils without paint, without erasers, and with only soft leads so they would not hold a sharp point. But consumers were outraged, and sales declined.

Then someone invented a machine that could measure crystalline silica below the parts-per-trillion level, and workplace, air emission, water effluent and waste disposal regulations required that the best practicable technology be used to reach this low level. The pencil company was threatened with financial ruin because of the large sums needed to purchase new control equipment. There were those who wanted to ban pencils entirely under the Toxic Substances Control Act, but the government decided that pencils were necessary, particularly since they were used to write new regulations. Besides, the Senators from the state where the pencil company was located declared that pencils were as American as baseball.

So the government bailed out the pencil company with a large guaranteed loan. But, of course, that was only a temporary measure, and to protect the pencil business, the government eventually nationalized it.

It is comforting to know that, after all, society is being protected against a danger that was so obvious we didn't even notice it for many, many years. There are still those who complain about paying $17 for a pencil, but you really can't put a price tag on health or safety.

TECHNOLOGY: THE FUTURE TODAY

Intertwining of capital investment and government policies is joined by tendrils from technology. Although the significance of technological innovation in productivity progress is unquestionably proclaimed, solid evidence is scarce.[11] Indirect measures correlate productivity growth with spending for research and development (R&D), number of patents awarded, and imports or exports in high-technology industries.

Following the national preoccupation with science in the 1960s decade, highlighted by humanity's first footprints on the moon, government inflation-adjusted spending on basic research declined some 14 percent from the 1969 peak to a 1975 low.[12] Since then it has increased slightly. Government funding accounts for about two-thirds of all spending for basic research, inclining toward areas that only obliquely support productivity—health, space, and defense.

Industrial R&D spending shifted away from basic research and toward more applied research until 1978, but threats from foreign competition based on fundamental science discoveries have since reversed the trend. International comparisons show that the United States spends more on total R&D than its major trading partners, but

Japan and Germany have been increasing their R&D investments more rapidly. Unlike the United States, their government R&D funding is concentrated in areas directly related to economic growth. Only Russia spends a higher percentage of its GNP on R&D than does the United States.[13]

Agriculture is a classic example of R&D's contribution to productivity. American farmers lead the world in productivity. Since 1950, land productivity has annually averaged a 1.9 percent gain, and farm labor productivity has enjoyed a whopping average increase per year of about 6.0 percent. These gains parallel the growth of agricultural research. A Cooperative Extension Service, established in 1914, meshes scientists advancing knowledge and scientists inventing technology with farmers producing food. The result, based on thirty-eight studies, is an annual average rate of return of about 50 percent on the investment in agricultural research.

The same conclusion about the value of R&D can be drawn from the performance of R&D-intensive industries. In highly intensive R&D-oriented companies—professional and scientific instruments, electrical equipment and communication, chemical and allied products—productivity gains are consistently good; low and medium R&D-intensive industries are consistently poorer.[14] Companies must increasingly look at their supply of technology in the same way that oil companies look at their reserves. Profits can be increased in the short run by depleting earlier discoveries, but over time they need new discoveries or they will run out of gas.

If the number of patents is a barometer of industrial innovation, storm clouds of foreign competition are gathering. The foreign-origin share of total U.S. patents increased from 20 percent in 1966 to 36 percent in 1977. Patents granted to U.S. inventors dropped from a peak in 1971 to a low in 1978 that was about equal to the number granted in 1961. While patents are a tangible output of R&D, and often a prerequisite for marketing a product or licensing a process, total number is an unconvincing measure of inventiveness.

Volume alone does not indicate value. Some experts believe that an increasing number of inventions are not being patented in order to protect trade secrets. Another plausible factor is the spread of the U.S.-based multinational companies that may opt to have their subsidiaries patent abroad. It is also possible that the U.S. industries' emphasis on short-term payoffs may have switched research from product to process innovations, which are less likely to be patented than new products. Finally, an actual decline in the U.S. inventiveness is conceivable.

American technology is still highly sought after around the world. The United States is by far the world's largest exporter of agricultural products and farm machinery. In 1940 one American farm worker fed

10.7 people at home and abroad; in 1980 he fed 65.0 people. The latter year also saw exports of $7.5 billion worth of computers, $10.0 billion in heavy construction equipment, and $14.1 billion in civilian aircraft and parts.

On the other side of the ledger, in 1960 the United States imported only 5 percent of its consumer electronic goods, 3 percent of metalworking machine tools, and 1 percent of all electrical components. By 1980 these percentages had soared to 51, 23, and 20, respectively.

Domestic debates put part of the blame for the current import deluge on prior export of American technology. The argument goes that U.S. capital investments abroad result in the loss of job opportunities at home. The counterview is that other advanced countries can provide most of the same technology and will get the benefit from sales if we do not. Exports help finance domestic R&D, and overseas investments open new markets otherwise inaccessible due to import restrictions. It is doubtful that the exportation of know-how could be stopped, even if it were advisable.

Strong signals radiating from Washington, D.C., and from high-tech companies suggest that a higher priority is being awarded to know-how and know-why. Recently passed tax-cut legislation includes specific incentives for R&D spending. General corporate tax reductions will also contribute. The Department of Justice has asserted that it will take into favorable account the prospects for enhanced technological innovation while considering mergers. Batelle Columbus Laboratories state a 3.6 percent increase in the nation's total R&D spending for 1981 and predict that such outlays will rise at an average constant-dollar rate of 3 percent annually, much higher than the 1 percent average in the 1970s.

WORK FORCE:
QUALITY AND QUANTITY

Labor is the cornerstone of productivity. All other considerations— investments in the production base, government taxing policies and regulation, advances in technology—support the performance of the work force. And that performance determines the nation's productivity.

A profile of the work force emerged from the 1980 census that partially explains some of the productivity difficulties during the past decade. The census was just a snapshot of demographics at a single point in time, yet a breakdown of the data is a springboard for abstracting trends. These indicate a fast-changing composition of the work force that should nourish future productivity.

•*Total U.S. population was 228.83 million in 1981, growing at 1.1 percent since 1980, the same rate as in the 1970s, but down from 1.3 percent in the 1960s and 1.7 percent in the 1950s.*

Birthrates from 1946 to 1964 spawned an influx of new workers that flooded the job market in the seventies. The baby-boom crop accounted for one-third of the U.S. population in 1980. It entered the 1970 decade largely inexperienced, increasing the work force annually by about 2.4 percent.[15] This rapid growth of young, less-trained workers, and the consequent decline in the amount of capital invested per worker, are believed to have contributed to the slowdown of productivity growth.

A larger proportion of females began working in the seventies. Their lack of experience probably had the same depressing effect on productivity as the infusion of youth. To the extent that women were less experienced than men, the experience differential should diminish in the future, as will the rate at which more women enter the labor market. The demographic shift to older, more experienced workers in the 1980s is expected to have a positive influence on productivity growth.

•*As the American population grows older, its occupational pattern is changing. While the number of children under 15 years of age dropped 11.5 percent, the 15-to-24-year age group went up 20 percent, young adults of 24-to-34 increased nearly 50 percent, and Americans 65 and over increased by 28 percent. As a result, the civilian work force jumped from 87.0 million in 1970 to 104.7 million in 1980. Nonfarm civilian employment has shifted to the following proportions:*

PERCENTAGE OF NONFARM JOBS IN —

Year	Blue-Collar Occupations	White-Collar Occupations	Service Occupations
1960	39.7	47.1	13.2
1970	36.8	50.3	12.9
1980	32.6	53.7	13.7

From the end of the baby boom in 1964 to 1980, employers opened a bountiful 28 million new jobs. Yet unemployment rose from 5.2 percent to over 8.0 percent. This job squeeze had many ramifications. Wage rates were held somewhat in check by the abundance of labor, rising only 78 percent between 1972 and 1980, slightly less than the 81 percent increase in the price of machinery, and far below the 244 percent jump in fuel prices. Compared with energy, labor became cheaper, focusing investment on energy conservation rather than labor efficiency.

At the same time that their inexperience and numbers were depressing productivity, baby boomers were borrowing a lot to finance the refinements of life they had grown accustomed to as children. Soaring consumer credit contributed to higher inflation, which in turn slowed technological advances by raising the cost of capital and uncertainties of investment. This triple whammy on the seventies will dissipate as the average age in the United States climbs from 30 to 36 over the next two decades.

Transfers from occupations of a blue-collar nature have been remarkably swift. In two decades the number of white-collar jobs rose by 78 percent to 51 million. Concurrently, service jobs grew to 13 million, a 62 percent jump, while blue-collar jobs gained only 28 percent to 31 million. *Increases alone* in employment since 1973 in eating and drinking places have been greater than the *total combined* employment in auto and steel plants. Today, McDonald's has more employees than U.S. Steel. This translocation reflects the growth in manufacturing productivity that produces more value per worker and society's inclination for more personal attention.

A Xerox machine has replaced the forge as a symbol of America's growth. It is also emblematic of our productivity ills. Heavy industry has been under the magnifying glass of industrial engineers for over half a century, probing for each tiny extra motion that can be eliminated to gain efficiency. Comparable scrutiny of white-collar operations is not yet under way, although engineers and management analysts are eagerly snipping at red tape. The direction employment has taken, away from higher-productivity factory work toward lower-productivity office work, is another partial explanation of productivity losses in the past decade and is a beacon for the productivity push of this decade.

•*Americans entered the eighties far better educated than ever before. Almost 69 percent have high-school diplomas compared with 55 percent in 1970. Roughly equal proportions of men and women completed high school and, significantly more blacks over 25 have high-school diplomas. At age 25 or older, 17 percent of the population had college degrees, over half again the percentage in 1970.*

Investments in education and training make workers more skilled and better able to adjust to new technologies. The time lag between the investment and its effect is quite long, obscuring its influence on productivity growth. According to Denison, educational upgrading has more impact on productivity development than physical capital.[16] Other analysts point out that employers sometimes use education merely as a screening device and that more schooling could even be counterproductive at an undefined saturation point.[17] They add that average scores in the Scholastic Aptitude Test given to students entering college have shown a downward trend since the mid-1960s, suggesting that schooling today apparently carries a lower educational performance than it did earlier. No one argues that better mental preparation can hurt job performance. The argument is about how well the needed skills are provided and whether job expectations associated with the development are excessive.

Disappointment from lofty expectations is most obvious in the ranks of college graduates who fail to find jobs in their specialties. Many frustrations arise from rapidly changing hiring needs. Recall the surplus of engineers in the early 1970s when the space program was winding down, and compare that with the shortage six years later. Educational and occupational imbalances prompt many degreed job seekers to accept positions below their aspirations. A trickle-down effect then disillusions the replaced workers who have less education. Resulting discouragement at each level may damage productivity.

Managers and supervisors occasionally complain that the quality of American workers is not what it used to be. They are generally referring to work attitudes. Their observation is valid to some extent, of course, because no two generations hold the same work expectations. Polls indicated during the 1970s that attitudes were changing. The proportion of people who agreed with the statement "Hard work always pays off" dropped from 58 percent in 1970 to 43 percent in 1976, and the proportion who agreed with "work is the center of my life" dropped from 35 to about 15 percent in the same interval. The survey in Exhibit 11 suggests that work attitude may still be deteriorating, reinforcing its status as a critical consideration in any plan to enhance productivity.

EXHIBIT II   *ATTITUDES ABOUT APTITUDES*

PERCENTAGE AGREEING WITH THE STATEMENT THAT TODAY'S WORKERS COMPARED WITH WORKERS 10 YEARS AGO . . .	Total Public	Business Executives	Labor Union Leaders	Industrial Engineers
. . . do not work as hard	62	62	62	90
. . . have less pride in their work	78	70	74	90
. . . are less loyal to employers	76	74	70	95
. . . exhibit worse workmanship	71	73	53	88
. . . have less motivation to work	73	77	67	91

Source: Combined results of polls conducted by Harris, Gallup, and the American Institute of Industrial Engineers reported in *Productivity Crunch,* AIIE, 1981. Reprinted with permission from "Productivity Crunch," 1981. © Institute of Industrial Engineers, 25 Technology Park/Atlanta, Norcross, GA 30092.

We have heard European managers express the same complaints as their American counterparts about a declining work ethic. This suggests either a generation bias or a cultural condition common to most industrialized nations. There are probably overtones of both. Television fantasy and political cynicism have been mentioned as causes. Elaborate financial cushions—unemployment insurance, union benefits, welfare payments, food stamps—now make it less catastrophic to be out of a job for a while. Personal shame of unemployment is displaced by a feeling of futility, being unable to cope with impersonal corporations that pass the blame for unemployment on to foreign competitors or the federal government. Company loyalty is diluted by company size. To many young employees, work is a means to a desired life style rather than a life style itself.

Logic dictates that employees' attitudes toward their work must reflect their performance. Logic also suggests that employers can improve the attitudes of employees. Yet there is little solid documentation of how much performance is affected by attitude, or the source of attitudes. Theories are plentiful, but which one should be followed to correct sloppy craftsmanship, idleness, or outright sabotage? Starting from the premise that American workers are capable and still believe work is intrinsically honorable, the task of finding what needs to be done in a certain situation resides with management. There is evidence that enlightened management can improve the attitudes of employees, not by temporary exhortations to excel, but by treating them as collaborators in a mutually rewarding exercise of betterment. When both parties recognize that productivity improvement is a win-win proposition, joint involvement commences, trust builds, and benefits flow.

ONWARD AND UPWARD

We are done with the 1970s now. They were years of disappointment as far as productivity is concerned, but their bleakness affords an ideal contrast to the brightness of the 1960s from which we can draw comparisons to guide productivity efforts in the 1980s. Any temptation to use unique events of the past decade as alibis is refuted by what happened to other nations. Some of them sailed through the seventies in fine shape, overcoming the same energy price eruptions, growing demands for government services, and population shifts that beset America.

Possible performance during the present decade by four trade competitors paints a sobering scenario in Exhibit 12. Based upon the per capita share of gross domestic product as a measure of national prosperity, the United States led other nations by a comfortable margin as it entered the eighties. Extrapolating a 2 percent growth rate after the dip in 1980, GDP per person would increase to a 155.3 index rating by the end of the decade. If Japan and West Germany enjoy growth rates of 6.0 and 4.5 percent, respectively, they will catch up with the United States in 1989. France lags behind at a rate of 3.5 percent, closing out the decade at 142.8 on the index. Britain's 1990 rating would equal Japan's 1980 score if it can muster a 2.5 percent growth rate for nine years.

The national growth rates in Exhibit 12 were selected partially for

EXHIBIT 12   EXTRAPOLATED INDEX OF REAL GROSS DOMESTIC PRODUCT PER CAPITA
FOR SELECTED NATIONS DURING THE 1980s (BASE INDEX: UNITED STATES 1967 = 100)

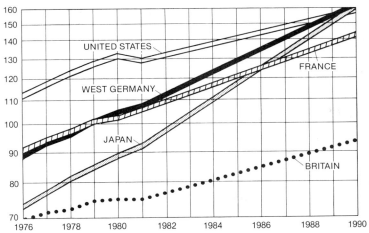

Index rating for years 1976-80 from *The Productivity Slowdown: Causes and Policy Responses*
(Staff Memorandum, Congressional Budget Office, 1981), p.42.

shock effect, but mainly as realistic estimates based upon past
achievements. The following sketches support the reasoning.

West Germany

The Federal Republic of Germany has followed an economic policy
aimed at maintaining full employment, industrial growth, stable prices,
and balanced foreign trade. It has had enviable success, engendering a
climate of investor confidence. To maintain its record, high-skill,
knowledge-intensive production is being emphasized to avoid product
competition from low-wage countries. Labor-management cooperation
has been institutionalized by seats for union representatives on corporate
boards. Bankers also sit on boards. As a result, German unions are inclined to support company strategies, large banks provide risk capital,
and the government has little need to intervene, confining its activities to
macroeconomic policy.

France

French industrial policy is at the other end of interventionism
from Germany. Following the concept of *dirigisme*—advocating strong,
centralized direction of the economy—the government has employed
various strategies over the years to promote selective industrial growth,
such as trade barriers, subsidies, tax concessions, price controls, credit
market intervention, and nationalization. However, its pragmatic side
has allowed troubled firms to go bankrupt. Technological competence of

French industry will bolster national productivity growth in years ahead unless it is strangled by the red tape of central planning.

Japan

This resource-poor, densely populated nation has indeed come a long way from its postwar position as an exporter of labor-intensive, low-tech products. Its marvelously integrated partnership of labor, business, and government has created an awesome industrial machine. The Ministry of International Trade and Industry (MITI) is the guiding force, persuading and facilitating industrial growth along forward lines. Its agenda for the 1980s includes technological advances in the areas of energy, medicine, and large information systems. Coordinated planning, combined with an adaptable work force and highly developed technology, puts Japan in the forefront of productivity expectations, notwithstanding a potential trade backlash if the world economy weakens.

Britain

The United Kingdom contrasts markedly with Japan. British industrial policies are inconsistent and scattered, tending to protect ailing companies and reinforce the existing industrial structure rather than reshaping it to accommodate emerging technologies. Unions, civil servants, and even managements seem to share a job protection mentality. North Sea oil has insulated Britain's economy from the worst consequences of its production ills. Whether the Thatcher shift to free-market economics—lower tax rates, removal of selected controls, cuts in public expenditures—can stimulate ailing industries remains to be seen. Antagonistic unions and a policy of continued subsidies to weak industries suggest that the 2.5 percent growth rate shown in Exhibit 12 is unduly optimistic.

United States

The U.S. trend line in the chart is conservative. After a drop in gross national product in 1974 and 1975, GNP per capita rose in real dollars for the rest of the decade at better than 3 percent a year. A comparable increase for GDP per capita would push the U.S. trend line to the top of the chart in 1988, effectively delaying catch-up by other nations until the mid-1990s. Just a half percentage point additional gain would secure U.S. supremacy for the rest of this century.

Our productivity performance will decide the growth rate. And that performance rests on the tripod of labor, business, and government. We have neither the Japanese symbiosis of labor and management nor the German institutionalization of cooperation. Direct government intervention to allocate resources toward favored industries has been used sparingly in the United States as opposed to French and British policies.[18] Steps by the Reagan administration to boost savings and ease regulations put the onus clearly on labor and business to build on these favors. If collaboration can displace the mistrust that has clogged labor-management dealings, and if consistent government policies can generate confidence by stabilizing a sound economy, the productivity cycle will progress from the 1960s bloom and 1970s gloom to a 1980s boom.

PATHS
TO PRODUCTIVITY

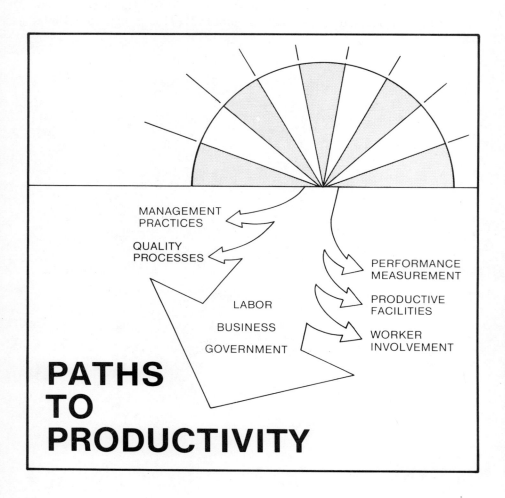

MANAGEMENT
PRACTICES

QUALITY
PROCESSES

PERFORMANCE
MEASUREMENT

PRODUCTIVE
FACILITIES

LABOR

BUSINESS

GOVERNMENT

WORKER
INVOLVEMENT

**PATHS
TO
PRODUCTIVITY**

3

Whenever someone talks about productivity, pay attention. What is said may not fit your situation exactly, but a small piece might be directly useful or, more likely, the concept could be adapted to your purposes. One of the most intriguing things about productivity is that there are so many ways to improve it, ranging from hard technology to soft behaviorals and all the mutations between. It is truly an interdisciplinary subject.

This immense lode of lore causes confusion. Where are the nuggets? Are they in the veins of engineering, psychology, business administration, politics, or whatever? "In all of them" is the unsatisfying answer. There is simply no single pocket of wisdom from which to extract all the right methods to treat productivity.

Several fertile fields for productivity activists are explored in this chapter. Together, these areas are the broad path to productivity depicted in the facing diagram. Only collective efforts can influence the ponderous movement of business, labor, and government. After a preview of coming chapters in the first section of this chapter, the other sections focus on episodes that could influence productivity nationally. Although it is easy to be intimidated by the scope of societal struggles, effective pressure can be exerted by business and trade associations, unions, service groups, and other organizations concerned with improving America's productivity.

BECAUSE AILMENTS VARY, TREATMENTS VARY

Seeking *the* method that works exclusively for a given situation, say, the service sector or just for supermarkets, is an ego trip that claims *my* problems are unique and no one besides me and my colleagues are close enough to them to realize all of the difficulties, and therefore we have to find our own yellow brick road. Not true. Any substantial endeavor relies on common resources—people, machines, capital, energy, service provided by others—all of which can be targeted for productivity improvement, as can the process by which they are integrated. Thus productivity science is not sector dependent, nor are its methodologies limited to exclusive applications.

Since there are myriad paths to productivity, signposts would ease the journey. A map is hinted at by the labeled arrows in the facing diagram. Subsequent chapters are devoted to each path. The topics are generic discussions of practices that can be applied by organizations in every manufacturing and service sector. The following examples indicate the types of productivity action proposed in each of the chapters.

Performance Measurement. A productivity program without benchmarks is a race without a timer. There is no scale of accomplishment, no feedback. Yet many organizations resist productivity measurement for such misconstrued reasons as distrust of accuracy, wariness of more paperwork, and lack of qualified people to do the measuring. A few claim that their operations are too complex or nebulous to quantify, and their reservations are somewhat valid in terms of quantifiable output. But they are neglecting inputs and other measures of results. Substitute benchmarks for output stated as desired levels of performance for input factors can provide quite accurate productivity indicators without adding layers of wheel-spinning bureaucracy.

The education system is a prime example of measurement difficulties and resistance. Counting the number of graduates is an oversimplified measure of output. Combining graduates and their scores on SAT exams, or any form of quality assessment, serves as a crudely weighted measure, better but still not definitive. An alternative approach is to delimit the generally accepted criteria of quality teaching and a qualified educational environment. At the university level, the measurable criteria for professors and their teaching climate include

- Average class size weighted by level, type, and subject area
- Support personnel and supply budget per professor
- Student ratings for each course taught
- Weighted student credit hours earned per professor
- Weighted number of publications by faculty
- Dollar amount of the research budget per year
- Annual expenditure for physical facilities—laboratories, equipment, library
- Weighted public and university service hours by faculty
- Scholastic and professional developments—patents, TV modules, etc.
- Student ratings for advising and assistance

Such measurements, not unlike those normally used for evaluating individual promotion and tenure for faculty members, track the accomplishment of a department, continually focusing on areas with improvement potential. The inherent assumption is that the quality of education increases with successively higher periodic scores.

If the productivity of education can be measured, any operation can be measured. The use of more conventional productivity indexes is presented in Chapter 4, and individualized productivity indicators are described in Chapter 11.

Management Practices. The mission of managers is to avoid problems or, if unavoidable, to solve them. Many of the opportunities are productivity oriented. A retail grocery supply chain had a knotty labor efficiency entanglement among its warehouse workers. New employees serve a twelve-hundred-hour probationary period before they gain "regular" status. These "casual" workers consistently produced well over the 100 percent standard for output. Once they became regulars, however, their performance invariably dropped to 90 percent of standard, or slightly above. By agreement, the cutoff rate for discipline was 89 percent of standard or below. Work standards were believed fair, and any change would surely intensify the hassle.

After several months of ineffectual jawboning, an informal survey was taken to find out what kind of added benefit would be most attractive to the warehouse "regulars." More fringes topped the poll, followed closely by more time off. The first choice was eliminated because pay was already high and raising it would do little for the work-efficiency problem. Instead, a clever time-off bonus was built into a novel incentive plan that awards weekly time-off credits according to a sliding scale based on increased output and decreased damage to items handled during a period. The current level of performance garners no bonus. Higher quality and quantity of output pays for the awarded vacation hours, and for a marginal increase in productivity.

More win-win management strategies are discussed in Chapter 5.

Productive Facilities. While computer-driven technology heads many shopping lists for productive assets, some firms tread a private trail to productivity. A new entry into the electro-sensing arena embraced an organizational structure that maximizes internal communications and comradery, and designed a small plant to complement it. Having been seduced by the Silicon Valley life style, and rich with venture capital, the young entrepreneurs established a three-tier organization chart and an open-door policy, enforced by removing all doors inside their renovated building. A balcony erected above a carpeted assembly line contained rest cubicles and exercise equipment. A communal sauna in a covered and glass-protected patio was the designated shoptalk site, accommodating afternoon imbibing and occasional midday celebrations. Everything, from bright murals to big cushions, was designed to foster the mellow mood deemed persuasive to productivity.

Plant and equipment options are considered in Chapter 6.

Quality Processes. Operations scheduling, inventory movement, and operators' activities in manufacturing processes are probably the most thoroughly examined portions of industry. For these analyses the primary measure of perfection is time, which is also an obvious factor of productivity. The supplementary criterion is quality.

Trade-offs between quality and quantity and time have fascinating economic possibilities. Savings acquired from sacrificing quality are invariably weighed against lost market value of the product. This trade-off faced the manager of a state motor vehicle registration department. In one phase of operations, information for registration is taken from application forms and entered into a computer. Errors occur in the original data and the transfer. A 100 percent inspection limited incorrect registrations to less than 1 percent, but it was expensive.

A revised plan set a goal of 98 percent accuracy. In the few instances when an error was serious enough to cause financial loss to the owner of a vehicle, the department accepted liability. Such losses proved to be much lower than the accrued savings. Operators now have the responsibility for inspecting their own work, and a check is provided by randomly sampling completed registrations. Only when an operator allows too many errors does more rigid 100 percent inspection begin again; it is continued until the operator is once more consistently producing at the 98 percent accuracy level. The modified process increased productivity and the pride operators took in their work.

Design of quality operations is the subject of Chapter 7.

Worker Involvement.   The idea of everyone working together and enjoying it is so innately attractive that nearly all managers succumb to the urge to implement some form of worker participation. When the anticipated harmony fails to emerge, it's back to the old grind. On-again, off-again campaigns naturally imbue cynicism in the work force.

We encountered a cynical crew, nicknamed "The Germans," while introducing a productivity-improvement program. The Germans manned the model shop of an electronics firm. Some of them had been with the company for twenty years and had seen enrichment promotions come and go. They characterized their swings from hot attention to cold neglect as averaging out to lukewarm toleration. There was only one way to convince the Germans that the latest involvement promotion was the real thing—longevity. All of the programs paled against their credulity about a continuing commitment by the company to its stated objectives.

Skepticism and other considerations for employee involvement are discussed in Chapters 8 and 9.

Firm-, department-, and team-level activities are featured in Chapters 8 to 11. In these chapters, aggregated actions are explored. The exploration begins with a side trip to Japan.

LAND OF THE RISING SUM

Successes by Japan in swelling its national product and increasing its productivity are providential examples for the United States. They are solid testimony for what can be done. If we did not have Japan for a prototype, we would have to invent one.

So much has been spoken, written, and televised about Japan in the past few years that there is danger of becoming jaded. Deprecating Japanese productivity accomplishments as aberrations, or attainments peculiar to an alien culture, misses the point that their remarkable record proves that productivity can be raised in a world of scarce resources and numbing politics. It would be foolhardy not to explore the workings of their success, screening out cultural differences to identify responsible traits and transferable techniques. Relationships between Japanese labor, business, and government are examined in this section; several additional aspects of Japan's industrial system are discussed in subsequent chapters.

U.S. business leaders are now trooping to Japan in search of productivity wisdom, mimicking the flow of the past two decades of Japanese executives seeking U.S. expertise. They are drawn by the riddle of how an overpopulated island country can leap from a purveyor of shoddy, labor-intensive goods to become an exporting dynamo of high-technology products while importing 100 percent of its aluminum, 99.8 percent of its oil, 98.4 percent of its iron ore, and 66.4 percent of its wood and lumber. But unlike popular riddles, there is no thinly disguised, simple solution to this puzzle. The answer is complexly rooted in centuries-old traditions and intricate industrial interdependencies.

Union-Company Cooperation

The cohesiveness of the Japanese labor force is legendary. It is overwhelmingly composed of one racial stock, sharing the same language and aspirations. Minor disturbances have arisen from calls for more equal treatment of female workers, but the prevailing importance accorded job dedication, teamwork, and company loyalty remains intact. Such allegiance and work conscientiousness is an outgrowth of employment policies that nearly avoid layoffs and a genuine concern by managers to include everyone in company activities.

The organization of labor unions along company lines also binds the workers' goals closely to management objectives. The health of the company is essentially the health of the union. The combination of close worker-management communication and continuous employment policies restrains a union from pulling the trigger when its members are unhappy. Instead, grievances may be expressed by armbands worn to work or wall posters decrying a work situation that needs correcting. Management's response is usually quick. More consequential issues, such as reductions in employees' working hours to help the company sweat out an economic downturn, are handled by consultation between union leaders and company executives. Because many of the union leaders have spent their entire working lives with the company, strong feelings of loyalty and attachment engender a cooperative atmosphere for settling disputes.

EXHIBIT 13   *PROTESTING WITH AFFECTION*

> Surprising similarities and striking differences between Japanese and American labor movements are pointed out by Tadashi Hanami in *Labor Relations in Japan Today*. (New York: Kodansha International, 1979. Reprinted with the permission of Kodansha International.) Union membership in Japan embraces about one-third of the work force as opposed to one-fifth in the United States. Dues, at one percent of wages, are comparable. Local administration is similar, and occasionally the fervor of negotiations is equally heated.
>
> At contract time, the so-called Spring "Shuntō" Offensive, a loosely knit federation of unions, may raise industry-wide demands but each organization's union usually ends up doing the bargaining to protect the competitiveness and prestige of "our company." Between contracts, armbands or headbands are occasionally worn, while work continues, to protest a general issue bothering company employees. Specific issues get a more dramatic treatment. Defamatory posters are messily pasted in conspicuous places and short stop-work sessions are staged unannounced. At one plant, barrels of paste were consumed in splashing more than eight thousand posters over building extensions in three days.
>
> Japanese workers have an "eternal and inviolable right to . . . act collectively" ensured by the national constitution (Article 28). Although strikes are legal, lockouts are not. In contrast to American labor agreements in which the *i*'s are dotted and the *t*'s are crossed, Japanese agreements are purposefully short, abstract, and obscure. Understanding rests on mutual trust and the honor of each side, placing a strong moral obligation on both. "Should a disagreement arise, both parties will consult each other in good faith" is the way Hanami capsulizes the grievance procedure.

Japan has fewer actual work stoppages due to strikes than any other major industrial power. In 1978 only 1.4 million workdays were lost, while the United States lost 39.0 million.[1] It may be difficult to maintain this record in the future. Akira Totoki, president of the Japan Management Association, believes that Japan's traditional seniority system is endangered. He observes that "in the last few years people have started wondering whether this lifetime employment system will survive. There is the possibility, in fact, that certain conditions that helped the system click in the past, have collapsed already. The economy is slowing down and average life expectancy is increasing."[2]

Until such economic and demographic distortions arise, if ever, Japan's labor peace will continue to be a paragon for other industrialized nations, especially the willingness of Japanese workers to accept advanced automation and labor-saving devices. To develop a comparable acceptance, other nations will have to find ways to equivalently relieve anxiety over unemployment and reluctance for retraining. Unless a company is an empire like IBM, GM, or AT&T, it lacks the resources to stabilize employment through in-empire transfers and gradual introductions of new technology. Public assistance may be needed for companies of modest size to buffer employees from technological shocks.

Government-Company Cooperation

Government policies in Japan serve as shock absorbers. Just as it is difficult to distinguish between the objectives of management and the objectives of labor, so also are the boundaries between government and business fuzzy. Public interests are protected by government regulations in areas such as pollution control and safety, but government intervention is less adversarial than in the United States and the European community. For example, antitrust enforcement is almost unthinkable in Japan. Cooperation among corporations is encouraged when it benefits the nation's social or economic goals, as in the common design of antipollution equipment. It was late 1981 before the U.S. Justice Department gave permission for General Motors and Ford to jointly develop and test antipollution devices.

Corporate capitalism has a unique Japanese flavor through relationships defined as "affiliation" and "corporate grouping."[3] Companies own shares of other companies in order to establish close relationships with one another. An "affiliation" occurs when a large company owns part of a smaller firm, sends its officers to hold key positions in the subsidiary, and extends financial assistance if necessary. The subsidiary firm is often a supplier of goods to the parent, which naturally contributes to high quality and prompt deliveries of contracted components. "Corporate grouping" forms a relationship of large companies through ownership of each other's stock. Today there are six such groups: Mitsubishi, Mitsai, Sumitomo, Fuyo, Daiichi-kangin, and Sanwa. Every company in a group owns shares of other companies in the same group. All are closely linked in their daily transactions and financial dealings. In the case of the Mitsubishi Group, members are said to hold equal status in regular gatherings, called *Kinyo-kai*, or Friday meetings.

Japan's government is a gentle governor over independent and interrelated businesses. It collects corporate taxes at a rate close to ours, and senior government officials often leave government to assume top positions in corporations, as in the United States. Businesses may similarly ignore government advice. For instance, in the 1950s the Japanese government suggested that automakers produce a low- cost car modeled after the Volkswagen to crack the American import market. While it is against Japanese policy to subsidize "sunset" industries such as shipbuilding, unemployment insurance and special government allocations ease the transition to healthier "sunrise" technology.

The Ministry of International Trade and Industry (MITI) has

produced a blueprint for Japanese industrial growth for this decade.[4] Three rather ordinary national goals are forwarded: contribute to international economic progress, overcome resource shortages, and improve the quality of leisure life. More concrete objectives apply to productivity. MITI wants the percentage of Japan's gross national product devoted to technology increased from 1.7 to 3.0 percent by 1990. Financial support in different forms would be directed at such growth areas as aerospace, electronics, and information processing. Energy consumption should drop by 15 percent during the decade through massive governmental capital investment. The report also warns against dangers of social unrest and unemployment that could accompany unrestrained business activities.

The value of MITI's report lies more in its existence than in its contents. It illustrates that Japan at least has an industrial policy, unlike the floundering that goes on here. There is no agency equivalent to MITI in the U.S. government. Instead, good intentions are fragmented among task forces, boards, foundations, and centers in various departments. It is doubtful if anyone wants a federal czar to dictate resource allocations for productivity, but minimal needs are coherent executive policies and a clearly designated departmental home from which to coordinate and promote productivity actions.

EXHIBIT 14   *IF SMALL IS BEAUTIFUL, JAPAN'S GOVERNMENT IS GORGEOUS*

The glow of productivity enlightenment radiating from Japan's government does not come from a large corps. In 1967 a limit was set on the number of white-collar workers available to the central government. The same limit applies today—506,571. The ratio for all national and local government employees, including defense forces, is 45 per 1,000 people in the population. By comparison, the United States has 82; Britain, 109; France, 83; and West Germany, 76.[5]

Control over the number of government employees is exercised by the Ministry of Finance. Periodic reviews, similar to U.S. "sunset laws," examine each program to determine whether it is functioning as expected. If not, it is closed down. A public body known as the Administrative Management Agency also audits government ministries, annually advising how many employees should be in each unit. The advice has never been overruled.

Conditions peculiar to Japan help hold the totals down. Only 2.5 people per 1,000 are in the armed forces, compared with 13.4 in the United States, 10.7 in West Germany, and 8.4 in France. Public groups perform functions done by governments in other countries. Trade and business associations collect statistics and help disseminate government decrees.

Perhaps reputation is also partly responsible. A Japanese bureaucrat is powerful and respected. Top-ranking students compete for civil service. Senior bureaucrats exercise political influence in their liaison with industry and by drafting legislation for parliament. Whatever the reasons, it is refreshing to see Parkinson's law violated: Officials make work for each other, and the work expands to fill the time available for its completion.[6]

GOVERNMENT OF THE PEOPLE,
BY THE PEOPLE,
AND FOR PRODUCTIVITY

No decree from government can possibly force people to ply their trades more efficiently. If it were possible, Communist countries would be exporting food instead of importing it. However, government policies can fabricate an environment in which productive practices flourish. We have already observed the importance to productivity of tax incentives, reasonable regulations, and a stable economy. These are essentially legislated conditions, subject to the tides of public opinion and political expediency. A productivity organ is needed in the executive body of government to read the tides and channel them toward national productivity.

Legislators are hustled by a flock of special-interest groups, many seeking privileges that negatively impact productivity. Since it is doubtful that productivity will ever become a popular cause in the mold of consumerism with a celebrated spokesperson, about all that can be hoped is favorable legislative fallout from lobbying groups whose interests are served by laws that also serve productivity. For instance, tax changes pushed by bankers and brokers to attract savings also promote productivity by making investment money available to modernize the production base. Conversely, some acts are counterproductive. A productivity advocate equivalent to Nader's Congressional Watch should be on duty.

A steady, but not necessarily strident, voice in government is needed to focus attention and act as a clearinghouse on productivity issues. The voice does not have to issue from a big body. A modest staff would write position papers, interface with industry and unions, and coordinate public committees working on specific issues. A federal secretary of productivity would attract press coverage, yet be a poor example of the subject. Nor is an undersecretary necessary. What is needed is a *"National Productivity Trust,"* not closeted in the Commerce Department or fragmented within dozens of federal programs stretching from GAO to OMB, as is the apparent want of recent administrations, but *conspicuous.*

A National Productivity Trust would not supplant ongoing productivity mechanisms. It would add to their credibility and visibility. Ambitious efforts by such organizations as the U.S. Chamber of Commerce would be recognized and their message enhanced by reducing any self-serving connotations, as would messages from organized labor. The impact of studies generated in both public and private sectors would be magnified. For example, the untrumpeted "1981 Midyear Report on Productivity,"[7] issued by a congressional joint economic committee, and reports from the House Task Force on Industrial Innovation and Productivity should have a larger audience. Leadership from a National Productivity Trust could also strengthen the embryonic network of regional productivity centers now emerging across America.

A PRODUCTIVITY NETWORK

A few years ago the United States had a productivity center. It was started in 1974 and abandoned in 1978. In the center's 1976 annual report, Nelson Rockefeller, then vice-president of the United States, said:

> One of the primary responsibilities of the Center is to provide an arena where varying points of view can be expressed. As an objective and neutral group, the National Center for Productivity and Quality of Working Life stands at the center of the effort to achieve a national consensus on productivity problems and policies. As is appropriate to this role the Center does not assume the responsibility of individual organizations to improve productivity. Rather it seeks to identify and aid in the removal of external barriers to those individual efforts.
>
> The Center has made progress over the last year under difficult circumstances. It is a small organization; its staff during the period of this report numbered less than 30, and its annual budget was only $2 million. . . . Obviously, there is much work yet to be done, and I urge that the highest priority be given to supporting the future activities of the National Center for Productivity and Quality of Working Life. Success in our efforts will yield important benefits to our Nation.[8]

The coincidental closing of the center and the nation's productivity decline was a happenstance, of course, but was also indicative of neglect by elected executives of an emerging debacle.

Irony gets thicker when the fate of our National Center for Productivity is contrasted with the Japan Productivity Center. At the urging of the United States to develop a nationwide productivity movement, the Japanese created their center in 1955. It is now a prominent national organ with regional productivity satellites and productivity councils in major cities. The center operates a Productivity Labor College where labor relations seminars and correspondence courses are offered on such subjects as the philosophy of productivity improvement and problems in labor-management cooperation. Thousands of study teams sponsored by the center have been sent abroad to become familiar with newer technologies and management techniques. A separate institution, the Asian

Productivity Organization,[9] assists productivity efforts in developing countries along the Pacific rim and inevitably strengthens economic ties among members. The organization's secretariat is located in Tokyo and Secretary-General Harumi Takeuchi is from Japan.

Today in the United States a number of loose confederations, advisory boards, professional institutes, business associations, consulting groups, and independent centers promote productivity. There is no coordinating body. Many groups are narrowly specialized, catering to specific applications, as in hospitals, or pushing specific programs such as flexible manufacturing and quality control circles. Others provide general information and limited on-site services. They speak with many tongues, each professing cures for certain productivity infirmities, well intentioned but collectively weak compared with national needs.

Some forty not-for-profit productivity, quality of work life, and innovation centers are scattered across the United States. Most of them are affiliated with universities. The most prestigious exception is the American Productivity Center, which was founded in 1976 by C. Jackson Grayson in Houston, Texas. It has splendid facilities and is bankrolled by a blue-ribbon roster of corporations. The Manufacturing Productivity Center is associated with the Illinois Institute of Technology in Chicago and is one of the largest university centers, having an annual budget of about $5 million, half of which comes from government contracts and grants, and half from industrial activities and affiliated institutions. Both APC and MPC offer many open-enrollment short courses or conferences and publish extensively. At the other extreme are small university centers operating on $25,000 to $100,000 per year with services confined to behavioral and technological advice.

These centers constitute a potential extension service for productivity. They could be assembled into a network of productivity stations modeled after the highly successful agricultural extension service. With leadership from a National Productivity Trust and some federal dollars, a *network of regional productivity centers* could engage in practical research, disseminate information, collect data, conduct sample projects, and directly assist productivity improvement in small businesses and local governments. Their cost effectiveness could be monitored by requiring that every federal dollar be matched by a dollar from industry for each type of service delivered; matching funds would have to be real dollars for real services, not funny-money fabricated from matching overhead or other grant money against a budget request. Each station in the network should be an example of productivity.

Beyond the basic drive to raise productivity, each center would have a distinctive mission compatible with the uniqueness of its region. A center in a region with an aging population directs its attention to the productivity of older workers, while a center in the midst of government employees focuses on their productivity. Then results from regional activities are exchanged to spread the wealth of gained experience. Network centers would leave basic research and business financing to units already in operation, favoring instead person-to-person contacts to overcome pragmatic difficulties.

An obvious deterrent to the creation of a National Productivity Trust and network of regional productivity centers is the danger of adding a layer of fat instead of muscle. To ensure leanness, a public review board convened by the National Productivity Trust should annually audit the performance of each center based on quantifiable criteria. An up-front ceiling on employment levels keyed to the number of people served would control proliferation, and sunset curfews would be imposed for dereliction, a la Japan. A productivity indicator matrix, as described in the next chapter, is a logical way to assess the worthiness of the network and its nodes. If productivity specialists cannot practice what they preach, they deserve to have their corks popped.

A PHILOSOPHER'S STONE
FOR PRODUCTIVITY—
EDUCATION

Education is today's equivalent of the ancient philosopher's stone. Alchemists in the Middle Ages sought a potion to turn base metal into gold. They failed. Modern tinkerers who seek a magic cure for productivity plights will also fail. The productivity philosopher's stone is education, slow in its effect but proven in its capability. The trick is rubbing the stone in a way that produces the desired effect.

The recommendation to install a network of regional productivity centers on campuses was not based on convenience resulting from the location of existing centers. A campus site has double-edged advantages. Faculty members are an underused talent resource that can be employed in selected areas where their expertise is most valuable, and, simultaneous with the employment, faculty become more aware of the practical aspects of their disciplines. Students conducting short projects for small companies, under guidance from a center's staff, provide and derive the same dual benefits as faculty. Just having a center on the campus reminds educators and the public of the role universities must assume in fostering industrial development.

Troubled Priests of Technology

Engineering education is in the spotlight because it molds the creators and maintainers of the machinery of technology. Its cycles are representative of changing attitudes in education. In the post-Sputnik era of the 1960s, engineering schools geared up for increased enrollment with science-oriented curricula. Federal money poured in to replace many hands-on shop courses with theory courses. Then job openings dropped in the early 1970s with the aerospace implosion, and a technology backlash from the prevailing counterculture movement discouraged enrollment in engineering schools. By the late seventies another shortage of engineers was looming. Demand was changing toward practical applications featuring computer-aided design and computer-controlled processes, but money was scarce for updating labs and lectures. Engineering schools are currently struggling with an overflow of students, insufficient faculty, and outmoded facilities.

Pleas for a bigger slice of the budget gush from every pore of the education system. Dr. Donald D. Glower, dean of engineering at Ohio State Univerisity, took shots at both science and liberal arts by noting that America and England win Nobel prizes while Japan and Germany apply the technology to corner world markets. As a remedy, "the U.S. must free itself from the grasp of traditionalists, the high priests of the liberal arts who yearn for a Utopia that never was, or at best seek to preserve a status quo more relevant to the Dark Ages than to the current age of technology."[10] Dean Glower might have exaggerated for effect, because science and humanities are certainly necessary ingredients in total education, but he fortified the argument that productivity is rooted in engineering.[11]

The inevitable comparison with Japan finds Japanese universities graduating eighty-seven thousand engineers in 1980 as opposed to about sixty-three thousand in the United States. Considering the relative populations of the two nations, that is quite a gap. Another comparison reveals a disturbing trend: The percentage increases in practicing engineers and lawyers in the United States over the past four decades are

    1940s: engineers, 83; lawyers, 0
    1950s: engineers, 59; lawyers, 19
    1960s: engineers, 40; lawyers, 25
    1970s: engineers, 15; lawyers, 83

If the trend continues, there will be more professionals involved in reslicing the national pie than enlarging it.

Acknowledging the need for engineering and technology graduates, there is still a question about the mix. Japanese managers are disturbed by the need to retrain engineers right after graduation. Their criticism is aimed at curricula that concentrate on abstract science. A gradual return to hands-on labs in American engineering schools has forestalled most complaints from industry about practicality. However, plenty of room for improvement remains, especially in manufacturing subjects. And two new needs are arriving. Means should be developed to deliver refresher courses on recent technological developments to engineers who graduated several years ago and are working at sites far away from a campus. Technician training also needs to be upgraded and expanded because employers increasingly rely on colleges to provide apprenticeship training, and more older workers are turning to community colleges to refurbish their skills. Expected financial support from business has not arrived as rapidly as hoped. Supplementary support for education is not exactly a choice between brains and butter, but it is getting close.

Awareness in Adolescence

The importance of productivity to the nation should be impressed upon students before they get to universities. "Business Week" programs conducted during the summer for high-school students and their teachers are an ideal platform for stressing productivity concerns. These industry-sponsored weeks could be improved by having a productivity pamphlet available to guide the program and to carry back to schools for reference during social studies classes. The Productivity Promotion Council of Australia has published such a text.[12] It is a forty-nine-page paperback, complete with discussion points that examine Australia's productivity performance and explain the causes.

In India even grade-schoolers hear about productivity. Dr. Krish Pennathur, former president of the World Confederation of Productivity Science, has written a book of fables about productivity.[13] In the Preface he writes: "In the ultimate analysis, Productivity is an *attitude of mind*. This attitude has to be cultivated from one's childhood. It must be inculcated in the formative minds of schoolgoing children so that it becomes a *way of life* for them. As a school subject, Productivity is more important than History or Geography. Yet, the subject of Productivity does not figure in the school curriculum!"

Number Trading

Another way regional productivity centers could contribute to education is by working with local trade and business associations. We have found that productivity-improvement short courses are much more effective when specifically designed for presentation to an audience from one industry. By working with directors of an association, the subjects are tailored to members' concerns, and participants have an opportunity to exchange gossip along with sharing their productivity successes.

Interfirm productivity comparisons are yet another possible service that can result from cooperation between regional centers and business associations. Interfirm comparison is a management tool. It is developed by gathering data in the form of selected production and financial indicators from each participating company engaged in similar production. Averages are then calculated, and each company receives a report comparing its performance with the group's average for each indicator. Confidentiality is achieved by having the data compiled by an independent agency, such as a productivity center, and reporting information back to firms as ratios; each firm receives an individual set of ratios pertinent to its operations.

Comparisons can be conducted in virtually any industry by categorizing firms according to size, product range, and method of operation. They are designed to answer a manager's question, "Am I using my resources efficiently?" Without a yardstick for comparison, any answer is purely subjective. Suppose, for example, that a manager budgets to reduce energy consumption by 2 percent and achieves 3 percent. On the surface this looks great, but if the industry as a whole has achieved a 5 percent reduction, the 3 percent accomplishment loses luster. Similarly, a budget that puts labor cost at 38 percent of revenue with an intent to trim it to 35 percent may appear commendable until it is learned that the rest of the industry operates at 31 percent.

Details about utilizing interfirm productivity comparisons are given in the next chapter. It suffices here to note that this technique is used far more extensively in other countries than in the United States, suggesting that it holds promise for our pursuit of greater productivity.

EXHIBIT 15   *PRODUCTIVITY ACTIVISTS ANONYMOUS*

The theme of this chapter is collective effort to influence policies and macroconditions that promote productivity growth. Many voices must rise in unison to produce any effect. What is needed most is a leader for the choir. A few years ago that position was filled by the National Center for Productivity and Quality of Working Life. No comparable leader has since emerged, although several organizations are trying nobly.

Notions of a united front for productivity have been bandied about in many circles. The accompanying cause-and-effect diagram summarizes the thinking about productivity awareness at one of the last conferences sponsored by the National Center before its demise.[14] Ideas galore inhabit the diagram. Many of them have been implemented, some spectacularly as TV specials and proclamations by eminent personalities, but the overall effect has been diffused and sporadic.

Assuming that no spiritual leader will arise to head a productivity crusade, advances will have to be ushered along by a band of anonymous believers. Each of the "cause" groups in the C&E diagram has a variety of options to pursue. The collective effect of a swarm of productivity activists may have the same effect as Adam Smith's "invisible hand" that promotes

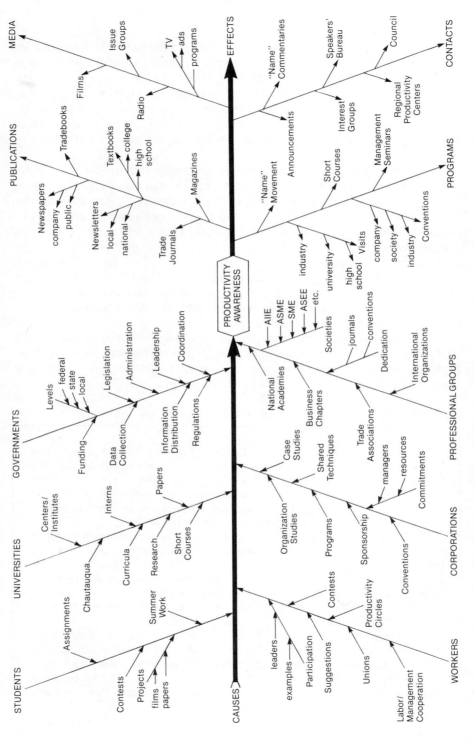

societal ends that differ from individual intentions: Pursuing productivity improvements as a selfish goal, only to improve one's own economic health, distributes benefits to everyone, perhaps more effectively than if pursued by society as a whole.

REVITALIZED LABOR RELATIONS

Only a few years ago the chances of a union being willing to bail out a faltering company by granting large wage concessions were nil. No more. Under the worst-case scenario, workers are forced to choose between having their entire plant close and taking drastic pay cuts. Less dire, but still loaded with the same implications, are demands to hold wages in check and drop some fringes or face massive layoffs because competitors offer lower prices—often the consequence of lower wages. Detroit carmakers point to much lower hourly pay in Japan's auto industry as a major reason why imported cars are stealing sales. One likely result of bailouts is an increase in labor leaders' representation in company decisions starting from mid-level union-management committees to a labor member on the board of directors.

Accommodation to the threatened closure of a Morrell Meatpacking Plant is a classic example of union-management adjustment.[15] Both sides tilted. Ignoring the disapproval of their international union, members accepted a $2-per-hour pay cut in return for a guaranteed forty-hour workweek, up from thirty-six, and a promised investment of $2 million in the plant, depending on its restored profitability. Additionally, a number of advisory groups patterned after Japanese quality circles were organized to give workers a say in plant operations. As a culminating bond of mutual interests, the company opened its books as a part of a profit-sharing plan that distributes a 20 percent share of profits among union workers.

The settlement at Morrell had a distinct Japanese flavor—no layoffs, QC circles, and a bonus plan. That style is naturally more pronounced at Japanese-owned and -operated plants in this country. Reports vary as to the success of imported management techniques, partly because their adoption varies from a full-tilt praise-the-company-and-pass-the-automation tune to a mild regimen of more personal attention by managers to workers' concerns. In rare instances company songs[16] and group calisthenics have found their way into American practice, but the most valued imports appear to be an emphasis on quality work backed by the tools to support it, more job training for workers and supervisors, and high priority for labor-management communications. A measure of acceptance of these traits is gleaned from the failure of most union attempts to organize Japanese plants, although there are a few notable exceptions.[17]

What Needed Unions Need

Organized labor is caught between a rock and a soft place. On one side is the incontestable reality that the nation needs a strong labor movement to balance the clout increasingly concentrated in huge corporations. Without organized labor as refuge for the abused, overzealous executives might be tempted to experiment impetuously. On the other side is the inescapable reality that union membership, as a percentage of the work force, has been declining since 1954 and rank discipline is not what it used to be. Part of the softness is owed to structural shifts that have seen flattening employment in highly unionized heavy manufacturing, transfers of industries from union strongholds in the East and Midwest to the mostly nonunion South and Southwest, and a burgeoning white-collar class that often resists union representation. The social climate also has an effect. Young workers, mobile and protected by government assistance programs, are generally less interested in the industrial class struggle. Having been exposed to lurid tales of skulduggery by both unions and corporations, their inclination is more toward the sidelines than the picket lines.

Labor relations must somehow become responsive to today's economy and today's work force. Instead of a rigid system of demands and counterproposals at contract time, labor and management should identify issues and problems, explore them together, and work out solutions that are sensitive to changeable conditions. They cannot afford to be in a state of war, yet they must retain adversarial roles to protect their constituents. When both actually realize that they are bound by a common purpose—success of the enterprise and welfare of the employees—the grating edges of conflicting positions will be blunted by empathy.

Productivity issues are attracting new attention to outmoded union practices that have repulsed previous assaults by management and to traditional boundaries between the front office and the production line. For example:

•*What is the union stance toward closer management-worker ties being promoted by quality circles and kindred involvements?* Some unions openly encourage the development of circles as a means to improve work conditions, but others fight the movement, fearing it is a management ploy to wean workers away from the union. It is quite possible that both outcomes will occur, which one depending on the union's posture.

•*Are give-backs really as dastardly as claimed, or are they simply corrections of inequities?* When flagrant make-work rules and costly special privileges are rescinded, the only losers are the privileged few. Society as a whole gains when managers act responsibly. Give-backs are not take-aways. In times of economic stress, managers legitimately question jobs and job practices that are not cost effective. When squeeze comes to crunch, union leaders owe it to their clientele to protect genuine jobholders.

• *How deeply should unions become involved in company affairs?* In the past, unions saw company prosperity as a challenge—"We want more because you have it." A more-rewarding challenge is to help the company get more so that there will be more to share. Collective bargaining can surely design a structure that resolves petty gripes before they fester to hurt feelings and waste time, while retaining a formal grievance procedure for serious contract violations. From this level, cooperation can extend as high as both parties see mutual benefits.

• *Where does productivity bargaining fit into the collective-bargaining system, or does it belong in it?* A decade ago when Peter Peterson was secretary of commerce, he pictured productivity bargaining as providing employee incentives to change work rules and methods to boost productivity. Since then the concept has expanded to include specified returns in labor contracts for specified increases in productivity. The hooker is how to measure productivity gains in a way that gives credit to those who earned them. Nonetheless, tying increases in wages and productivity together is fundamentally sound for *both* workers and managers.

Labor-Management Productivity Committees

The idea of labor-management cooperation is certainly not new. During World War II, labor-management plant committees dealt with material conservation, work performance, and morale. Since then, joint committees in many organizations have worked on training, alcoholism, retirement, drug abuse, and safety. Such committees are increasingly addressing issues of worker participation in operating decisions, gain-sharing plans, waste avoidance, job training and self-direction, cooperative projects involving plant layout, and other means to enhance productivity.

Joint committees are not a substitute for collective bargaining or good management. Contract bargaining typically centers on economic issues and often sets aside work problems, which are the primary interest of joint committees. By providing channels of communication between bargaining periods, joint committees may lower tensions by looking into recurring problems; they do not supplant the formal grievance procedures. Furthermore, a year-round bargaining relationship paves the way for the next series of contract negotiations. It is unfortunate that consultations through labor-management committees is often viewed as a court of last resort, installed only for a crisis.[18]

A crisis in the construction industry has fostered closer cooperation between management and building trades in several cities. The large productivity losses recorded by the construction industry have been puzzling because there is no ready explanation for their cause.[19] However, the productivity drop probably had less effect on the creation of joint committees than the growth of open-shop operations, which reached over 60 percent of all construction in 1980, up from 30 percent in 1973.

A 1972 unemployment rate of about 30 percent in St. Louis building trade unions spurred the formation of a labor-management group that also included architects and engineers.[20] Its goal was to arrest escalating construction costs and restore customer confidence in time and cost schedules. For their part, unions agreed to eliminate artificial work restrictions and jurisdictional strikes. Contractors pledged to have materials and equipment available when needed. Other parties also promised to do their part. The cooperative venture produced many changes in restrictive work practices, sometimes painfully given up, but rewarded indirectly by no desertion of contractors from closed shops. By many measures the goals of the group were achieved—greater productivity.

KEEPING SCORE:
Productivity
Measurement

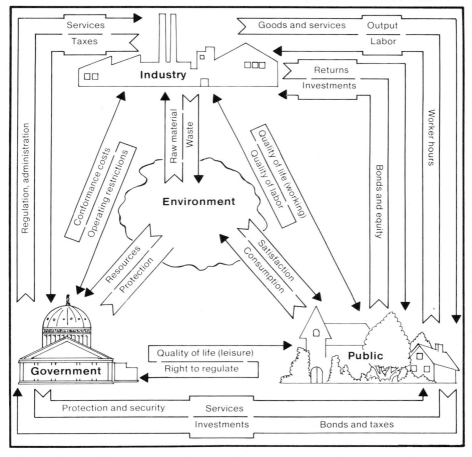

Source: James L. Riggs, *Production Systems: Planning, Analysis and Control*, 3rd ed. (New York: John Wiley, 1981), p. 604.

Without realizing it, we all use productivity measurements in our daily lives. Drivers rate automobiles by the miles per gallon they deliver—the output is distance and the input is fuel. Investors measure their success by the rate of return earned on investments—output profit divided by input capital. A student's grade-point average is the output rating given for the work done to obtain a certain number of credits. These ratios and innumerable others are adaptations of the fundamental measure of efficiency:

$$\text{EFFICIENCY} = \frac{\text{OUTPUT}}{\text{INPUT}}$$

When the ratio is confined to units of production, it becomes

$$\text{Productivity measure} = \frac{\text{Goods and services produced}}{\text{Resources consumed}}$$

The purpose of measuring productivity is to keep score, to see how well something is being done. Some people, however, dislike keeping score, preferring instead to dwell on outcomes without referencing them to the resources consumed in their creation. "There are some things you can't measure," they say, "human feelings and perceptions such as pain, beauty, and affection are intangible effects that have to be interpreted individually." But the inability to register personal feelings on a scale does not detract from the utility of measurements.[1] In fact, statements of feelings lack meaning until they are compared with specified reference points. The difficulty of assigning numbers to subjective considerations is a scarecrow erected to avoid the real issue—How well is something being done?

An overwhelming need for adequate performance measures is manifest in the preceding diagram of the public-government-industry triad and its dependence on the environment.[2] All the pictured flows are represented as output/input ratios. Each bears monitoring, even though some of the measurements may lack preciseness, to detect any abrupt change before it becomes a run in the socioeconomic fabric.

Consider, for instance, the factors involved in the public's "quality of life." The flows show that availability of goods and services, and the capacity to buy them, are functions of working hours in facilities provided by investments. Time spent working is made more or less pleasant by material gains derived from production outputs. The attractiveness of leisure time relies strongly on the services provided by government agencies, which in turn are supported by taxes. These agencies, in concert with the public and industry, attempt to manage the environment. Distortions in any of the relationships impinge on the other factors, which reinforces the importance of auditing flows to maintain the balance of the entire system.

It will be a long time before we have a measurement system sophisticated enough to track all the sensitive factors in a nation's economy, but productivity accounting at sublevels can improve the performance of all the pieces that together constitute the socioeconomic system.

National measures of productivity are considered first in this chapter, followed by methods of measurement for successively smaller organizations. At first glance the methods may seem too demanding, perhaps not worth the effort to obtain the numbers. A good manager should harbor such reservations about all management techniques. Good managers, however, are already measuring performance, so the described methods are just potential refinements of activities that heretofore have not been given deserved attention. But the refinements are not casually acquired. It takes diligence. What follows is heavy reading for the uninitiated. Scanning the chapter furnishes a surface familiarity with vocabulary and concepts, but honest understanding requires sincere study. A plea for stamina is issued in the "PBO Creed for Productivity Measurement":

TO IMPROVE PRODUCTIVITY, YOU MUST MANAGE.
TO MANAGE EFFECTIVELY, YOU MUST CONTROL.
TO CONTROL CONSISTENTLY, YOU MUST MEASURE.
TO MEASURE VALIDLY, YOU MUST DEFINE.
TO DEFINE PRECISELY, YOU MUST QUANTIFY.

VOCABULARY
AND PRECAUTIONS

Productivity measurement is by no means an exact science. Different nations, different corporations, and even different departments within the same organization apply different formulas to measure their productivity. This variation is less serious than it appears because the measurement that counts is the *rate of change*. That is, by whatever tabulation the first count of productivity is established, progress is measured thereafter as a percentage gain or loss from that reference point. *Consistency* is thus a law for productivity measurement.

The difficulty of switching from one measurement procedure to another gives weight to the choice of the initial design. Every well-run organization keeps track of its finances. If it is a profit-making enterprise, the telltale marker is on the bottom line of the income statement. Nonprofit organizations budget equivalently. But these financial numbers only imply how specific resources were utilized. Profitability is *not* a measure of productivity. The former focuses on the short-term flow of funds, and the latter on the long-term utilization of resources. To get the most out of productivity measurement, it is therefore logical to select a design that includes the most critical resources and reports their consumption in relationship to prime operational objectives. Productivity measurements examine the basic efficiency of operations.

Types of Productivity Measures

Since there is no consensus about how productivity should be measured, or definitions for the exercise, we will adopt the following terms and practices.

Total Productivity Measure (TPM) is a ratio of real gross output to all real inputs. Gross output includes all goods and services produced by the organization during a given period. Inputs constitute everything used to generate output—labor, capital, materials, energy, and purchased services.

Partial Productivity Measure (PPM) is the ratio of real gross output to one type of real input. For example, the productivity record cited in Chapter 2 for the United States was based on a partial productivity measure:

$$\text{PPM (U.S.)} = \frac{\text{Gross domestic product (U.S.)}}{\text{Total hours worked}}$$

This is the ratio of output to labor-hours, which is probably the most widely quoted productivity measure.

Total Factor Productivity (TFP) is the ratio of net output to the sum of labor and capital inputs. Net output, also called *value-added output,* equals gross output minus materials (intermediate goods and services consumed in production, such as raw materials, fuel, and containers). Mathematically, TFP just rearranges TPM by taking materials, energy, and services from the denominator to subtract them from gross output in the numerator:

$$\text{TFP} = \frac{\text{Gross output} - \text{Intermediate materials}}{\text{Labor and capital}}$$

Conceptually, intermediate materials are considered to be a throughput representing someone else's productivity, so their elimination gives recognition to the actual value added to a product by the most critical factors of production—labor and capital.

A productivity index is the ratio of successive productivity measurements, usually expressed as the percentage difference between the measurements for two periods. For example, a productivity measure of 142 for 1982 that increased to 149 in 1983 has an index of

$$\frac{149}{142} = 1.049, \text{ or an annual increase of } 4.9\%$$

An index is also used to compare the productivity of one organization with that of another organization or the average rating of several organizations. Thus one company's partial productivity measure for energy consumption could be 0.13 while the industry average for the same PPM was 0.11, yielding an index of 0.13/0.11 = 1.18, or 118 percent. Somewhat similarly, an index is used to describe a figure derived from weighting several components. For instance, a grade-point average is an index of scholastic performance calculated by weighting the grade received for each subject by the number of credits assigned to that subject, and then averaging the weighted grades:

SUBJECT (PRODUCTIVITY CRITERION)	GRADE (PRODUCTIVITY RATING)	CREDITS (WEIGHT)	GRADE POINTS (WEIGHTED RATINGS)
Mathematics	A = 4	4	16
Physics	C = 2	3	6
Geography	B = 3	3	9
Literature	B = 3	3	9
Physical Education	C = 2	1	2
		14	42

$$\text{GPA} = \text{Productivity Index} = 42/14 = 3.0, \text{ or B}$$

A comparable industrial productivity index based on criteria that indicate relative performance against the reported averages of other companies doing like operations can be demonstrated as follows:

PRODUCTIVITY CRITERION	INDUSTRY AVERAGE	COMPANY ACTUAL	PERCENT OF AVERAGE	IMPORTANCE WEIGHT	WEIGHTED RATING
Passenger Miles Employee	84,512	91,014	107.7	0.45	48.5
Freight Received Employee	27,472	16,889	61.1	0.30	18.3
% Occupancy Vehicle	71	78	109.9	0.25	27.5
				Productivity Index =	94.3

The ratios in the table above are *productivity indicators*—measures of performance that indirectly affect the productivity of operations. They are premier characteristics, believed to provide reliable evidence of efficiency, that do not necessarily relate the output of a process directly to its input. They are useful in assessing the productivity of an operation that has no readily discernible output, as in offices, R&D labs, management staffs, and any intermediate stage of a process handled by a distinct organizational unit. Typical characteristics include reject rate, accident severity, absenteeism, calls made, error rate, waste, damage, machine downtime, and turnover. Measured characteristics are combined to get a composite index by assigning an importance weight to each criterion, weighting each rating, and summing the weighted ratings of all the criterion. Several examples of this versatile technique are given later in this chapter and in Chapter 11.

"Real" Dollar Value

Most of the outputs and inputs are measured in dollars. It would be nice if we could always use physical units rather than money value because there would then be no need to correct for inflation. Physical units are generally translated to cash amounts because dollars are used as weights to differentiate unit values. For instance, a pound of grade 1 apples is worth more than a pound of grade 3 apples. An output showing just total pounds of apples could be misleading. In the same way, total labor-hours does not account for differences between skilled and unskilled labor; this is corrected by weighting each class of labor by its wage rate to obtain a total dollar value for the labor unit.

The term *real output* means that the output is stated in constant-value, or "real," dollars. Constant-purchasing power has to be referenced to a base year. A convenient procedure is to call the year in which the first productivity measurement is made the *base year*. Then actual dollar values in subsequent years are converted to their base-year equivalents by applying an appropriate price deflator. As an example, assume that the initial productivity measurement was made last year when gross output amounted to $10 million and the price index number was 195.4, increasing to 214.1 this year. If actual gross output this year is $12 million, the equivalent output in real dollars is

$$\$12,000,000 \times \frac{195.4}{214.1} = \$10,951,891$$

This means that output really increased only 951,891 constant-value dollars during the year, because 214.1/195.4 = 1.0957 dollars are needed this year to buy what could have been purchased last year for one dollar.

Adjustments for inflation should be treated carefully because they may distort productivity ratios. The first decision is to select the price index most representative of the measurements. All inputs are unlikely to be affected identically by price changes, and output price variations will probably differ from input cost variations. When individual price indexes are available for each category, they should be applied accordingly. The Bureau of Labor Statistics publishes price-index numbers for several industrial sectors, and individual corporations sometimes track their own prices. However, the most commonly used deflator is the Producer Price Index, PPI.

The forerunner of the PPI was the Wholesale Price Index, first published in 1902. The Labor Department decided in 1978 to replace it with three price indexes, one each for finished goods, intermediate goods, and crude goods. The Finished Goods Index has been popularized as being *the* Producer Price Index. PPI is not as well known as its more glamorous sister, the Consumer Price Index, CPI, but it is more appropriate for productivity studies because it does not include such extraneous factors as used-car and housing costs. A plot of PPI percentages in Exhibit 16 shows how they vary from month to month. Subsequent discussions of productivity measures assume that all monetary values are deflated to base-year worth; that is, they utilize *real* dollars.

EXHIBIT 16   *THE PRODUCER PRICE INDEX DEFLATOR*

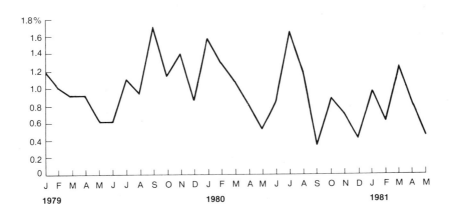

MONTH-TO-MONTH CHANGES IN THE FINISHED GOODS INDEX
Source: Bureau of Labor Statistics.

Who Measures What

Before examining the innards of all the different productivity measures and indicators, a quick assessment of which techniques are most used in industry should help guide the study. In contacts with hundreds of companies, we have found that most of them employ some form of productivity measurement, but very few use a broad, systematic procedure. Where engineered standards are available, companies tend to concentrate on labor efficiency through comparison of actual times with predetermined times for operations. Where energy or raw material is a major expense, productivity measures deal mostly with conservation or yield. In government agencies productivity is generally equated with paper flow and people's performance. Subcontractors tend to focus on quality, reject rates, and waste control as their yardsticks for productivity. Only in large corporations that have sections assigned to productivity control have we encountered comprehensive measures.

These observations are upheld by a survey of large corporations.[3] Less than 0.5 percent of the corporations used either total-productivity or factor-productivity measurements. About 19 percent of the measurements were of partial productivity with their application most often in word-processing, manufacturing, sales, distribution/warehousing, finance/accounting, and marketing functions. The remaining 80 percent were nonstandard productivity indicators such as

> Factory cost per unit produced
> Manufacturing expense per direct labor dollars
> Percentage downtime of production facilities
> Percentage of deliveries made on time
> Labor standard hours per $1,000 of sales

The main drawback to such a hodgepodge of productivity indicators over more complete measures is that indicators may be misleading unless used discriminately. However, this reliance on key indicators is evidence of a hard-nosed approach that focuses on the most worrisome operations.

NATIONAL MEASURES OF PRODUCTIVITY

Do you ever wonder where those productivity statistics that appear in newspapers come from? Or wonder how reliable they are? The information is compiled by the Bureau of Labor Statistics in the U.S. Department of Labor. Data are secured from many sources and are reasonably accurate, but insufficient understanding of the concepts involved often leads to misinterpretation of reports.

Measures of productivity have been kept by the government since the 1880s. Dimensions of the basic measure are output per labor-hour input. This ratio is now computed quarterly and annually for five economic sectors: private business, farm, nonfarm business, manufacturing, and nonfarm nonmanufacturing business. Ten industry groups are measured annually, as are a few individual industries. By the middle of this decade additional ratios will be published that break out the separate components that contribute to productivity. The value of current and forthcoming statistics lies in their application to economic planning.

Planners would like to have more detailed and precise measurements. But data-collection problems are enormous. Not only must such things as "number of hours worked" be collected from all over but the number must also be collected quickly to be put to best use. Consider just the partial productivity measure for the private business sector to observe the complexities.[4]

The output for the business sector is the gross national product with certain exceptions. It includes the market basket of goods and services produced by labor and capital that generate observable income transactions, and imputed values for certain resources without observable market transactions such as food produced and consumed on farms. This information is collected by government agencies, trade associations, and corporations. All revenues are converted to real dollars.

Input is the *unweighted* sum of the *paid* hours of all workers who produced the measured output. Hours-paid-for include holidays, vacation, and sick leave in addition to hours at work. The unweighted sum does not account for differences in workers' skills, education, or experience. Labor data are obtained primarily from current employment records and current population surveys.

The impossibility of obtaining irrefutable figures is easy to appreciate. Measures for the manufacturing sector are most accurate, but these constitute only about 30 percent of total output. Delivery of services is far more difficult to measure. Shortcomings from not being able to measure the ultimate effect or mission can be illustrated by reference to physicians' services: Ideally, improvements to health should be measured, but a lack of dimensions for "health" forces such substitute measures of service as the number of office visits by patients or procedures performed by physicians. Therefore physical measures of output and input are best viewed as approximations of more appropriate measures that distinguish quality as well as quantity.[5]

The measure of the nation's total productivity does not include all workers. General government is the largest excluded sector. Neither the output nor the input of federal, state, and local government employees is counted. Again the measurement difficulties are manifest, yet the Bureau of Labor Statistics has developed measures that cover about 65 percent of the federal civilian work force.[6] Private researchers have developed equivalent measures for certain identifiable services provided by local governments, such as police protection, waste collection, and education.

Not-for-profit institutions are also excluded from measurement. Demonstrable outputs are scarce for hospitals, universities, and churches, but the sheer size of their cash flow begs for some form of representation in productivity statistics. An almost undetectable cash flow occurs in home production—child care, meal preparation, home repairs by owners—and it too is excluded in productivity accounting.

The subtle effect of these exclusions is the creation of bugaboos: "If the experts from BLS can't measure nonmarket activities, how can I expect the productivity of our office staff or legal people or janitors to be measured? They don't have clear outputs other than paper, briefs, and trash."

A more blatant hazard of national productivity measures is misinterpretation. The BLS publishes cautionary statements warning readers not to attribute changes in output-per-hour to labor alone, but these statements seldom make the news releases and may even be ignored by users, as is the warning from the surgeon general on cigarette packs. Output-per-hour is also affected by changes in technology, influx of capital, rates of capacity utilization, and many other factors. An added complexity is that our productivity data cannot be compared directly with other nations' data because of structural differences in the way measurements are taken and vagaries due to monetary exchange rates.[7]

A final caution is to be aware that both national and local productivity measures need to be handled delicately, drawing conclusions carefully to avoid embarrassing or damaging encounters. If the office staff's productivity is measured, *which it can be,* ups and downs have to be put in perspective with external and internal influences. A sudden rise might be owed to a new word processor. A drop might not signal sudden laziness, being caused instead by a flu epidemic or the introduction of new procedures. As Thomas Carlyle said, "Conclusive facts are inseparable from inconclusive except by a head that already understands and knows." Or, as the old Persian proverb goes, Trust in God, but tie your camel.

OTAL PRODUCTIVITY MEASUREMENT

Measuring the total productivity of a firm is immediately below national measurements in complexity. The output of a firm might be called its *gross corporate product* because it is an inclusive summation akin to GNP. Input comprises labor, as in the familiar national measure, plus all the other factors that contributed to the output:

Calculating TPM is an exhausting exercise. Judging from the

Total Productivity Measurement (TPM) =

$$\frac{\text{Products} + \text{Services} + \text{Value added to plant}}{\text{Labor} + \text{Capital} + \text{Energy} + \text{Materials} + \text{Other inputs}}$$

survey reported earlier, not many companies undertake the exercise. Bypassing momentarily all the number-crunching snags, the naked value of a total measure is still questionable. If all corporations calculated TPMs, using the same assumptions and formats, the results could be compared to determine relative efficiency. But all of them do not. A complete set of measurements provides an overview of operational effectiveness, clinically assessing all the resources used in the productive process to reveal the consequences of trade-offs, as in the substitution of capital for labor. But partial measures more readily disclose specific dysfunctions.

Although a few organizations may find total productivity measurement helpful at the firm or plant level, we do not recommend its use. Well-selected productivity indicators or partial measures furnish comparable information at less expense; expensive calipers are wasted where a cheap ruler is sufficient. Nonetheless, the measurement components are worth discussing, since they may be employed individually in confined ratios.

Output

When output is homogeneous, or nearly so, a pure quality measure is sufficient. This is the case in production of a raw material of essentially constant quality—corn, ice, or one grade of coal. When quality varies, as in a combination of anthracite and bituminous coal, weighting is needed—each ton mined is weighted according to the price it fetches. Service organizations that repeatedly perform the same type of work can measure quantity by the number of their output deliveries. Unfortunately, the likelihood of having just one class of output decreases as the size of the organization increases.

Regardless of the size of the unit being measured, it is easy to overlook part of its output. For instance, a firm or department that primarily produces goods or services for outside customers may also have a small fraction of its output delivered to customers inside the corporate shell. Excluding an output resulting from consumption of an included input(s) registers a spurious productivity figure. Equivalently, a reverse effect is caused by including an unearned output.

Changes in product mix during a measurement period have to be accounted for. This situation may require that the reporting period be divided into intervals, one for each change in the mix. Because output is normally limited to the number of units produced, *not* units sold, partially completed units should be counted, their value set by the percentage completed. Both the product-mix and partial-completion irregularities are avoided by expressing output in dollar values. *Real* dollars, that is.

Inputs

If output is the labor of labor, all laborers should be registered. Managers and staff specialists are labor too. A conventional limitation is to include only direct labor with a supplementary figure noting the ratio of direct workers to indirect workers. When the numerator of a productivity measure comprises the total output of a firm, all employees should logically be in the denominator. Any deviations from either total should clearly be stated to avoid misconstructions.

Several reasons support the belief that the common practice of treating labor-hours as a homogeneous input is misleading. It is argued that different kinds of labor make different contributions to output. For instance, differentiating between skilled and unskilled labor is supported by reasoning that more-skilled labor represents a larger labor input per hour of work. Weighting by a skill-related dimension (years of experience, training, etc.) also accommodates recognition of a change in labor mix or wages. This type of weighting helps explain a situation like that of a retail-store chain that closed several stores, keeping its more senior employees by transferring them to the retained outlets. The chain improved its productivity but still had higher labor costs; changes in labor productivity act as a sobering check on trade-offs in labor mix.

Capital investment is conceptually analogous to labor, sometimes called human capital, but there is less agreement about how it should be measured and weighted. The monitoring difference between human and physical capital is the difficulty in tracking the depletion of dollar investments and establishing their earning rates. Four basic methods of capital productivity accounting are in use, with numerous variant forms proposed to overcome perceived inequities.

Perpetual Capital Inventory.   An estimation of capital stock based on asset service life is followed in many nations. It inventories the years of service that an asset possesses productive capacity, and the value of that service each year. At purchase, an asset's annual service contribution is estimated to establish a schedule of depreciation based on actual use, *not* tax life. The perpetual inventory is then a summation of the worth of different vintages of capital assets available in a given year. Each year the portion of an asset's worth that has been "consumed" is dropped from an updated inventory.

To illustrate perpetual capital inventory, assume that a new business purchases a machine for $100,000 with the expectation that it will provide adequate service for four years and then be retired at no additional cost or revenue. Further assume that the machine becomes less efficient with longer ownership, its end-of-year values decreasing to: year 1, $60,000; year 2, $35,000; year 3, $15,000; year 4, $0. According to this schedule, the capital input during the first year is $100,000. In the second year of ownership, $60,000 of the investment capital is left, $40,000 having been expended to produce the first year's output. Next, assume that a second identical machine is purchased one year after the first one at a cost of $110,000. If productivity is measured according to a base year taken as the year the business began, all capital inputs are deflated to that date. Therefore the $60,000 value for the first machine in year 2 is already stated in base-year worth, but the second machine's price must be deflated to its base-year, real-dollar value. Assuming that the price index during the second year went up from 213 to 238, the total capital input in year 2 for both machines is

---

$60,000	(remaining value of three more years of service from machine one)
+ 98,445	$= 110,000 \times \dfrac{213}{238}$ (first cost of machine two, deflated by the price index to the same real-dollar value as machine one)

$158,445	(total capital, stated in base-year value, that contributed to production of the firm's output during its second year of operation)

The perpetual inventory thus tracks the amount of investment funds employed each year in operations.

Annual Capital Cost. A conceptually different and simpler approach is to charge a consumption plus return percentage against total, real-dollar capital stock to obtain the annual capital input. Instead of considering the aggregate investment accounted for in a perpetual capital inventory, only the decrease in total capital attributable to operations is counted. Calculation is simplified by assuming an average life for all physical assets. An assumption of twenty years means that 5 percent of the assets are "consumed" each year; a fifteen-year average service life implies that each asset annually loses 6.67 percent of its value. In addition to the charge for depreciation, a charge is also made for the cost of using the capital. In theory, capital earnings are held to be equivalent to wages paid for labor. If a rate of 13 percent is deemed to be a reasonable return for investors, and a fifteen-year asset life is assumed, annual capital input is calculated by multiplying the total investment by 19.67 percent, that is, 13 percent + 6.67 percent.

Working capital may also be included. Sometimes the value of inventory is lumped together with the amount of cash, accounts receivable, and notes receivable. This total is deflated by an appropriate price index to obtain its real-dollar, base-year value and is then multiplied by the

selected rate-of-return percentage to obtain the working-capital portion
of the capital input.

As an example of the annual capital cost method, let total investment this year be $10 million in physical assets and $1 million in working
capital. Assume that the price index deflator for the current year is 0.83,
a fifteen-year average asset life is applicable, and a realistic *rate of return*
is 13 percent. Then the capital input is

$$
\begin{array}{lll}
\$10,000,000 \times (0.0667 + 0.13) & = \$1,967,000 \\
1,000,000 \times 0.83 \times 0.13 & = 107,900 \\
\text{Annual capital cost (this year)} & \overline{\$2,074,900}
\end{array}
$$

Next, assume that another year has passed in which inflation has pulled
down the price index deflator to 0.76, working capital has increased to
$1.2 million, and another $500,000 has been invested in capital assets.
The value of physical assets is the preceding year's real-dollar investment
total minus the amount depreciated last year, plus the current year's additional real-dollar investment:

$$\$10,000,000 - \$10,000,000(0.0667) + \$500,000 \ (0.76) = \$9,713,000$$

Capital input for the next year is thus

$$
\begin{array}{lll}
\$9,713,000 \times (0.0667 + 0.13) & = \$1,910,547 \\
1,200,000 \times 0.76 \times 0.13 & = 118,560 \\
\text{Annual capital cost (next year)} & \overline{\$2,029,107}
\end{array}
$$

The sum is considered to be the capital input for the second year,
down slightly from the preceding year.

Rental Price.   The rental-price approach visualizes all capital assets
as being leased, including working capital. A rental value could theoretically be determined by going to the marketplace to see how much it
would cost to rent each item used in production. But for many productive
assets, there is no rental agency. Who rents pot lines for producing aluminum or almost any piece of specialized equipment? The alternative is to
calculate a "rental" value by deflating the purchase price of an asset to
its base-year value and then annualizing its cost over its expected life.
The cost includes a profit for the leasor, which is equivalent to the rate of
return expected by an investor.

For an individual asset, the calculation of its annual rental cost is
quick, but collectively the procedure is tedious. After deflating an asset's
purchase price, its base-year value is multiplied by an annuity factor that
determines an annual charge large enough to recover the invested capital

plus a desired return on the investment.[8] If the real-dollar price of an asset is $100,000, its life is ten years, and the expected rate of return is 15 percent, its annual "rental" cost is

$100,000   (annuity factor
            at 15% interest   = $100,000 (0.19925)
            and 10-year life) = $19,925

The sum of the annual rental costs for all assets employed is the capital input for that year.

Book Value.   The simplest way to estimate capital input is to use book values taken directly from accounting records. A total capital investment is then the book value of the complete company, and capital cost is just the sum of all depreciation charges in a year; either figure could be used as the capital input, depending on the analyst's preference for aggregate or annual figures. This simplicity is gained at the expense of accuracy. Book values are less likely to represent the physical consumption of assets than to be write-offs taken to maximize tax advantages for depreciation. The value of capital is distorted by eliminating base-year adjustments. Nonetheless, the convenience of book values allows a rough fix on capital input that might otherwise be forfeited to data-generating difficulties.

None of the methods for determining capital input is completely satisfying. For the sake of convenience and consistency, we recommend the annual capital cost method.

Intermediate Inputs

All other inputs besides labor and capital are classified as intermediate goods and services—things consumed in the process of producing the firm's output. Included are raw materials, operating supplies, semifinished goods to be further refined, purchased services, and all forms of energy. Consumption is measured in real terms by deflating the current year's nominal prices to their base-year equivalents.

Notable productivity gains can be achieved in the handling of intermediate inputs. A small increase in the percentage of finished products obtained from raw or semifinished materials can yield a big boost in productivity, especially in material-intensive industries. Trade-offs between energy consumption and other production inputs are being reexamined as fuel costs climb; conventional wisdom about substituting energy for labor is being questioned, as is the relationship between energy consumption and material acquisition policies.[9]

The conceptual issue about where to include intermediate goods and services in calculating a productivity measure is more cosmetic than cardinal. Consider the following sample data given in real dollars:

	LAST YEAR	THIS YEAR
Gross output	$21,000,000	$23,000,000
Labor input	4,000,000	5,000,000
Capital input	6,000,000	6,000,000
Intermediate goods	10,000,000	11,000,000

Based on these figures, the Total Productivity Measure (TPM) and Total Factor Productivity (TFP) for the firm are

$$\text{TPM}_{(\text{last year})} = \frac{\$21,000,000}{\$4,000,000 + \$6,000,000 + \$10,000,000} = 1.050$$

$$\text{TPM}_{(\text{this year})} = \frac{\$23,000,000}{\$5,000,000 + \$6,000,000 + \$11,000,000} = 1.045$$

$$\text{TFP}_{(\text{last year})} = \frac{\$21,000,000 - \$10,000,000}{\$\ 4,000,000 + \$\ 6,000,000} = 1.100$$

$$\text{TFP}_{(\text{this year})} = \frac{\$23,000,000 - \$11,000,000}{\$\ 5,000,000 + \$\ 6,000,000} = 1.091$$

from which the productivity index for this year is calculated as

$$\text{Productivity Index (TPM)} = \frac{\text{TPM}_{(\text{this year})}}{\text{TPM}_{(\text{last year})}} = \frac{1.045}{1.050} = 0.995, \text{ or } -0.5\%$$

$$\text{Productivity Index (TFP)} = \frac{\text{TFP}_{(\text{this year})}}{\text{TFP}_{(\text{last year})}} = \frac{1.091}{1.100} = 0.992, \text{ or } -0.8\%$$

Both indexes show the same trend, declining productivity. The role of labor and capital receives greater emphasis in the TFP index because only the value added by the factor inputs is considered in the firm's output. Swings in a productivity index are generally larger when a value-added ratio is evaluated; proportionately high intermediate inputs have a damping effect on fluctuations in total productivity measurement. Another example of firm productivity measurement is demonstrated by the tabular format in Exhibit 17.

EXHIBIT 17   *A PRODUCTIVITY PROFILE: TOTAL, FACTOR, AND PARTIAL INDEXES*

> The good news about a total productivity measurement is that it examines all resources used in the productive process. The bad news is that data are needed about all the resources used in the productive process. Obtaining readily available data from accounting records mitigates the bad aspects but compromises the good aspects by delivering a less than complete picture. A profile is better than no picture at all.

Productivity analysis of annual operations

	1 9 8 2			1 9 8 3			Productivity Rise (82-83)
	Current Dollars (in 100s)	Price Index (1981 = 100)	Constant (1981) Dollars	Current Dollars (in 100s)	Price Index (1981 = 100)	Constant (1981) Dollars	
1. Net sales	$1,831	108	$1,695	$2,293	122	$1,880	
2. Labor	295	107	276	352	120	293	
3. Materials	880	105	838	1,161	131	886	
4. Services	301	106	284	365	118	309	
5. Depreciation			96			122	
6. Total inputs (2 + 3 + 4 + 5)			1,494			1,610	
7. Net output (1 − 3 − 4)			573			685	
8. Factor input (2 + 5)			372			415	
9. Labor Productivity (1/2)			6.14			6.42	4.6%
10. Factor Productivity (7/8)			1.54			1.65	7.1%
11. Total Productivity (1/6)			1.13			1.17	3.5%

Source: James L. Riggs, *Production Systems: Planning, Analysis and Control,* 3rd ed. (New York: John Wiley, 1981), p. 582.

> In the accompanying table, five categories represent a firm's productivity posture. Four of the categories are deflated by their associated price indexes to legitimatize year-to-year comparability. The other category, depreciation, represents capital inputs as the sum of the year's depreciation charges, based on book values that are assumed to be nonresponsive to current price changes. These five categories, listed numerically as 1-5, are combined in different patterns to produce three productivity ratios, numbered 9-11, which conform to previously defined productivity measures:

Partial Productivity(9): PPM (labor = Net sales/Labor

Factor Productivity(10): TFP $= \dfrac{\text{Net output/}}{\text{Labor + Depreciation}}$

Total Productivity(11): TPM   = Net sales/Total inputs

Calculations are straightforward. Real-dollar values for 1981 result from Constant dollars = Current dollars $\times \dfrac{100}{\text{Price index}}$.

The productivity indexes in the lower-right column are for the 1983 production year and are calculated as

Productivity Index (1983) =
$$\dfrac{\text{Productivity ratio (1983)} - \text{Productivity ratio (1982)}}{\text{Productivity ratio (1982)}} \times 100\%$$

For example:

$$\text{Total Productivity Index (1983)} = \dfrac{1.17 - 1.13}{1.13} \times 100\% = 3.5\%$$

All of the partial productivity indexes, except capital, indicate improved productivity for 1983:

Labor Productivity Index	=	4.6%	(1/2)
Capital Productivity Index	=	−12.5%	(1/5)
Material Productivity Index	=	5.0%	(1/3)
Services Productivity Index	=	1.8%	(1/4)

The positive Factor Productivity Index (10) masks the negative effect of capital productivity.

Once the ratios have been calculated, the critical phase of interpretation begins. Perhaps expenditures for equipment nourished the gains in labor and material productivity. The workings of such trade-offs are not explicit from productivity measures, but the consequences are evident.

PARTIAL PRODUCTIVITY MEASURES

Classical measures of partial productivity are derived from dividing total output of a firm by any single input factor. These are illustrated in Exhibit 17. A more revealing measure may be the output of a department or any individual operating unit of an organization; for instance, circuit boards prepared by one department are naturally the output of interest for that unit. Similarly, the number of deliveries made in one geographic area by a division of a service agency tells more about that division than total deliveries by the whole agency. Outputs and inputs from separate operating units are simply scaled-down versions of firm productivity measurements, harassed by the same difficulties of proper weighting, but somewhat smoothed by better access to data.

A formula that looks forbidding at the first glance, but is really quite reasonable, conveniently accommodates both real-dollar equivalence and output-input weightings. In verbal form it is

Partial Productivity Index (PPI) =
$$\frac{[(\text{Constant-price output})/(\text{Constant-cost input})]\text{ current period}}{[(\text{Constant-price output})/(\text{Constant-cost input})]\text{ base period}}$$

Replacing words with symbols:

$$PPI = \frac{[(\Sigma O_1 P_0)/(\Sigma I_1 C_0)]}{[(\Sigma O_0 P_0)/(\Sigma I_0 C_0)]}$$

The symbol Σ is a summation sign that indicates a total value for weighted output or input during a certain period. The symbols O and I indicate, respectively, output and input quantities; and P and C indicate, respectively, output price and input cost. Subscripts attached to each symbol refer to the period in which each measurement is taken; zero and one, respectively, refer to the base period and the current period. Thus $\Sigma O_1 P_0$ is read: "Sum of the products obtained from multiplying each quantity in the current period by its base-period price." Rewriting the ratio to collect outputs in the numerator, the working equation takes the form

$$PPI = \frac{(\Sigma O_1 P_0)/(\Sigma O_0 P_0)}{(\Sigma I_1 C_0)/(\Sigma I_0 C_0)}$$

The formula above is applied to data from the following table to demonstrate its applicability. Two types of products, Models A and B, are produced by workers in two wage categories, Rates 1 and 2. The number of units produced and the hours required to produce them in the base year (0) and the current year (1) are shown in the table.

PRODUCTION DATA, BASE YEAR (0)					
OUTPUT	Model A	Model B	INPUT	Rate 1	Rate 2
Units produced	5,000	2,000	Labor hours/Unit	9,000	7,500
Price per unit	$ 50	$ 90	Labor cost/Unit	$ 12	$ 16

PRODUCTION DATA, CURRENT YEAR (1)

OUTPUT	Model A	Model B	INPUT	Rate 1	Rate 2
Units produced	6,000	2,000	Labor hours/Unit	11,500	7,000
Price per unit	$ 70	$ 100	Labor cost/Unit	$ 13	$ 18

Substituting figures from the table into the formula

$$\text{PPI} = \frac{[6,000(\$50) + 2,000(\$90)]/[5,000(\$50) + 2,000(\$90)]}{[11,500(\$12) + 7,000(\$16)]/[9,000(\$12) + 7,500(\$16)]}$$

$$= \frac{\$480,000/\$430,000}{\$250,000/\$228,000} = \frac{1.116}{1.096}$$

$$= 1.02, \text{ or } 2\% \text{ increase}$$

indicates that labor productivity has increased by 2 percent during the year when output and input quantities are weighted by their economic worth. Note that the value of output in the current year increased slightly less than 12 percent strictly from production of more Model A units, since both years' outputs were weighted by the same base-year prices. Meanwhile, labor cost increased 9.6 percent, as a result of more hours worked and a change in labor mix that shifted toward lower-wage workers. The formula only insinuates the relationship between changes in product mix and corresponding changes in labor mix, yet the index is a significant score by which performances in different time periods are equivalently compared, though it alone does not explain the cause of a high score, nor does it more than imply potential remedies for poor performance.[10] More explicit readings about causes of high or low productivity are likely from scoring operational characteristics, called productivity indicators.

HANDY PRODUCTIVITY RATIOS

Scratchpad jottings about production performance have undoubtedly been fixtures of management as long as there have been managers. These impromptu measures are now receiving acclaim. They are known as *productivity indicators*.

An *indicator* is usually a ratio of two physical quantities that characterize the performance of one portion or one mission of a production system. Its limited scope distinguishes it from a partial-productivity measure, although indicators for a total firm may utilize quantities that constitute a substantial portion of total output and input. For example, total output of a newspaper publisher includes many printing projects in addition to issuing a daily paper, yet the nation's largest newspaper chain, Gannett, gauges its productivity by an indicator ratio of the number of worker-hours expended per newspaper page printed. Conversely, Texas Instruments has developed a whole family of indicators, ranging from the physical amount of goods produced per worker to net sales billed per non-production-line employee.

The selection of productivity indicators is guided by productivity objectives. *Each indicator should reflect a controllable facet of production to disclose how efficiently a particular resource is used to meet a specified objective.* While most indicators pertain to internal operations of designing, producing, and marketing a product, external indicators measure customer service, as in ratios of complaint per-product-sold, and late-versus-total deliveries. Indicators are especially useful for service and government organizations that do not produce an easily identifiable product. Various measurable functions that are conducted regularly represent the output, and the resource associated with each function is the input: bills collected per employee, clients served per caseworker, patient-days per capacity, paid miles per taxi, revenue per service slot, and so forth.

The difference between financial ratios and productivity ratios is that the former measure financial flows and the latter physical flows. In some instances, the same ratio measures both types of flow: rate of return is simultaneously a financial and a capital productivity ratio (net profit/investment), and an inventory turnover ratio concurrently measures dollar flow and physical flow of materials (Net sales/Inventory). Some additional productivity ratios in common use include the following:

$$\frac{\text{BTUs}}{\text{Weight of product shipped}} \qquad \frac{\text{Weight of product shipped}}{\text{Employees}}$$

$$\frac{\text{Net sales}}{\text{Sales employees}} \qquad \frac{\text{Units produced per day}}{\text{Machine-hours}}$$

$$\frac{\text{Output}}{\text{Area of space utilized}} \qquad \frac{\text{Loss of produce}}{\text{Total commodities sold}}$$

$$\frac{\text{Total revenue } - \text{ Interest income}}{\text{Total cost } - \text{ Interest expense}} \qquad \frac{\text{Premiums} + \text{Investment income} + \text{Paid benefits}}{\text{Staff payroll } + \text{ Office equipment cost } + \text{Overhead}}$$

Endless variations are possible from the core ratios based on properties included in the total-productivity formula. An indicator, for instance, may substitute floor space or machine time for the capital input of the total productivity measure. And the ratios may be inverted for forensic purposes, as in BTU/Output rather than Output/Energy.

Two precautions hedge the substitution of indicators for sanctioned productivity measures. Foremost is the omission of deflators in most indicators, precluding year-to-year comparisons when inflation is rampant, which it has been irregularly. Second, too much reliance on one or two indicators may yield a deceptive impression, casting blame in the wrong direction or glossing over weaknesses. Nonetheless, a full array of well-understood ratios forms a robust menu for productivity promotion.

EXHIBIT 18   *THE TIME-STANDARD STANDBY*

Engineered work standards have been used and abused, lauded and lambasted, since the turn of this century. The stopwatch put the science in "scientific management" and industrial engineers became the architects of work design. The discipline has matured since the infamous era of "efficiency experts," benefiting from advances in mathematics and cross-fertilization from psychology and anthropometrics, but suspicion lingers.

Aside from the notion that people tend to distrust any system that measures their personal performance, and criticism from the direct labor sector that only its work is exposed to timing, the basic issue of fairness exists. Time standards rest on the definition of a "normal pace" that can be attained and maintained by an average worker during a typical working day without undue fatigue. Trouble comes when the adjectives in the definition are put into practice. Until "average," "typical," and "undue" are blessed with consensus, there will be tension, and this anxiety is the antithesis of high-quality work life. Building trust is therefore the prerequisite to productivity improvement in organizations that rely on time standards to measure work performance.

The ratio of actual hours to standard hours for work accomplishment is a superb productivity indicator when its accuracy and reliability are accepted by both workers and management. A 1:1 ratio means that workers are achieving the level of output that satisfies management, assuming that the integrity of the standard has not been bargained away. A mutually approved standard is both a floor and a ceiling. Performance below standard is grounds for discipline, and performance above is open to suspicion—why do more than is expected? Then the corollary question is, How can productivity be improved beyond the stated level of satisfactory achievement? There are ways.

Ignoring the desperate resort of renegotiating standards, a frequently used tactic is to offer incentives for output above 100 percent of standard. There are abundant incentive plans to choose from. A more fundamental approach is to penetrate into the structure of standards to identify ways to improve work methods, reduce delays due to machine stoppages and lack of materials, provide equipment that raises quality, and redesign the workplace to make it more conducive to high performance. Most of these improvements cater to the familiar "work smarter, not harder" philosophy, minimizing resistance to changes in standards by adding to the output without accelerating the work pace. Most fruitful implementations are the result of a joint effort between workers, supervisors, and industrial engineers.

Engineered standards will surely continue to be the basis for most direct labor measurements and they will increasingly be applied to measure indirect labor, even in the realm of "knowledge" workers.[11] The expertise to do so is being refined. Still, it must be acknowledged that whatever is capable of being done well is also capable of being done poorly.

INTERFIRM PRODUCTIVITY COMPARISON

Comparison of selected productivity indicators among firms within a limited industrial sector is a potent tool for management. The mechanism is simple. Data about common operations are exchanged by firms through a third party to ensure confidentiality. Each firm receives a report tabulating its performance in several categories and its standing in these categories relative to other participating companies. By comparing a firm's standings with competitors' standings, managers locate their firm's weaknesses and strengths, enabling them to concentrate their attention and resources where most needed.

Interfirm comparisons are conducted in many countries. They were instituted by the United Kingdom Centre for Interfirm Comparison in 1959 as an activity of the British Productivity Council; studies were undertaken in more than fifty industries covering over one thousand firms. The Australian Department of Productivity arranges comparisons among fifteen hundred firms in sixty industries. An Australian businessman strongly endorses interfirm comparison (IFC): "We thought we were efficient in the employment of resources but after having taken part in the last two IFC's, we have been shown numerous avenues for improvement, we are now convinced that directing a business without IFC is like driving at night without lights."[12]

In contrast to the government-sponsored studies in other countries, trade associations run most of the interfirm comparisons in the United States. But there are not many of them, perhaps fifty or so. Typifying the associations involved in comparative measurements are Air Transport, North American Wholesale Grocers, National Screw Machine Products, and American Railroads. Productivity ratios are featured for intrinsic operations and are supplemented by general financial ratios, as illustrated in Exhibit 19.

EXHIBIT 19   *RALLY ROUND THE RATIOS*

A "Business Index Report," issued monthly by the National Screw Machine Products Association, reports industry averages from over two hundred member companies for such ratios as

Sales/Screw machine-hours   Capacity usage/Machine-hours
Sales/All machine-hours   Orders received/Screw machine
Sales/Man-hours worked   Average backlog/Company

The annual "Management Ratio Report" provides ratios categorized by
sales dollar volume (four levels) and equipment type (three kinds) that
allow companies to compare their performance with that of other companies of the same size and similar facilities. Also included are broad ratios
for

Turnovers (Net sales/Total employees,
          Net sales/Total assets, etc.)
Operations (Direct labor/Value added,
          Administration/Value added, etc.)
Finance (Current assets/Current liabilities,
          Long-term debt/Working capital, etc.)

The information exchange is perhaps most valuable to smaller companies. Seth Young, general manager of Enoch Manufacturing which
employs about eighty-five people, says, "Interfirm comparison data keeps
us finely tuned to the rest of the industry. I would feel very handicapped as
a manager without access to this information on a regular basis."[13]

General Genealogy

Distinctions between cost ratios and productivity ratios are not
always obvious. Every business manager is intimately concerned with
financial figures and is likely to believe that this concern automatically
embraces productivity. Profitability is the punch line to the story, but
productivity is the theme. Cost ratios tell whether gross margins
adequately cover costs; they do not tell whether an operation is as efficient as it could be, or whether it is as efficient as the industry norm.
Only productivity ratios give this information.

The relationships between financial and productivity ratios are outlined in Exhibit 20. From the number one ratio that relates profit to
investment, progressive differentiations lead to economic indicators, cost
indicators, operating indicators, and so on. The family of ratios shown
within each indicator classification has many relatives that are not listed.
Additional entries customize the comparison with specific industry sectors or service agencies.

The closer a ratio comes to representing the formative stages of the
product, the more clues it reveals for productivity improvement. Each
ratio in Exhibit 20 bears a message. For instance, a figure higher than the
median ratio for

Ratio 4   indicates that manufacturing expense is disproportion-
           agely large.

EXHIBIT 20   *FAMILY TREE OF RELATIVE RATIOS*

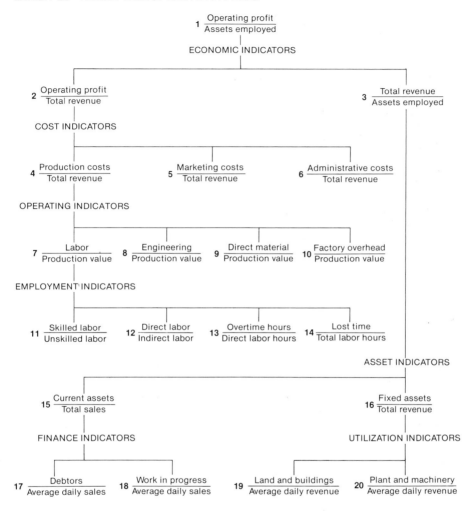

Ratio 9   suggests excessive spoilage, lack of standardization, or inefficient purchasing.

Ratio 10   implies higher than average energy costs, maintenance, or level of depreciation.

Ratio 14   suggests the possibility of unpleasant working conditions, poor staff relations, unattractive factory location, or personality problems.

Ratio 18   recognizes the problems in work flow, plant layout, length of the production cycle, or number of "rush" orders received.

Ratio 20   indicates ownership of more capacity or more expensive plant and machinery than other companies, which should be compensated by significantly lower labor cost, ratio 7.

A single corporation or government agency with several organizational divisions may benefit as much from internal as external comparisons of productivity indicators. The ratios locate areas of excellence in different divisions and may explain reasons for favorable readings. Just paying attention to financial ratios can obscure long-run effects on productivity, making a manager temporarily look good by sacrificing future productivity capability for current profits, or conversely, not giving a manager credit for laying the foundation for future productivity growth. Cost ratios show today's competitive standing. Productivity ratios foretell tomorrow's position.

Struggle to Start

Appreciating productivity comparison is a gulf away from applying it. A few consulting firms offer comparison services in which they visit the participating companies to extract necessary information directly from company records. Most associations that do comparisons provide a set of directions and preprinted forms to assist their members in collecting the data themselves. Completed forms are checked for superficial errors before submitting the data to a computer. Printouts of the digested data, and possibly a supplementary analysis of results, are returned to the participants. The mechanics of the comparison process are simple compared to the difficulties of getting started.

Companies first have to be convinced by missionaries to participate. Imre Bernolak, director of the Canadian Productivity Analysis Branch, recalls that the way to get firms to cooperate was to concentrate first on analysis of their profitability, and then to build in productivity measures. Questions about confidentiality of information and the legality of sharing it with competitors may also deter participation.[14]

Definitions are the most frustrating start-up problem. A pound is not a sufficient designator of weight, nor is an hour simply an hour. A pound must be defined as dry weight, dead weight, unpackaged weight, grade weight, or some other weighty classification. Should a labor-hour include coffee break, vacation time, supervisory time, and other hours that are paid but not actually used in production? Can everyone agree to the same line between direct and indirect labor? What is included in maintenance cost? In setting up interfirm comparison arrangements, we have seen these issues debated exhaustively.[15] And it was worth every minute of debate to achieve complete agreement, because one piece of rotten data rots the rest when figures are averaged.

After the survey design has been approved, data have been submitted and audited, and the computer run has been completed, the final step is analysis. A trained analyst should provide commentary on significant numbers. A printout minus explanation comes close to being an index without a text.

TEAM PRODUCTIVITY
MEASURES

While winding through the maze of productivity measures, indexes, and indicators, the purpose of the trek is blurred by the interminable number manipulations. *The mission of productivity measurement is to improve productivity*—not to control operations, scale profits, set wages, reward or punish managers, or reduce costs. Success or failure of the mission indeed affects operations, profits, wages, and costs, but these are outgrowths rather than contributions to productivity. The contributors are those who organize resources and produce the output.

An ideal productivity measurement system would be equally applicable to skill-based and knowledge-based activities. Output from the former is physical and consequently amenable to measurement. So-called knowledge-workers—engineers, computer programmers, executives, purchasing agents, etc.—exercise judgment to plan, schedule, control, and analyze things, making their contribution to productivity difficult to assess. Moreover, there is often a lengthy lag between the time a decision is made by a knowledge-worker and the effect of the decision is evident. Yet both types of workers share many performance characteristics that determine how well their work is done.

Keeping in mind the mission of measurement, and the need to measure all kinds of productive activity, the following attributes appear desirable for an effective measurement system:

1. Output should be directly attributable to its source. Reciprocally, the people who do the work should be credited with what they produce.
2. Only output that contributes to the organization's goals deserves recognition. Little or no credit is bestowed on activities unrelated to the primary thrust of production or service. People tend to work toward what is measured, so what is measured should be what will do the most for productivity.
3. Wherever possible, use objective rather than subjective measures. Simple, imperfect measures are usually preferable to complex, closer-to-perfect measures: Unadorned gauges are better understood by those being counted and by those doing the counting.
4. The performance of cohesive groups or teams of workers should be measured rather than that of individual workers. Team measures are perceived as less threatening and encourage cooperation among members.
5. The same measurement procedure should be applicable to working teams at all levels in the organization. "Workers" include managers and professional staff. Uniformity enhances acceptability, given it is rational.
6. Team members ideally select the attributes by which their performance is determined or, at a minimum, participate in the development of the measurement plan. Thereafter, workers should be able to monitor their own performance according to the procedure they have helped design. This closes the feedback loop.

7. Each attribute of team performance must be controllable by team members. Corrective action to improve performance cannot be initiated by a team if it cannot influence the inhibiting factors.

8. Quality of performance should be linked to quantity of output. Trade-off proportions between quality and quantity should be expressed as clearly as possible. Timeliness of output is considered to be a measure of quality.

9. Productivity indicators must direct performance toward achievable goals without implying a ceiling on accomplishment. Evaluation of indicated performance should be scaled to realistic expectations. An unreasonably high objective discourages any drive for improvement, an embarrassment to both the drivers and the driven. Alternatively, easy-to-reach objectives offer no challenge. Every indicator should serve a purpose, exposing a specific pathway to improvement.

10. Every designated group of employees or naturally formed team should have its own set of indicators with each indicator weighted according to its importance to the company's productivity objective. The end result is a single score for each organizational unit, a mini version of a total firm productivity measure. Different indicators are needed for each team because teams have different responsibilities. Weights are applied to each set of indicators to inform team members of the activities that they should emphasize to promote overall performance. Scores are kept to determine progress from one period to the next, *not to compare one team with another.*

No measurement system is going to fully satisfy all ten desirable features listed above, or any other list of theoretical musts. As operation researchers say, the solution is to "satisfice"—to strive for perfection while being willing to settle for a less ambitious eminence that gets the job done. The first forfeiture in satisficing for a practical productivity index is the substitution of performance attributes for actual outputs and inputs. These substitutes are called "surrogate measures" because they represent output and input quantities by measurements of productive performance that contribute to the real quantities. Also forfeited are consistency and equivalence that allow one-to-one comparison of results between independent organizations and between deflated values from one year to the next. But gains from this satisficing include versatility, workability, and goal orientation that foster more personal involvement by all concerned with the measurement process.

We recommend a multifaceted measurement system, based on productivity-by-objectives principles, which we call the *Objectives Matrix* because it objectively measures performance, sets objectives for future team accomplishments, and incorporates quantitative recognition to management objectives.

Construction of a Team-
Performance Measurement Matrix

By definition, a *matrix* is "that within which something originates, takes form." The Objectives Matrix molds performance in ways that promote better communication and stimulate productive behavior. No measurement device can accomplish these objectives if it is forced on a group and applied dictatorially. The people whose performance is to be measured should participate in the construction of their matrix and become immersed in its application. They must realize and accept the purpose of measurement and then be willing to adapt their activities to attain objectives from which they will benefit.

Team measurement is an exercise in mutual trust. If management measures with the intent to use the scores to whip people into line and to discipline weak performance, the exercise misfires. Management by threat leads to failure by revolt. If team members scorn the measurement system or ridicule it, nothing worthwhile will be accomplished and conditions may even be worsened by its introduction. Therefore the first phase of matrix construction is to build a firm foundation of confidence.

When both parties act in good faith, understanding each other's concerns, the structural properties of the matrix format can institutionalize cooperation. Four phases in the development of an Objectives Matrix are described next. Each phase contains one or more of the ten desirable features listed previously for a measurement system.

1. Selecting Performance Criteria.   A group of workers engaged in any part of manufacturing, providing any type of service, or performing any function that supports an organization's output has certain characteristics that distinguish poor performance from good performance. These are the criteria of performance for the team. Criteria are usually stated in the form of a ratio, but the ratio need not be a conventional productivity ratio of output per input. Many criteria for white-collar and knowledge-worker teams do not include output quantities. Instead, surrogates for output focus on measurable modes of behavior that are known to affect the output of the unit. For example, team personnel performance criteria could include the following:

$$\frac{\text{Hours missed from irregular absences}}{\text{Total possible work-hours for the team}} \qquad \frac{\text{Number of quits}}{\text{Average team size}}$$

$$\frac{\text{Number of appointments missed}}{\text{Total appointments}} \qquad \frac{\text{Number of calls made}}{\text{Number of callers}}$$

$$\frac{\text{Overtime hours required}}{\text{Total regular working hours}} \qquad \frac{\text{Number of hours lost to accidents}}{\text{Total paid hours}}$$

Criteria that represent results of team activities include such ratios as the following:

$$\frac{\text{Equivalent vehicles unloaded}}{\text{Labor-hours}} \qquad \frac{\text{Weight handled}}{\text{Labor-hours}}$$

$$\frac{\text{Number of orders processed}}{\text{Number of department hours}}$$

$$\frac{\text{Number of drawings}}{\text{Number of drafting-hours}}$$

$$\frac{\text{Volume of caseloads}}{\text{Employee day}}$$

$$\frac{\text{Number of pages completed}}{\text{Employee day}}$$

Quality of performance is assessed by the following specific ratios:

$$\frac{\text{Number of defects}}{\text{Units produced}}$$

$$\frac{\text{Hours of rework required}}{\text{Units produced}}$$

$$\frac{\text{Number of customer complaints}}{\text{Orders delivered}}$$

$$\frac{\text{Number of late deliveries}}{\text{Total number of deliveries}}$$

$$\frac{\text{Number of data entry errors}}{\text{Number of data lines}}$$

$$\frac{\text{Number of policy errors}}{\text{Number of new policies}}$$

Team members have responsibility for helping to generate the criteria by which team performance will be judged. Their decisions are guided by three rules:

1. Criteria pertain only to team activities that contribute to the accomplishment of the whole organization's productivity goals.
2. Achievement of criteria relies on actions controlled by team members.
3. Criteria must represent all aspects of team responsibility, including quality of performance.

The number of criteria selected usually ranges from four to seven per team.

2. Establishing Performance Scales. When team members understand that they are going to collect the measurements for the performance criteria they select, the ratios are almost always quantifiable. Occasionally a team insists that an intangible characteristic such as loyalty or enthusiasm be included as a criterion of productivity. In most cases it is possible to associate tangible outcomes from loyal or enthusiastic performance that satisfy the team's concern for these intangible attributes, thereby substituting objective indicators for subjective impressions. When a team believes a criterion with no natural measure of results is a vital indicator of its performance, an artificial scale can be established. A rating form is devised in which each level of accomplishment is described by a written statement. Carefully crafted statements make the assignment of a score relatively easy.[16]

Performance scales in the Objectives Matrix run from 0 to 10. There are thus eleven levels of accomplishment for each criterion. Assignment of results expected at each level is the crucial part of scaling because the results set specific accomplishments that reflect a team's productivity objectives. The scale is anchored by designated numbers at three levels:

Level 0   The lowest level of performance over a recent period, say the last two years, in which normal operating conditions existed.

Level 3   Operating results that represent the current level of performance by the team.

Level 10   A realistic estimate of results that can be attained with essentially the same resources available to the team in the foreseeable future, say two years.

Levels 0 and 3 are clearly defined benchmarks. Level 10 is the challenge. An overly optimistic estimate of improvement may later prove to be discouraging, and a conservative estimate may put a lid on accomplishment. A trained facilitator to assist the team in setting objectives is almost indispensable at this stage and is valuable throughout the matrix construction process.

Comparing the rating scale with a thermometer is a useful analogy. As depicted in Exhibit 21, the 0-to-10 scale for a performance criterion stretches from the bulb to the top of the thermometer, and each interval between markers is associated with a range of numbers from the productivity indicator for that criterion. The measurement in the example is based on the ratio of rejected units per thousand units produced during the period and represents the quality of output for the team. By consensus, the team has agreed to shoot for a quality level of ten defective units in every thousand produced, reducing the present defect rate by 78 percent.

Equal intervals of measured results are commonly assigned to each

EXHIBIT 21   *TEN-POINT "THERMOMETER" REJECT-RATE INDICATOR OF QUALITY*

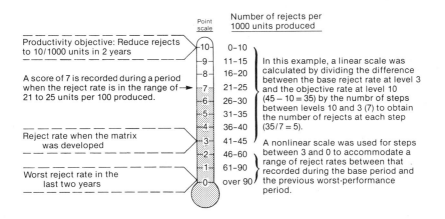

Productivity objective: Reduce rejects to 10/1000 units in 2 years	Point scale	Number of rejects per 1000 units produced	
	10	0–10	
	9	11–15	In this example, a linear scale was calculated by dividing the difference between the base reject rate at level 3 and the objective rate at level 10 (45 − 10 = 35) by the numbr of steps between levels 10 and 3 (7) to obtain the number of rejects at each step (35/7 = 5).
	8	16–20	
A score of 7 is recorded during a period when the reject rate is in the range of 21 to 25 units per 100 produced.	7	21–25	
	6	26–30	
	5	31–35	
	4	36–40	
Reject rate when the matrix was developed	3	41–45	A nonlinear scale was used for steps between 3 and 0 to accommodate a range of reject rates between that recorded during the base period and the previous worst-performance period.
	2	46–60	
	1	61–90	
Worst reject rate in the last two years	0	over 90	

point on the scale, as shown for points 3 through 10 in Exhibit 21. These seemingly linear proportions actually represent increasingly larger percentages of improvement for each upward step in the scale. To progress from the midpoint of level 8 (eighteen rejects per thousand units) to the midpoint of level 9 (thirteen rejects) is a $(18 - 13)/18 \times 100$ percent $= 27.7$ percent improvement, as opposed to a $(43 - 38)/43 \times 100$ percent $= 11.6$ percent improvement gained by going from level 3 to level 4. Linear or nonlinear intervals can be utilized for any of the criteria, and a single criterion may even use both. The vital issue is complete understanding of the whole measurement process by all team members.

3. Rating the Relative Importance of Performance Criteria. Management has responsibility for assigning an importance weighting to each criterion developed by every team. Weighting factors reflect the relative contribution, as perceived by management, of each type of performance to the organization's productivity objectives. For instance, if reducing the amount of wasted raw material is a critical problem, the "waste reduction" criterion would be weighted most heavily.

Weight assignment is not a trivial undertaking. It provides managers with the opportunity to direct attention to areas that they feel have greatest potential for productivity improvement. Ambitious teams naturally concentrate on the criteria that tender the most recognition. A weight for "waste reduction" twice as large as "out put per hour," for example, encourages a team to conserve raw materials, perhaps at the expense of lowering output to avoid scrap. Importance ratings thus establish values for trade-offs between productivity improvement efforts.

A small committee can adequately determine the importance factors. Committee members should be familiar with the firm's long-range productivity objectives and current operating conditions. The same members should serve fairly long terms to ensure consistency in the weighting process. Continued association also improves the efficiency of the weight-assignment process. We suggest that 100 points be distributed among the criteria selected by a team, each point suggesting one percent of the team's productivity-improvement emphasis. By this reasoning, a criterion that possesses a 40-point weight should receive 40 percent of the team's attention. After the first couple of weighting sets have been hammered out by the committee, subsequent assignments become easier. But they become no less important.

4. Calculating the Team Productivity Indicator. The final phase of team measurement ties together criteria points and weights to determine a performance index. Periodically, once a month or quarter, a team meets to calculate its weighted productivity score. Performance results are secured from appropriate departments (accounting, personnel, quality control, computing, etc.) to supplement the tallies the team has accumulated. Results are translated to points earned in each criterion according to a "thermometer" reading, as shown in Exhibit 21. Then each point rating is multiplied by the weight assigned to that criterion by the management committee. The sum of the weighted criterion scores is the team's productivity index for the period.

The calculation procedure is illustrated below and is identical in concept to the grade-point average calculation demonstrated on page 63:

CRITERION	RESULTS	POINTS	× WEIGHT	=	WEIGHTED SCORE
Quality: Rejects per 1,000 units	22 units	7	25		175
Yield: Wastes per ton of raw material	410 pounds	3	40		120
Output: Completed units per 100 labor-hours	27 units	5	25		125
Safety: Hours lost per total labor-hours	0.004	6	10		60
			Productivity Indicator	=	480

This is the unique productivity indicator for one team; it has no relevance to indicators for other teams based on different criteria.

Implementation of Team Productivity Measurement

To say that "you have to have teams before you can measure their performance by the Objectives Matrix system" is a redundant reminder, considering the nature of matrix construction. A nominal group gathered together just to formulate a measurement system, and then disbanded, seldom has as much concern as a permanent team in making the system succeed. Systems similar to the Objectives Matrix are in use in organizations that do not have a team structure. We have helped implement customized versions in which managers determined the criteria, rating scale, and weighting factors for operations they felt could not be measured adequately by traditional methods. We believe, however, that the full benefit of the Objectives approach is obtained only through full involvement among and between workers and management.

The weighted indicator system is perhaps most attractive for non-manufacturing activities where measurement is generally more difficult, but it nicely supplements engineering standards when these are available. Output measured by time standards might be one of an array of criteria for which the ratio is "Actual time/Standard time." The weighting for this criterion would probably dominate other criteria, but including additional considerations in an overall assessment of performance creates a stronger management tool. If combined with team involvement, it can also create motivation.

A series of team productivity scores must be collected before they can actually become useful. One team score is about as valuable as a single shoe. The first one calculated is simply that—a score, nothing more. What counts is the rate of change from one period to the next:

$$\text{Team Productivity Index} = \frac{\text{Score this period minus score last period}}{\text{Score last period}} \times 100\%$$

The perspective provided by continuous indexing is destroyed by changes in the rating scale or weights. Maximum usefulness is therefore obtained by correctly setting up the initial measurements and continuing them over several periods.

A suggested format for the Objectives Matrix and detailed examples of its implementation are given in Chapter 11.

SETTING EXAMPLES: Management Practices

Action to Improve Productivity	Ranking for Probable Success	Type of Improvement Expected				
		Improved efficiency: lower total operating costs, savings in labor and machine time, less waste of material, etc.	*Improved effectiveness*: growth in total revenues and/or profits, better decision making and communications, etc.	*Higher performance*: improve quality of output, increased flexibility, fewer breakdowns and accidents, etc.	*Greater organizational vitality*: more initiative and involvement, more worker stability, greater co-operation and job satisfaction, etc.	
Machines: Replace manual labor by machines, get faster or more reliable equipment (automate).	4	82% 13 5	64% 29 7	71% 19 10	17% 47 36	Positive effect No effect Negative effect
Management: Better coordination and budgeting, more inspiring leadership (motivate).	1	82% 36 2	83% 15 2	56% 42 2	85% 13 2	Positive effect No effect Negative effect
Processes: Improve scheduling and material flow, more accurate--faster data flow (computerize).	2	78% 19 3	75% 22 3	62% 36 2	34% 55 11	Positive effect No effect Negative effect
Work design: Modify job content, improve work methods, restrain workers (enrich jobs).	3	75% 21 4	63% 33 4	69% 28 3	70% 24 6	Positive effect No effect Negative effect
Environment: Make safer or more pleasant working conditions, reorganize structure (innovate).	6	28% 55 17	27% 56 17	42% 52 6	59% 37 4	Positive effect No effect Negative effect
Programs: Raise pay, revise policies, try goal-setting (MBO) programs (all participate).	5	36% 52 12	49% 42 9	37% 55 8	70% 26 4	Positive effect No effect Negative effect
Rating for improving productivity (rating scale is shown below).		7.2	6.6	6.1	6.0	

Rating scale for types of productivity improvement:

Decrease or no change	May produce a small improvement	Certain to make a small improvement	May raise productivity significantly	Certain to yield large improvements
1 2	3 4	5 6	7 8	9 10

Source: James L. Riggs, *Production Systems: Planning, Analysis and Control*, 3rd ed. (New York: John Wiley, 1981). p. 594.

The busy table on page 93 is packed with productivity messages. Opinions were secured from a survey of businesspeople who had attended national productivity conferences.[1] Six types of actions to improve productivity are listed on the left side of the table, where *management* is ranked as the action area with the greatest probability of success. Across the top are listed four types of improvement expected from implementing the actions; *improved efficiency* was judged the most promising for productivity gains. The highest ratings are split between machines and management: Machine assistance is most useful in securing operating savings and quality gains, while better management is the preferred path to performance effectiveness and greater organizational vitality.

More revealing than the match-up of top vote-getters is the spread of votes. *Work design* and *computerized processes* are awarded prominent positions across the table. Attention to the *work environment* and *special programs* excelled only as morale builders. *Management* had a robust showing everywhere, probably because it is the wellspring of all other actions.

This confirms the creed: *TO IMPROVE PRODUCTIVITY, YOU MUST MANAGE.*

To manage in a business sense is to direct, conduct, and administer. The breadth of this activity is reflected in the survey report by the span of improvements imparted by management; even in those areas where technological advances and technical practices are judged most effective, managers still direct and administer. In most cases, managers do not actually produce the goods and services that appear in a productivity measure. They nonetheless account for a big chunk of labor cost while their direct contribution to output is tenuous. They don't do; they facilitate doing. They are suspect.

The work scene is seemingly bifurcated into "management" and "workers," them and us. Bosses, staff, and everyone else in the front office are collectively regarded as a distinct social group with special interests and characteristic economic views. Workers are the doers with dirty hands and regimented schedules. This demarcation castigates management by inference that only the workers work while managers ride along extracting an unjust share of labor's reward. Such misgivings are often vocalized during a drive to increase productivity when workers ask, "What are *they* [managers] doing? What's their contribution?"

The questions have to be answered, even if the doubts are not expressed verbally, because misgivings about who shares in a shared mission can scuttle it. The bold solution, more convincing than any number of sermons on beneficial management, is to lead by example. What is good for the troops is good for the commanders.

Effectiveness of an example depends on how it is perceived by the audience. Fine efforts that go unnoticed have no multiplier effect. Token efforts are deservedly disdained. A staged production risks suspicion.

Example setting should be guided by the old preacher's code: Tell them what you're going to do; do it; then tell them what you did.

"Follow me" is an instinctive exhortation by leaders. Exceptional leaders are those who strike a responsive chord in their followers; their declarations are heard with sympathy and their actions are appreciated. What attracts followers in one instance fails in another. An influential leader has the ability to view his or her behavior from the perspective of the other person. This *outsider's viewpoint* is difficult to attain and may be embarrassing to witness, but it clarifies that which produces the strongest impression and exerts the greatest influence.

Management-by-example from an outsider's perspective is the theme of this chapter. In the following sections examples are advocated that appear to be sensible practices to those who are outside the corporate machine and government honeycomb: consumers, union leaders, taxpayers, shareholders, and employees at each level looking upward at the organization. Each example supports contentions being expressed about what needs to be done to rectify productivity ailments, and some run against the grain of traditional managerial thinking. Recent productivity results by the directors, conductors, and administrators of commerce suggest that some rethinking is advisable.

EXHIBIT 22   *THE JAPANESE MANAGEMENT EXAMPLE*

Koji Matsumoto argues that "because the superior qualities of Japanese management, as well as the factors which give rise to them, are all of such an objective nature, Japanese management may thus be said to have an intrinsic universality."[2] He bases his claim on the "initiative" and "cohesion" fostered by the structure of Japanese corporations and the nature of Japanese management practices.

Freedom to initiate productive practices is owed in part to Japan's unique corporate ownership pattern.[3] Individuals own 10 percent or more of just 3 percent of the major corporations. Banks and other companies are the principal shareholders. These institutional investors are more interested in the *stability* of a company, which affords continuing mutual business relationships, than the dividends provided. In fact, Japan consistently has the lowest dividend rate among all developed capitalistic nations. Japanese managers regard dividends as a capital cost, similar to interest payments, instead of an obligation of the corporation and a yardstick of management competence; consequently they are free to reinvest more earnings in productive assets. Encouragement to do so is further enhanced by corporate boards composed largely of directors who have worked their way up through the company ranks, as opposed to a majority of outside directors in 80 percent of American corporations. It is therefore not surprising that 95 percent of the general shareholder meetings in Japan last less than half an hour.[4]

Management's accountability to shareholders in Japan is largely replaced by responsibility to employees. Should a choice arise between dividends and dismissals, dividends are sacrificed for continuous employment. This concern for employees builds an allegiance that reduces absenteeism, job hopping, and general unrest, freeing managers to court productivity. Workers feel they have a personal stake in management decisions because most of the managers rose from their ranks and their union representatives sit with managers in labor-management councils at company, factory/office, and shop levels to work out differences and achieve consensus for company actions. The resulting cohesiveness, bonding employees to employers by mutual confidence, eases the introduction of new technology by removing fears of unemployment and creating a we'll-make-it-work climate.

Japanese management is shaped by long-term convergent interests between workers and management. The mold is social "companyism." Managers plan for the future, unrushed by demands for dividends and stock-boosting short-run profits. Company oneness acquired from stable employment and cooperative unionism allows versatility in solving production problems and ensures that a solution will be carried out by the marshaled strength of all employees' energies. Whether these characteristics of Japanese management style can be universalized is debatable, but they are beacons for relief from capital and labor constraints that hamper productivity efforts elsewhere.

TOP-TIER MANAGERS

Boardroom strategies set the framework for middle-level management.

> **Objective:** *Develop and publicize a detailed long-range plan for increasing the organization's productivity: a productivity proclamation.*

Five-year plans issued for the controlled economies of socialized countries may be a mirage of propagandism, but they at least set objectives and marshal support. Equivalent five-year plans by American companies tend to be economic boasts designed more for market consumption and internal motivation than blueprints for performance. A productivity proclamation should include commitments to

- Provide job security for employees
- Utilize developing technology to protect employees and customers, as well as to increase the efficiency of operations
- Strengthen R&D, either through scientific investigation or innovations by employees, or both, if feasible
- Devote a significant share of financial resources to the acquisition of productive assets
- Create an organizational entity that encourages cooperation between workers and managers in pursuing corporate productivity goals

✔ Provide new, or unclog old, communication channels to improve the upward flow of ideas and downward flow of concern for employees

✔ Survive

Comparable commitments are appropriate for the executive boards of government agencies, especially the creation of a permanent productivity-improvement entity within each agency that solicits advice from experienced workers, rewards superior performance, and encourages group activities that boost morale and build loyalty.

The composition of a board influences its concerns about certain corporate activities, emphasizing those aspects that board members are most familiar with. When the only tool you have is a hammer, every problem is treated like a nail.

> **Objective:** *Select directors who have expertise in production and productivity for membership on the board in proportion to the importance of production and productivity to the corporation.*

In many organizations, the proportion should be large. Directors with the desired expertise do not necessarily have to be promoted from within the company, but that is a logical source. They should be selected for their proven ability to look ahead and be innovative, as well as for their knowledge of corporate resources and operations. Dangers of inbreeding are reduced by selecting one or more outside directors who have either broad-based experience that provides a leveling perspective or a narrow speciality in knowledge that is needed but lacking in home-grown directors. A short rotation period of outside experts educates the holders of relatively permanent board positions for institutional investors.

Many boards have been enlarged in recent years to accommodate outside directors representing diverse interests relevant to, but outside of, the mainstream of corporate operations—consumers, women, minorities, educators, politicians. In some cases, proponents of special interests have had a distracting effect, diluting attention from the business of producing products to the politics of social responsibility. While a corporation dares not overlook its societal obligations, its board of directors must not stray from its obligation to be a tough, independent master that keeps management alert, planning for the future by anticipating market changes, transforming new technology into operational realities, and developing products and practices that promote productivity.

In addition to advice from the directors, the chief executive officers and other top-tier executives should have financial incentives that direct their efforts toward sustained corporate productivity. Productivity by objectives should start at the top with people who are productively oriented.

Objective: *Base top executives' pay on their achievement of challenging long-term goals.*

Much has been made of American management's concentration on short-term profits. The classic example is our aging production base caused in part by corporations maintaining a reputation-building dividend rate at the expense of modernization; much of the technology employed by foreign competitors to undercut prices for products delivered to the United States was invented here, but ignored. Many factors played a part in the decline of U.S. industrial competitiveness, including some unavoidable lapses in R&D and incorrect trend readings, but three managerial pressures are prominent:

1. Top managers are graded by their short-term results—how the stock of the company behaves, this year's earnings compared with last year's, a return on investment better than that of the CEO's predecessor. A farseeing board of directors insulates managers from these short-term pressures.

2. Business risks exaggerated by inflation tend to shorten managerial time horizons, tilting investments away from new product and plant development toward quick financial coups obtainable from marginal changes in products and acquisition of existing assets. While CEOs are seeking safe but glamorous acquisitions, or fighting off a hostile takeover spawned by a depressed stockprice, immediate subordinates are trying to maximize quarterly profits for their independent profit centers, all of them trying to protect their careers from being slapped by inflation.

3. Both of the pressures above can be relieved or reinforced by an executive's pay package. As stock options lost attractiveness in the sideways stock market and tax reforms of the past decade, bonuses have become the favored sweeteners of executive compensation. Bonuses geared to annual earnings or returns on investment may tempt an executive to lease rather than buy equipment to boost this year's ROI percentage, or to delay cash outlays until the bonus year is over, costing the corporation payment penalties and forgone discounts for prompt payment. It is hoped that such manipulations are uncommon, but bonuses inevitably invite myopic behavior by linking a significant portion of compensation to the here and now. Few CEOs can be expected to resist short-term maximizing when their typical tenure in office is five or six years. The following executive compensation options are proposed to reduce the short-term bias of incentives:

✔ Drop incentives and pay a straight salary based on the manager's qualifications, and add fringe benefits plus perquisites appropriate to the job and industry. Japanese and most European companies appear to believe that top managers do not need special incentives to ensure full commitment to their work.

✓ Base incentives on a well-defined set of strategic objectives that include inflation-deflated earnings measured against the performance of comparable companies and a set of criteria for internal company development, such as new-product introductions, improved product quality, corporate diversification, and production efficiency. Directors of the company have responsibility for establishing realistic performance objectives that avoid target levels set so low that inflation alone makes them fail-safe.

✓ Base bonuses on the earnings of the firm over a series of years after the executive has departed. An alternative is to give top managers contracts for a certain number of years, say three, and pay annual bonuses for the same number of years after each contract period; a three-year contract would yield bonuses during years 4, 5, and 6 if the firm's performance in those years meets contracted objectives. Basing incentives on long-run profits theoretically lengthens resource-commitment horizons, and a guaranteed employment period removes some of the pressure of an immediate shake-up to produce clearly observable activity.

Underlying all executive pay packages is the need to maintain credibility of the firm's total compensation schedule. Extravagance at the top of the scale may be tolerated during periods of prosperity, but in hard times the same incentives will be criticized as unfair giveaways. It is difficult for stockholders to swallow hefty bonuses to executives when profits are plummeting. More pertinent to productivity, lush rewards to top executives undermine austerity proposals to low-ranking employees. Fastening bosses' pay to measured productivity gains is a powerful example, and possibly a clinching argument for a companywide commitment.[5]

If the proof of manufacturing productivity stems from the factory floor, it deserves acknowledgment in the boardroom.

> **Objective:**   *Promote more-experienced production people to top positions in the firm when manufacturing is a fundamental part of business.*

The shock of markets lost to imports and faltering productivity has led to painful introspection in many manufacturing firms. Has the company lost contact with the bread-and-butter business of putting products out the door? Has production management been overshadowed by concern for financial management? If the answers are yes, it is time to rediscover the factory.

Many executive suites are filled with financial wizards who know how to juggle all the P&L numbers, but very little about the processes represented by those numbers. These professional managers often have financial or legal backgrounds and almost no experience with the nuts and bolts of manufacturing technology, production operations, and factory workers. They can observe the avalanche of new technology, but they lack confidence about its internal workings and cannot champion bold ventures for its adoption. In an era of technological tumult, every top-management team needs production prophets.

The shortage of production virtuosos is attributed to the vapidity associated with grind-it-out manufacturing. Graduate students shun production management. M.B.A.'s seek the go-go glamour of money management, missing what Martin Starr, professor at the Columbia Business School, slyly calls "insurmountable opportunities." The isolation of manufacturing from the corporate mainstream is manifested by lower salaries and slower promotion of factory managers in many corporations.[6] Until production specialists get the respect they deserve, and manufacturing expertise gets the attention it merits, factory productivity is the loser.

Distance from the factory floor to the executive suite is conventionally counted by steps on an organizational chart. Each level is occupied by a superior directing a number of subordinates. The number varies. When it becomes too large, overstaffing is a pungent possibility.

> **Objective:** *Increase people-productivity by slicing surplus layers from the organization.*

Span of control—the number of subordinates per superior—is an anomaly. A boss with many subordinates is conventionally held in higher esteem than one with a smaller flock but is criticized for not providing enough personal attention to the staff. Fewer levels in the organizational pyramid increase the number of people in each tier, which shortens lines of communication from top to bottom but decreases opportunities for promotion. Stricter control allowed by smaller span sizes is balanced against more erratic coordination caused by added supervisors. Productivity discipline advises fewer levels of command *and* smaller spans of control.

A lower and leaner profile for an organization probably demands major surgery. Slicing out a level of management is a morale-quaking exercise. But it can be done. Experts claim that three or four levels of management in a manufacturing plant are preferable to the typical six or seven. Japanese auto companies have five levels compared with eleven or twelve in their U.S. counterparts.[7]

Surplus staffing is white-collar featherbedding. Not only is it a waste of talent and a drain on company resources but properly staffed units are contaminated by envy of the featherbedders' lighter workloads, or fretfulness, caused by nuisance antics of employees with too little to do. The following ramifications can evolve:

- When each manager has a span of control of four or five and there is one secretary for every two managers, secretarial costs mushroom. Data processing and report proliferation correspondingly expand.
- Staff work becomes a crutch for weak management when there is an over-

population of staff slots. Any question in doubt is shunted to staff specialists for study. The bigger the staffs, the easier it is to blame someone else for a missed deadline or a dumb decision.

✔ Managers placed into positions having only half a job are apt to strive to create a whole job, asking for assistants to do so. Frequently they succeed, and pretty soon another whole layer is in place that requires additional supervision.

✔ An organization with more levels of management has more reports written to tell each level what is happening above and below. As the proportion of people who physically produce shrinks in comparison to those who manage and administer, more criticism is aimed at the upper end of the pay scale.

If future productivity gains are sought in the upper tiers of management, upper managers will have to seek them. But who leads the search? It contradicts the principle of lean staffing to create a new level of management to promote productivity. Although productivity is everyone's responsibility, any job that is everyone's job tends to get lost in the shuffle. A focal point for productivity is needed.

> **Objective:**   *Establish a productivity-management council with a designated leader and specific responsibilities.*

Some companies have crowned a productivity czar whose kingdom is the entire organization, but a shortage of vassals often undermines the czar's effectiveness. Other companies have assigned productivity responsibility to an agent in each major operating unit; but lacking centralized support and direction, isolated agents wonder what to do and whom to do it with. State and federal departments sometimes form interagency boards to tackle productivity concerns; but middle-level boards may have neither the horsepower to back strong program proposals nor the horse sense about actual operations to develop worthwhile proposals to boost work efficiency. However, either centralized or decentralized productivity networks can be effective if they are backed by authority and resource commitments.

Attaching a productivity assignment to a staff position has great vogue. It is written proof that management is concerned about productivity. We have seen these "productivity coordinators" wander about trying to define their mission, well intentioned and enthusiastic but desperate for guidance. They turn to literature, short courses, and consultants for assistance. Those with sufficient stamina eventually discover promising options for their organization, but then they have to sell their plans to upper management. Much wear and tear on junior executives is avoided by a senior council that sets strategy and outlines tactics.

A productivity council should be more than a showcase, yet its commission is the marrow of existing managerial obligations. Organizations have always struggled to be productive. A council just localizes the struggle, giving it more visibility and concentrating efforts to maximize their effect. The role of a productivity council, and its composition and duties, in a total firm PBO program is described in Chapter 9. A council involved in general productivity concerns should benefit from the following considerations:

- ✓ A very large organization may utilize a task force to initially define its productivity drive, but a permanent V.P.-level council is likely to be a redundant structure. Those holding top offices surely earned their office-door keys by stressing productivity, so their advice is more useful in setting up the total program to allow lower managers to gain experience by directing activities.

- ✓ A plant or division productivity council is conventionally chaired by someone immediately below the top rank, and a half dozen or so members are drawn from leaders of operating and support units: production, administration, engineering, maintenance, purchasing, etc. Membership reflects the thrust of the council's efforts. If worker participation is a critical issue, worker or union representatives should be included.

- ✓ Early meetings may have to be devoted to distinguishing productivity activities from pure cost reduction and personnel development interests. Measurement is sure to be a hot topic. Quality of work life must also be high on the agenda. In the formative stages, assistance from corporate or bureau headquarters and other outside advisers is very useful.

- ✓ A shotgun approach by the council may pepper a lot of targets, but it makes only small dents. After arranging ways to increase productivity awareness of the total work force, resources should be concentrated on one area at a time to maximize forcefulness. If quality is a problem area, one production line or one office operation is provided with new lights, equipment, procedures, or motivation to improve performance. Good results will, it is hoped, infect adjacent operations. One small company blocked off part of its cafeteria to provide a little "productivity-thinking" room in which posters adorned the walls, including some sheets on which ideas could be scribbled, and productivity literature was available. Free coffee and occasional finger snacks enticed people into the room.

After a productivity campaign is functioning smoothly, the council has to keep recharging it by starting new activities and publicizing previous successes. Providing tangible recognition to especially successful efforts is also a council duty. A municipal department organized a productivity picnic, inviting the mayor who later proclaimed a citywide productivity day, during which both serious and humorous productivity awards were made. Intel installed a "125 percent solution" to emphasize its management's responsibility for productivity; all salaried employees were expected to put in fifty hours a week to hasten the development of new products during a bleak sales period. These types of creative events and solutions are needed to keep productivity in the spotlight.

EXHIBIT 23   *CARRYING THE BALL FOR PRODUCTIVITY*

Planning for a corporate productivity push shares many of the considerations used for a football game plan. Both coaches and productivity planners know that the game will be won or lost in the lines (scrimmage and production). Game strategy is resolved before the kickoff: a running game to steadily grind out small gains through the line, a passing game to get occasional big gains at some risk of big losses, or a mixture of the two. These football strategies correspond to productivity strategies of relying on production supervisors for small, consistent productivity improvements, initiatives from corporate headquarters for heavy resource commitments in selected areas, or plant-level activities that combine limited resource investment with employee-involvement programs.

Sideline coaches offer plenty of advice. Consultants note that some corporate productivity committees are formed just to impress stockholders, and that productivity czars often have a nice title but not enough clout to make significant changes occur. This line of reasoning supports grunt-it-out gains at the line level where every worker plays a part. Somewhat opposite reasoning suggests that line operators need direction and support from above to get started, and that the appointment of a corporate productivity manager is evidence of the high priority accorded to productivity.

Westinghouse Electric Corporation has tried to capture the best of both strategies. A position was created for a vice-president of corporate productivity. Money has been committed too. Big chunks of productivity-fostering technology are expected from a new thirty-five-acre, $10 million productivity center for robot, laser, and computer development. The center also contains an extensive library covering all the productivity subjects. As the vice-president of productivity, Mr. Hudspeth, explains: "We felt we needed a mechanism in place to assess developing technology outside the company, as well as ideas happening within separate Westinghouse business groups."[8]

From a multimillion dollar productivity improvement "seed fund," Westinghouse has committed $30 million to more than 120 separate projects. By late 1981 the corporation also had seven hundred quality circles operating in about 150 locations with over ten thousand employees participating. Recognizing that managers and white-collar workers represent half the corporation's work force and 70 percent of its payroll, productivity improvements are pursued in every area, from offices to drawing rooms to construction yards.

MONEY MANAGERS

To imitate or to innovate? That is the question. The answer ultimately rests on willingness to take risks. And risk is related to time. Copying products and practices that already enjoy success reduces the investment gamble and the time required for development. *Imitation* is a safe, comfortable management strategy that avoids most second-guessing and long waits for results. *Innovation* entails a wholly different mind set: a disposition away from the turtle shell of risk sharing and toward bolder initiatives for long-term advances that jump instead of crawl.

American managers have a well-deserved reputation for efficient utilization of existing assets. Day-to-day operations are carefully coordinated and analyzed in grueling detail. Medium-range planning, however, is handicapped by institutionalized controls that discourage innovation at decentralized profit centers by unduly penalizing short-term financial setbacks. Managers are reluctant to risk their corporation's money and their own reputations on highly promising new ventures when reasonably profitable, low-risk options are available, particularly when they are being judged on their ability to produce reasonably profitable, consistent quarterly earnings. The same reluctance affects long-term planning for the development of new products and processes. Recent comparisons of American and foreign management practices, spawned by souring U.S. productivity, deplore the get-results-now orientation of American managers that tends to make them less technologically daring than their overseas counterparts.

The following three objectives are directed respectively at long-, medium-, and short-term economic planning for productivity.

> **Objective:** *Look beyond immediate markets and current processes to secure cutting-edge technology: basic discoveries by big corporations, basic product and process refinements by all manufacturers, and major innovative improvements by government and service providers.*

Where the top tier of big corporations is dominated by executives with financial and legal skills, it is not surprising that cash hoards are accumulated for corporate acquisitions and mergers. The corporate takeover battles of 1981 were labeled "merger mania" and "big business feeding frenzy." Lines of credit and cash reserves were committed to thrusts for, or protection from, acquisition. Executive time spent on takeovers is time unavailable for operating problems. Investment money plowed into acquisitions is dollars unspent for upgrading existing operations. These time and money allocations are completely defensible from financial and legal viewpoints: Total corporate risk is reduced by distributing it among diverse product lines and businesses, and decisive actions produce moderately quick outcomes. But they seldom improve productivity.

Acquisitions are not necessarily unproductive, sometimes creating symbiotic conditions, and asset diversification is a cushion against normal business tides, yet such investments provide little shelter from tidal waves of technologically superior competition. Investments in R&D high-tech equipment can also reduce risk—failure owed to manufacturing obsolescence and noncompetitive products or services. Managers with hands-on experience have the necessary insights to further minimize risk by keeping new developments on track, avoiding waste, and economizing time. A policy to attain in-house technological superiority is a long and generally arduous commitment that involves both money and operations managers; the ante is long-term planning and the stakes are organization vigor and competitiveness.

> **Objective:** *Modify capital-budgeting procedures to give priority to expenditures for productivity improvement.*

Medium-range proposals for capital expenditure cluster around cost-reduction, product-enrichment, and regulation-mandated requests. Required outlays to satisfy government regulations receive top priority because ignoring them could shut down operations or result in fines. Cost-reducing proposals are attractive because results can be accurately predicted and successes directly boost profit. Product-improvement proposals are a bit riskier than the others but are needed to protect earnings. Many of the proposals in these categories also favorably affect productivity. Most investment selection processes, however, do not award special priority to proposals that contribute to technological innovation and higher work-life quality. Potential adaptations that favor productivity-oriented proposals include the following:

- A percentage of capital funds available each year for internal investment could be set aside for productivity projects. Within this mandated allocation, preference among the productivity proposals could be determined either by vote of a productivity council or by ranking proposals according to their expected rate of return.

- Larger organizations usually have a preprinted "request-for-expenditure" form that is filled out for each proposed project. One of the categories on the work sheet should be a required explanation of what effect the project will have on productivity and, if pertinent, on the quality of working life. The factors listed in this category should then receive special attention by the committee that selects the proposals to be funded.

- A "seed" fund could be established to encourage workers to develop their ideas for improving products or processes. It would provide time and materials for them to experiment with their inspirations. Unceremonious application forms coupled with ceremonious acceptance announcements increase participation. One company boarded off a small section of a shop, put a lock on the door, which was opened by a very large key, and issued keys to workers who had been awarded "research contracts" to work in the "think tank annex."

✓ A version of the seed fund, called a "sapling" fund, can be established for staff members who are regularly assigned to R&D or product development. If allows them to spend time on offbeat projects that do not conform to the edict that marketability supersedes makeability. The intent of a sapling fund is to relieve some of the market-driven pressure to work only on products that already have consumer acceptance.[9]

> **Objective:** Create incentives that provide positive feedback for productive performance. Money is a powerful stimulus.

"Behavior modification" is the buzzword for directing people's performance toward organizational goals. Although it sounds Machiavellian, Orwellian, and Pavlovian, the concepts have been in force since primitive people first collected into groups to play, learn, live, and work together. Money managers have a role in behavior modification because money can be a potent influence as a reward for desired behavior.

A purely incentive wage scale is a time-honored and excessively criticized way to stimulate work performance. Equaliterian pressures limit the use of most piece-rate payment plans. Group incentives are better accepted but are inefficient behavior modifiers because the groupings are usually too large to have any personal effect and the rewards are too small to matter much. Profit sharing and blanket bonuses are ineffective when workers get the same reward irrespective of individual performance. Perhaps simple but sincere praise for a job well done is more effective than any uniform reward, so long as it is given atop adequate monetary compensation and delivered personally. But praise has the greatest impact when given in conjunction with tangible and timely awards.

The following aspects of productivity-activated performance modifiers are worth noting:

✓ Wages can act as disincentives for productivity. Slow work performance is frequently rewarded by overtime pay. Departments that go over their budget in one year are likely to be awarded a higher budget the next year. Salary goes up for an empire builder who hires more people than are really needed. Just spending more time or dollars is not an automatic indicator of more work accomplished, but compensation arrangements too often treat it so.

✓ The behavior to encourage is that which contributes most to productivity. If products are rolling out the door at a satisfactory rate but material costs are frightening, no genius is needed to concentrate on material waste reduction. Yet inflexible incentive plans may continue to award only faster output.

✓ Rewards should be tied to well-understood activities. If you do *this*, then *that* will happen. For instance, *if* a worker is neither absent nor tardy for a month, *then* the worker's name is dropped in the hat for a monthly $100 lottery.

- Scheduling is a critical factor in behavior modification. The reward, whether a pat on the back or a wad for the wallet, should be provided as soon as possible after the desired act has occurred. And rewards should be frequent enough to sustain interest. Fast feedback is important.
- Size of monetary incentive should reflect the financial importance of the activity and how much improvement is recorded. Small and frequent rewards are usually associated with improvements up to a satisfactory level of performance. Thereafter a reinforcement schedule is started in which rewards coincide with peak activity periods or occur at random intervals. Randomness discourages bursts of activity to meet a fixed reward schedule, avoids having rewards taken for granted, and reduces employees' feelings of being overcontrolled.
- The Objectives Matrix described in Chapters 4 and 11 can be modified to accommodate classes of individual incentives instead of a group incentive. The first step is to compare the behavior of those who do certain activity well with those who do it poorly. The discovered traits are the performance criteria. Then an incentive scale is formulated in place of the 0 to 10 scale of the matrix to associate rewards with performance of each higher level of achievement; the point scale is replaced by actual monetary reward values, similar to sales commissions. From this table, employees can monitor their own performance. They will catch their mistakes faster and will be reminded of the objectives they are working toward. Self-monitoring also enhances trust, the vital ingredient in any incentive plan.

MIDDLE MANAGERS

Being in the middle is an uncomfortable position. On an organizational ladder, the halfway rungs are high enough for the climber to be hurt if bumped off and far enough from the top to be excluded from the perquisites of power. Studies of stressful occupations place middle managers firmly in the ulcer zone, below the tension-reducing indulgences of bossdom but too high to blow off steam in face-to-face confrontations with subordinates.

Being all things to all people, the personal skills recommended for middle managers are endless. Advice on how to acquire and use these skills is given interminably from mother's knee to professors' lectures. From the seemingly inexhaustible inventory of desirable talents, only two productivity-oriented abilities will be discussed: thinking productivity and using time productively. The scope of this discussion is further constrained by not including first-line supervision; the criticality of first-line management-worker interfaces and associated foreman foibles are discussed in Chapters 8 and 9.

> **Objective:** *Think productivity. Talk up productivity. Learn more about productivity.*

When top management decides to gear up for productivity, middle management has to grease the gears and control the tempo. When such

an upfront commitment is lacking, middle managers still command resources sufficient to create islands of excellence in a sea of productivity
apathy. To do so incurs risk and requires uncommon dedication, but
these qualities are the essence of professional competence. Generating
productivity through subordinates is the age-old proof of managerial
artistry.

The overall attitude or *culture* of an organization affects its management style. A laid-back manager who was successful in the Silicon Valley
culture finds the same management style inappropriate in a military-
mold company. Individual talents are no less valuable; they just have to
be applied differently. Productive practices, however, can generally be
transferred intact from one culture to the next. Both authoritarian and
egalitarian managers subscribe to output/input maximization. Transferable practices are explored in the following options:

✓ **Start a middle managers' productivity team.** The arrangement can be as informal as a weekly bull session to exchange ideas over coffee, or as structured as the worker teams described in Chapters 9 through 11. Regular
low-key meetings fan the flames of productivity, but an organized, PBO-
type program can ignite a dazzling blaze. We recommend that middle-man-
agement teams be formed before or concurrent with a company's move into
an involvement mode.

The difference between a worker-involvement team and a management-
involvement team is occupational interest. Workers focus on their piece of
the production process. Managers rally around their professional specialties. In a small company an inclusive team represents all operations, putting a productivity stamp on gatherings that previously had a general
agenda. Larger organizations are better served by cohesive teams that
share interests, such as R&D or an integrated team of managers from marketing, production, and engineering who are engaged in a common project.[10] Once organized, management teams, like workers' teams, benefit
from training, facilitation, objective setting, and performance monitoring
by productivity indicators. Although measurement may be resisted, the
dictum still holds that what's good for the troops is good for the commanders.

Talking productivity to fellow managers beats talking to oneself but
limits discussions to local ideas. Attending seminars and reading productivity literature broadens in-house horizons when the nuggets obtained
from outside are disseminated. An automatic requirement for anyone who
attends a company-paid presentation should be a brief digest of what was
said, its pertinency, and whether attendance by others is worthwhile. Similar reports of valuable ideas gleaned from periodicals should be prepared
and distributed. Some management groups circulate a scrapbook into
which members insert their latest readings or musings as it reaches their
desks. A centralized arrangement relies on a "librarian," a rotating position in the group or an actual company librarian, to collect submitted items
and issue a regular "rumor rag."

✓ **Alleviate idea inbreeding by hiring consultants to come on-site to expound
their pet approach to productivity.** Short presentations representing several different approaches are most useful during the formative phase of a

company productivity program. Once a course of action has been selected, the preferred consultants can return to provide implementation details and program demonstrations. Delivering the right advice at the right time is a problem for both consultants and clients. Sponsorship by a management team makes selection of the "right" consultant more likely, because the team is responsible, and delivery of the "right" material is assisted by input from the team about what is expected.

Some government agencies have tried in-house consulting by managers who visit each other's operations to look for possible improvements; this is in addition to consultations provided by the regular management analysis staff. Visiting managers learn about related activities, even if they fail to discover any productivity bonanzas.

✓ **Get out of the office and mingle.** Managers in manufacturing traditionally spend considerable time on the plant floor mixing with workers and observing firsthand the effects of their decisions. Some companies rigidly enforce a rule that managers have to work a given number of days each year in factory jobs. Those who are really conscientious visit the night shifts and are usually rewarded by enlightenments that are not apparent in the bustling day shift. Managers of administrative units are less inclined to venture out, reasoning that things do not change much in white-collar jobs and they already know what is happening. They could be surprised. Seclusion from the operating staff not only eliminates a valuable information channel but diminishes respect for administrators. Who has faith in a faceless department head, especially when the going gets tough, as in cases where a push for productivity necessitates belt-tightening reorganization and a reduction in force (RIF).

Sensitivity to current operating conditions probably does more to avoid bad decisions than to steer good decisions. In deciding what can be done to boost productivity, managers often remember the things that were, or become enamored with what will be, forgetting how things are now. They see the big picture and overlook all the tiny figures in the panorama. These little figures are the doers. Fun is poked at educators by the gibe that those who can't do, teach; and those who can't teach, administer. The subtle thesis in the taunt is that administration is weakened by its distance from reality. It leads to such decisions as

Elimination of a "gofer" in the secretarial pool, which then required secretaries to chase paper and do errands instead of concentrating on their more productive regular duties.

Rearrangement of assembly tables to reduce distractions that also reduce conversation among workers, which was later held to be the reason for a sudden jump in absenteeism and turnover.

These unwise decisions would have been avoided by more familiarity with the operations they affected. Eyes-on experience helps abort mistakes and abets better solutions.

> **Objective:** *Assuming that the ratio of decisions/time is a provident indicator of management productivity, reducing the time input increases productivity when the quantity*

> *and quality of decisions are un-*
> *changed. So, get rid of time wast-*
> *ers.*

The advice above can be taken two ways. There is no place in a productive organization for inveterate, hopeless time wasters who fritter away their own capacity and pollute the schedules of their colleagues. Before crossing off such individuals, however, salvage should be attempted. The second interpretation of getting rid of time wasters is to eliminate time-wasting practices. Reams of recommendations for time management have been published and are worth reading, and then rereading at a later date, because it is so easy to fall back into bad habits. Middle management can lead the assault on productivity-inhibiting time dissipators by the following actions:

- **Make people aware of the cost of wasted time.** Twenty to 40 percent productivity improvement is not an unrealistic expectation from more efficient time utilization, and an extra bonus of higher morale is possible from eliminating institutional delays such as having to wait in line to get to the copying machine.
- **Abhor duplication of effort.** A company found that its auditors were checking freight invoices while it was paying a verifying agency to do the same thing. It is middle management's job to dig out duplications.
- **Get rid of built-in time wasters.** Nothing is much more frustrating than the hurry-up-and-wait syndrome. Every queue in an organization represents an opportunity to save time. An idle operator waiting for machine repairs or incoming material is a target for time conservation. A study by Booz, Allen, & Hamilton, management consultants, found that clerical employees lose 18 percent of their workday waiting for work.

  Managers are also regularly exposed to these hurry-wait-hurry situations. Some delays are inevitable due to the natural randomness of events, but many can be engineered out of the system. Perhaps the foremost offender is the manager who sets unrealistic deadlines. Personal promises to get results unrealistically soon cause tension and mistakes that have to be corrected. Hasty deadlines imposed on other people are disruptive to regular operations and create a storm of uncoordinated antics at the eleventh hour.
- **Be a time watcher.** Note how time is parceled out all day and ration it to the best uses. This means prioritizing activities. It also means not wasting other people's time. Managers can help each other by mutually scheduling an open-door period for exchanging visits and calls; only red-flag interruptions are allowed at other times.
- **Prepare a schedule.** Everyone knows that the most important things should be acted upon before mundane matters get attention. The trick is to divide those important things into small goals that can be accomplished one after the other: divide and conquer.
- **Know how to conduct a meeting:** posting the agenda in advance, starting promptly, maintaining the pace, summarizing at the end, and abiding by the social amenities Robert had in mind when he set the rules. What may be forgotten is that essentially the same preparations improve one-on-one

meetings. The tremendous potential for managers to manage meeting time is demonstrated in Exhibit 24.

EXHIBIT 24   *HOW MANAGERS SPEND THEIR TIME*

Comparisons of the way managers allocate their time are interesting but not very definitive because individual styles and duties vary so much. A little extra spice is added by comparing times from two cultures. Modest surveys were conducted by the Japanese Management Association and IBM to study time management by middle- to upper-level executives.[11] Results are listed in the following table according to inclusive activity blocks.

	PERCENTAGE OF TIME SPENT ON EACH ACTIVITY BY	
MANAGEMENT ACTIVITIES*	Japanese Managers	American Managers
Scheduled meetings	24.4%	13.1%
Conferring with others	21.6	25.2
Reading	15.7	16.6
Writing	16.3	20.0
Planning or scheduling	5.7	4.7
Traveling outside hqtrs.	8.5	13.1
Other	7.8	7.2

*Each activity category includes related operations. For example, the 20 percent allocation for "writing" by American managers includes actual writing (9.8%), dictating (5.9%), proofreading (1.8%), calculating (2.3%), and copying (0.2%).

Japanese managers spend more of their time in meetings, as expected in a culture that values consensus. American managers, in contrast, spend the largest chunk of their time on unscheduled meetings, over half of which are by telephone. The popular conception that managers devote a major share of their time to thinking and planning is shattered by the low percentages, 5.7 percent in Japan, and 4.7 percent in the United States. The Japanese survey reported that an average working day for managers lasted ten hours and nine minutes.

ENGINES OF EFFICIENCY:
Productive Facilities

6

Run. Run. The robots are coming!

Run which way? A race to embrace worker-machines is a marathon for the winners' purse of international dominance. At risk is a backlash from displaced human workers.

While robots are the histrionic forerunners of rampant technology, computers and associated electronics are the driving force. Advances are paraded out of development labs at a pace that prohibits even dedicated managers from fully appreciating the potential impact on their operations. Productivity implications of the high-tech parade are inescapable for the developments already available, and overwhelming for designs still being developed.

Experts say it takes twenty to twenty-five years before a new technology is assimilated by industry. Computers are of age.[1] Machine-paced automation is also a mature manufacturing medium. The following technologies are still in the adolescent range:

> *Lasers.* Already engaged in cutting steel, welding metals, and performing delicate eye surgery, more uses for lasers will be found in hardening metals, making precise measurements, reading video disks, and performing many data-oriented operations.
>
> *Fiber Optics.* Future applications of fiber optics technology will expand to many areas beyond its proven worth in telephonic communications.[2] Even now, it is being applied to information processing and to quality control inspections for a wide variety of products.
>
> *Energy Technology.* Fuel scares in the 1970s spawned a deluge of energy research projects that created exotic products that are now nearly ready for commercial application. Changing sunbeams into electrical energy (solar photo voltaics) is a proven process waiting for a means of low-cost production. Strange-shaped, more efficient windmills in "wind farms" are generating electricity. Fuel cells that produce electricity through electrochemistry show promise. The tongue-tying technology named magnetohydrodynamics sends gases from superheated fossil fuels through a magnetic field to create electrical current.

No one expects all of these technologies to burst on the marketplace in the near future, yet they are far enough along to put a gleam in the eye of a forward-looking manager. Of more immediate concern to most managers is which type of technology to grab hold of now, the new designs that will retrieve or build a competitive edge.

A study by the Office of Technology Assessment[3] on what needs to be done to improve the competitiveness of steel, electronics, and automotive industries noted that "while the United States retains technological superiority in many industries, it has no across-the-board advantage." It stressed the importance of modernizing facilities and restructuring priorities to promote competitiveness, and it acknowledged the difficulties. To catch up with technology already installed in foreign steel mills would require capital spending at rates approximately double those of the past few years. Even this level of investment in new integrated mills might be insufficient to overcome the price advantages that result from the lower labor costs of steelmakers in developing countries. Cheaper labor has also contributed to imports' domination of consumer electronics,[4] increasingly causing U.S. firms to relocate their production to foreign soil. As a consequence of these and other factors, the report concluded that much of the drop in employment in steel, consumer electronics, and automobile industries is irreversible.

The loss of jobs to foreign competition is a growing emotional issue. Soon it may instigate legislative actions to counter the competition. A better solution is to reverse our declining share of world sales and protect our own markets from greater import penetration by boosting our productivity. Gains from self-regulating machinery and processes will unquestionably eliminate some jobs and arouse vitriolic censure that ignores the jobs generated by manufacturers of the new equipment and overlooks all the downstream benefits that accrue from greater production efficiency.

Vigilance owed to decisions about physically upgrading production facilities is the gist of this chapter. Each industry has its innate technology and unique requirements, but all employers share similar considerations for competitiveness, employment stability, and managerial strategy. These considerations are explored with respect to robots, factory technologies, and computer-assisted office operations.

EXHIBIT 25   *ROBOTS MAKING ROBOTS IN THE DARK*

Japan manufactures and uses more robots than any other nation. Industrial robots imported from the United States were first displayed in Japan in 1967. By 1981 Japan had nearly seventy-five thousand robots working in factories—more than the rest of the world combined—and was producing new machines at the rate of almost twenty thousand per year.[5] Approximately thirteen thousand of the robots are programmable, over four times the number in the United States.

At the Fujitsu Funac factory on the slopes of Mount Fuji, robots are constructing parts for more robots. The plant draws over one hundred thousand visitors a year, who gaze in awe at the premier example of unmanned manufacturing. They see some two dozen five-foot-tall yellow boxes with protruding arms feeding parts to other machines. A robot picks up a piece of metal, positions it for machine tooling, and then puts the finished part onto an unmanned trolley that delivers it to the assembly area. So far, people still assemble new robots, but Japanese engineers are working on that phase of manufacturing too.

At night, lights are dimmed and the robots continue to work. The trolleys no longer sound warning beeps as they trundle along their dotted paths. Only two humans are in the factory, confined to a control room where they monitor TV screens. Other than breaks for occasional maintenance, robots labor twenty-four hours a day with no vacations, strikes, lunch hours, or absenteeism. Fujitsu says it take three years to train a human in the skills needed on an assembly line. A robot, with its built-in memory, takes twenty minutes.

The automobile industry in Japan is loaded with robots, partially explaining why fifty-two cars are produced annually by each human worker, as opposed to about twenty per worker in Detroit. Toyota alone plans to introduce 720 new spot-welding robots in its body assembly lines. General Motors had about 450 robots operating in 1981 with plans to increase the number to 14,000 by 1990. Roger B. Smith, chairman of GM, has noted that "every time the cost of labor goes up $1 an hour, 1,000 more robots become economical."

The Japan Robot Leasing Company was established in 1980 to promote the use of robots in smaller companies. Employing older, fixed-sequence robots can be hugely profitable for a small factory. For $90 per month, a rented robot welder can do the work of three human welders whose average pay is about $400 per month. As Taguchi Takahiro, head of the leasing company's operations department, puts it: "If smaller businesses do not introduce robots, they will find that their costs will exceed the prevailing market prices of their products."[6]

Japan's romance with robots is already deeply rooted. Films and comic strips have featured mechanical men for years. Actors with plastic skin give performances in stores, and uniformed robots beckon customers into restaurants. Flag-waving robots direct street traffic. Some experts attribute the Japanese acceptance of automatons to beliefs of the Buddhist religion that all of nature is fused together—insects, rocks, sky, and even pseudo-humans.

The first recorded fatal accident involving a worker in a roboticized factory occurred in 1981. The sensationally reported death happened when a Japanese worker went into a zone restricted to robot operations and was struck by a transport robot. Journalists speculated about a future when human survival is dependent on machines. Conjectures once limited to science fiction pulps are now actual headlines, and the coming wave is still just a ripple.

AUTOMATONS ANONYMOUS

The word *robot* was coined by playwright Karel Capek in 1920 from the Czechoslovakian word *robota*, meaning "forced work." More practical definitions say a *robot* is a machine that performs certain functions according to computer programming, or simply is a tool to save labor and advance automation. Whatever the name, the age of the automaton— anything that can move or act of itself—is sure to have a profound effect on the entire industrial scene in the immediate future.

It all started with the development of a mechanized industrial manipulator by George De Vol in the 1950s. Joseph Engleberger brought the concepts to reality through Unimation, Inc., a worldwide supplier of industrial robots. Developments are now happening on many fronts. When sensory capacity is perfected, robot employment will emerge from narrowly repetitive operations in dirty, hot, and dangerous jobs to more skillful occupations. Remarkable inventiveness is leading to "smart" robots that have the ability to make basic decisions.

A robot "thinks" according to its programmed memory. Work routines are stored in the memory for a variety of jobs, and more jobs can be added by reprogramming. A robot gets "smarter" when it is equipped with apparatus for seeing and touching. A TV camera provides sight; coded signals are reported to the computer brain which allows the robot to respond to the shapes it perceives. The brain acts similarly on data reported from a tactile claw about the size, shape, temperature, softness, and vibrations of any grasped object. Sensing devices for hearing, tasting, and smelling could also be added. Moreover, perceptions would extend far beyond human abilities to detect very high and low light waves and ultrasonic waves. While these capabilities are remarkable, they are still very limited. A robot looking for objects of a certain shape must examine each one, discarding—one at a time—those that do not conform. For the time being, industrial robots will be employed to work rather than think.

The potential for spectacular productivity gains from robotization is undeniable. The inhibitor is social cost.

RAMIFICATIONS
OF ROBOTIZATION

Financial costs of robots are attractive. A typical model is priced at $40,000 and can be operated for about $5 an hour.[7] But there is a catch. The cost of associated machinery to feed and service a robot may be double or triple the first cost of the robot itself, and operating costs are reasonable only when a company has a skilled staff maintaining several robots. From an economic standpoint, having a single robot is simply tokenism.

Overestimating what robots can do for an operation is a dangerous management inclination. In general, robots are not appropriate for labor-intensive, low-unit output. When a high-volume, low-labor-content-per-unit process appears to be a likely candidate for robotization, it should still be questioned whether the work could be done more cheaply by simple machinery than by sophisticated robots. It is also worth remembering that robots never do more than they are told to do, and no robot has ever offered an innovative idea.

More than the equations of economics, the social imponderables will probably control the implementation pace of robotics. At the national level the advantages of robot-assisted production are clear-cut. Factories that operate around the clock with only a few human attendants are relatively immune to global economic pressures and remain competitive even in harsh times. Military strategists see the capability of producing high-quality weapons in virtually unlimited quantities at very low cost. Military applications evolving from robot research are mind-boggling, conjuring up memories of fifteenth-century battles fought by metal-clad mercenaries, stirring Capital Hill economists to envision robots leading the nation in its battle for world markets. These advocations follow the line that what is good for national policy is good for the citizenry.

At the corporate level the social benefits are less convincing. Freeing workers from boring, strenuous, and unsafe jobs is the rallying entreaty for accepting robotization. Lower-cost, higher-quality products for consumers are the second chorus. Retention of jobs that would otherwise be lost to foreign competition, and new jobs created to manufacture and service robots, are the clinchers. The obligatory rebuttal is that the net effect will be fewer blue-collar jobs in manufacturing.

STEEL-COLLAR
CO-WORKERS

Making amicable arrangements for more steel-collar workers in blue-collar slots may be the most severe management task of this decade. A few years from now the declining population coming into the labor force will help ease the transition to robotics, but by then the pattern will have been set. Management's response to the following directions will determine the pattern:

- Place robots in jobs that workers do not like. Even in Japan workers have been alienated when robots took away pleasant and easy jobs, leaving the dirty and unpleasant ones for people.
- Be sure the production process is ready for robotization before attempting changes. An embarrassing beginning will undermine further attempts, convincing workers that robots are a wasteful indulgence.
- Involve blue-collar workers in the planning. Make it clear that provisions have been made for their future. Start early and keep everyone informed.
- Make provisions for displaced workers. Retraining should be provided. Robot maintenance is an ideal type of training. If other positions in the company are not available for robot-replaced workers, hold off the implementation until normal attrition has provided vacancies.
- Point out the advantages robots provide for other employees. During depressed market conditions robot-run operations can be limited to a single-shift, preserving other jobs. Completely predictable robot movements contribute to a safer working enviroment.

- Seek understanding outside as well as inside the plant for the long-term gains that robotization can provide. Workweeks can be shortened and more social services can be supported from the wealth generated by robots. The robot revolution will be peaceful only if it is understood by all the participants.

ELSEWHERE
IN THE FACTORY

Robots are actually just one front in the computer invasion of manufacturing. Another revolution in factory productivity is under way. It involves the design of products and the associated tooling to coordinate material flow, production, and testing. Calling this swing to integrated systems a "revolution in manufacturing" smacks of an overused hyperbole, but it is an accurate assessment of how computer-based mechanisms are overthrowing conventional manufacturing practices. Foreseeable productivity gains are enormous. How soon they materialize depends on industry's willingness to find the funds and fortitude to implement the technology that is currently available.

EXHIBIT 26   *CAD/CAM/CAT: CIM*

Computer-integrated manufacturing (CIM) is the amalgamation of computer-aided design (CAD) with computer-aided manufacturing (CAM) and computer-aided testing (CAT). This triad of computer-inspired advances was cradled in the United States and is now shaping the future of manufacturing worldwide. An offshoot in the metal-working sector, flexible machinery systems (FMS),[8] is well established in Europe, Japan, and the Soviet Union. The world's first fully automated factory is expected to be in operation by the late 1980s, probably in Japan.

Computer-aided designing takes place on a screen. CAD substitutes computer graphics for laborious manual drafting to put pictures on a terminal that enables designers to study various views of an assemblage before it is actually built. Different designs can be on-screen tested, seeing how they react to changes in operating conditions such as overloads, sudden shock, and partial damage. But these displays are not inexpensive. Besides the costly equipment, scores of programmers are necessary to write millions of lines of coded instructions to create the sophisticated design images.

Once a program is in place, however, design changes can be done in minutes instead of weeks, as was required for pencil-and-paper revisions. The consequent reductions in time from product concept to hardware can go a long way toward averting time overruns that have plagued manufacturers in recent years. CAD also makes it possible to instantly exchange design data by computers between contractors, vendors, and subcontractors. As manufacturers increasingly ask vendors to accept parts specifications in the digital languages understood by computers, the relationship between customer and supplier will be dramatically altered. CAD adoptions in big companies will result in a chain reaction of supporting CAD implementations in smaller companies that should improve productivity in every link.

CAM and CAT are a bit less exotic than CAD. Computer-controlled production machines are quite commonplace. In many factories the machines are served by computer-controlled material handlers, and computer-aided testing and inspections are increasing as new devices become available. Expenditures for CAM and CAT are justified by studies that indicate that a part spends 5 percent of the time being machined and 95 percent moving or waiting in a standard manufacturing process.[9]

The linkage of CAD, CAM, and CAT into a fully integrated system is what excites productivity dreamers. Ideal computer-integrated manufacturing would allow anyone in the factory to tap the common pool of production data to deal with scheduling, inventory, purchasing, and other planning problems. Operational CIM would reduce material waste, improve quality, shorten development time, and maximize output of labor and capital inputs. In short, CIM spells productivity.

Contrary to the wilder claims of CIM proponents, all of the nation's productivity problems will not be solved by computer-controlled mechanisms. However, CIM impacts a large proportion of the industries that constitute the nation's industrial base, and from that base flow the products that determine the health of the economy. Although most of the heralded applications of CIM are concentrated in the metal-working sector, the concepts and machines are readily adaptable to many other sectors—wood products, textiles, mining, food processing, and so forth. The crucial point is that CIM is here and is available now. It is no longer a vision to be dealt with in the future.

Both management and labor must adjust their thinking to accommodate the benefits obtainable from CIM while minimizing the pain of its exploitation. Aches will be felt by companies that lack resources to upgrade their facilities and consequently become uncompetitive, and by people who are forced to relocate or learn new trades. Unattended aches could inflame to jolting spasms of protest that deprive everyone of technological blessings in order to appease vociferous critics.

*CIM*ULATION

Moves toward CIM involve more than just buying new machines. Professional staffs must know how to use a computer-integrated system. Business planning and support must be able to take advantage of all the additional information provided by real-time computer reports to improve customer services and inventory management. Designers must be able to employ advantageously the time-saving features of interactive computer modeling. Not all members of the current management class possess the qualifications to thrive in a CIM environment.

"CIMulation" of production will have a larger effect on management positions than most managers realize, but most objections to it will come from organized labor. The considerations given for introducing robotics into a plant apply equally to CIMulation. These considerations were addressed by a resolution adopted by delegates to the 1980 UAW convention: "With their vast memories and 'real-time' analysis capabilities, computers could become the 'Big Brother' watching every worker every minute; and so-called efficiency gain produced by that approach is not worth the cost in self-respect and other human value."

No fair employer wants or expects a computerized eye in the ceiling to spy on employees and sound an alarm when the work pace slackens.[10] Such degrading practices deserve scorn by management and union alike. But a movement to defend every job threatened by CIM defeats the whole intent of technology-based productivity improvement.

Without doubt many current work skills will be devalued by technological advances, and the need for new skills will grow commensurately. Accommodations are necessary to ease the adjustment. Suggestions made by the UAW include the following:

- Strong contract language to deal with bargaining-unit erosion, job assignments, and training
- Prenotification to the union of plans to introduce new technologies
- Reduction of worktime without loss of pay, so that more job opportunities are created
- Public assistance for income maintenance of victims of job displacement
- Standards set for health and safety hazards associated with new technologies

Where the suggestions protect human dignity and social welfare, they are valid. Where they subsidize individual or class gains at the expense of general social gain, they are discriminatory. Confining benefits from CIM to those directly involved with it, by awarding more pay for less work, is as unfair as neglecting employees who are adversely affected by CIM. Negotiations to decide how smart machines will be assimilated into each production process should include, at least in spirit, a representative of the general public, because CIM fuels the production base from which productivity achievements radiate to strengthen the whole economy.

MEANWHILE, BACK AT THE OFFICE . . .

The extravagantly advertised office of the future is under construction. Its reliance on computers is no less than the factory of the future. The entire service industry is becoming ever more computer conscious, enough so to earn its own monogram: CIS—computer-integrated services. Assuming that the office is a microcosm of the service sector, the deluge of devices described in Exhibit 27 confirms the renovation now under way in white-collar territory.

EXHIBIT 27   *AUTOMATED OFFICES*

A productivity audit conventionally notes that an office is notoriously labor intensive and supports the observation with figures that compare capital investment per office worker with that of factory and farm workers: respectively, about $2,500, $45,000, and $65,000. Even if investment per worker stays in the same proportion, big bucks will be spent on offices just to keep pace with the increasing number of white-collar employees, now well over half the work force and rising. Those dollars are under siege by an

FUNCTION	ACTIVITY	TYPICAL COST PERCENTAGE
Information creation	Generation of ideas and words by an author: thinking, analysis	28%
Information capture	Putting thoughts and words into a process-ible medium: notes, dictation	14
Entry and editing	Entering the system: keyboarding	13
Materialization	Output and duplication: printing, copying, micro-filming	10
Distribution	Disseminating data: mail, cable, facsimile, elec-tronic mail	19
Storage and retrieval	Safeguarding and accessing stored data: index, search	15
Disposal	Purging the storage files	1

Source: Adapted from Robert M. Dickinson, "Exxon: How a Major Corporation Is Coping with the Pressures of an Office Automation Program," *Industrial Engineering,* July 1980. Reprinted with permission from *Industrial Engineering Magazine,* July 1980. © Institute of Industrial Engineers, Inc., 25 Technology Park/Atlanta, Norcross, GA 30092.

army of vendors offering a bewildering variety of products: desktop computers, word processors, management work stations, electronic in-baskets, electronic calendars, and teleconferencing.

Vernacular confusion is diluted by examining the functions of business communication systems. Shown on page 121 are seven components and associated cost proportions for information generation and handling.[11]

If CIM and robots are indeed causing a revolution in manufacturing, office automation exemplifies the seemingly perpetual electronics revolution. A 1980 survey by Booz, Allen, & Hamilton indicated a 15 percent improvement in productivity by 1985 for companies that aggressively pursue office automation. The following guidelines can help achieve this prophesied jump in productivity:

- Improve existing manual procedures and paper flow before trying to automate. A manual mess converts to an automated mess.
- Start small and proceed gradually. Swallowing computerization too fast causes electronic indigestion.
- Integrate the new technology gently into the existing office structure. Finding what people want beats telling them what they need, especially if they do not need what experts want them to have.
- Persuade rather than force. Provide training and let satisfied users sell the technology to the reluctant ones. If an electronic work station becomes a status symbol, it sells itself.
- Start soon, but be patient. Allow users to adjust to the new system at their own pace. If "old hands" resist the change, pamper the generation that accepts change until the resisters see by comparison how they are disadvantaging themselves.
- Don't get discourgaged. Remember that some people who profess to be 100 percent for progress are 100 percent against change.

CRITIQUE OF COMPUTER-INTEGRATED SERVICES

A roll call of operations affected by computerization would last interminably, the list always lengthening. A discouraging list could also be tabulated of the companies that have been disappointed by some of their computer experiences. Many computerized systems have been justified by the amount of manual labor they would replace, but the replacements never took place. Instead, new positions were often created to serve the new machines. Where business increased enough to utilize the expanded capacity, a productivity gain did occur. But when the same information was simply transferred from file storage to computer memory, paper reports were just converted to printouts, and data for decisions became more voluminous but no better; the technology was wasted.

Savants of computerology stress that the setting must be ready for the insertion of new technology, or the frustration of its implementation will destroy its value. For example, many small, old-fashioned lumber mills have been modernized by computerized sawing systems, at considerable consternation to old-fashioned lumber workers. Although the old hands realized the wood- and time-saving advantages of the new cutting technology and seldom forcefully opposed the change, they were not enthusiastic. After working out the bugs of installation, company engineers expected the new machines to operate smoothly. Seldom did they do so. Breakdowns were frequent, and quality fell below expectations. Many of the failures were traced to well-intentioned mistakes. The new electronic machines were treated like the old mechanical machines they had replaced: Settings were not quite precise enough, maintenance was not strict enough, repairs were crudely done, and operating difficulties were overcome with more brute force than the sophisticated equipment could stand. Behind these difficulties is the simple fact that newly labeled "knowledge-workers" have to be given enough knowledge to squeeze productivity out of sophisticated gadgetry.

A different kind of difficulty has frustrated the adoption of computer-assisted checkout counters in supermarkets. Electronic scanners use a tiny laser beam to read the price encoded on nearly all product labels to record and total a customer's purchases automatically. Besides speeding up the checkout lines, the scanning process eliminates the chore of marking prices on each item and keeps closer track of grocery inventories. Resistance to their wider use has arisen from customers, not employees. Many shoppers get angry when they cannot find a price marked on a box or a can and have pressured legislators in several states to pass laws requiring grocers to keep using individual price tags. Technology is trying to come to the rescue with a "talking" electronic scanner that vocally tells customers how much cash they paid and how much change they have coming. Whether a friendlier machine can counter the resistance is still unknown, but it illustrates the value of customizing technology to the situation, even if it means creating new technology to get the old technology adopted.

The banking industry has gobbled up new technology and absorbed it swimmingly. Computers have been processing funds since the mid-1950s, laying the groundwork for the introduction of automated tellers and word processors. "Big Eye" machines electronically scan seventy thousand pieces of paper money an hour, detecting worn and counterfeit bills while counting and bundling the good ones. Some banks now have electronic mail by which "written" messages are transmitted on telephone lines to computer screens. These technology-driven advances in productivity have been procured mostly from ready-to-use devices implanted in congenial knowledge-worker environments, making gains affordable and convenient.

Industries hard pressed by competitors have turned to computerized assistance in desperation. Textile manufacturers in the United States have rebounded amazingly from a 1971 low when their share of the world market dropped to 6.7 percent from a previous level of 11.1 percent. A 10.4 percent slice was captured by 1981 on the strength of heavy investment in new equipment. Much of the technology was purchased from foreign sources. Many ailing industries find that the equipment they need to catch up with foreign competitors was specially designed for them and is available only from foreign vendors. Reliance on foreign and ready-made technology almost forecloses any chance to push ahead of competition. Breaking out of this Catch-22 circle—needing the newest technology to get ahead but not being able to afford its development until the lead is won—is going to require risk taking by both the ailing industries and the U.S. suppliers that have the capability to produce the needed technology, or some of the suppliers will also be caught in Catch-22.

Warehousing and distribution industries have been quick to profit from domestic technology. During the past decade warehouses have evolved from "barn" to mechanized marvels of computer-directed storage. The movement has been spurred by spiteful jests:

CONTROLLER: A warehouse is a massive repository of goods procured with money that should be invested at a higher rate.

PURCHASING: A warehouse is a boundless area waiting to be filled with endless bargains, most of which are lost in the labyrinth too long to be appreciated.

MANAGER: A warehouse is a sink into which you pour good products that come out damaged or disappear down the drain.

SALESPERSON: A warehouse is a forbidding building overstocked with none of the products my customers order.

The warehouse, as a critical buffer between the production place and the marketplace, is buffeted by rising labor, land, utility, and energy costs. To counteract these costs, computers have been employed to keep track of inventory items, control material-handling equipment, guide fixed-path vehicles and picking heads, and coordinate shipping and receiving activities. The most spectacular development has been AS/RS—automated storage and retrieval systems. It has spawned such new products as automatic code readers for machine positioning, radio data links, and computer-controlled carousels. It has also fostered a new way of thinking about the total material-handling systems, thoughts that were ridiculous before the era of smart machines.

The systems-oriented thinking that has modernized energy conservation was force fed. In response to soaring fuel bills and government largess, thoughts went in every direction in pursuit of BTUs. Many of the grander thoughts are still just gleams in inventors' eyes, while more modest designs now monitor and direct energy consumption:

- *Sensors* detect indoor and outdoor temperatures to allow microprocessors to regulate heating and cooling as changes occur. As the sun moves around a building, the computer makes adjustments to maintain comfort levels.
- *Time-of-day* programming has microcomputers lowering nighttime temperatures, switching off lights, and shutting down or turning up production equipment in response to variable demands.
- *Duty cycling* optimizes the time furnaces and air conditioners run in response to outdoor temperatures and space utilization. Dampers also benefit from sensory computer controls.

Many technologies besides computers have contributed to the drop in energy usage, of course, and all of them deserve credit as productivity boosters because energy is a major component in the total productivity measure. Application of computer controls illustrates, however, the potential of *knowledge transfer*—use of technology developed for another purpose—to provide immediate productivity gains.

TUNING UP THE ENGINES
OF EFFICIENCY

At the same time that people revel in the achievements of technology, they distrust the consequences. In general, managers look toward new hardware for part of their future productivity growth and workers have misgivings about the future effects of labor-saving machines. Neither group fully appreciates the ramifications of the rapid movement toward smart machines and computer-aided processes because no one can accurately forecast the eventual directions the movement will take. Both groups must work together to shape events to protect employees' occupational livelihood, preserve or enhance the quality of work life, and forward productivity improvements that strengthen the national economy.

In search of greater productivity, organizations can build, buy, or borrow technology. Building from scratch is an expensive and lengthy undertaking, but its reward could be exclusive ownership of a new device, or even the founding of a new industry. Buying ready-made technology means upgrading production facilities by acquiring modern machines and structures from vendors, and possibly modifying them to perform new functions or doing designed functions better. Technology is borrowed by taking something that has been designed for another purpose and adapting it to solve a different problem, often at the suggestion of people who are facing the problem.

Whether technology is built, bought, or borrowed, its acquisition involves capital risk and transfer of knowledge. Trying anything new is risky and exposes managers to the money auditors who, according to managerial lore, enter the fray after the battle is lost to bayonet the wounded. Chances of escaping a bayonet are improved by fielding knowledgeable recruits. However, it is still possible to win the battle to implement technology and lose the war to improve productivity. The recruits have to want to win both engagements.

Finally, the adoption of labor-saving technology neither begins nor ends with its implementation. The work environment must be prepared for its introduction, especially the affected blue- and/or white-collar workers. Continuous productivity growth depends on continuing worker approval of the technology-enhanced workplace.

QUEST FOR QUALITY: Process Improvement

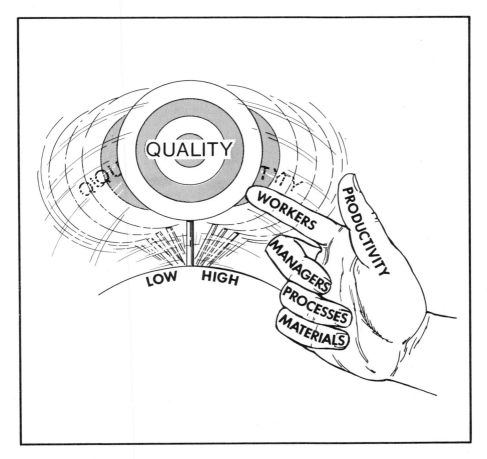

7

Quality is a moving target. It goes up and down, sometimes for no apparent reason. It is sought by every production line supervisor, office administrator, agency executive, and government official, yet some employees seem oblivious to its value, caring more about quantity quotas or looking busy than the quality of their output. When quality deteriorates, it drags productivity down with it.

In the drawing on page 127, the hand is analogous to an organization aiming at the elusive quality target.[1] The thumb represents productivity because it operates in conjunction with each finger. Workers index the way to quality, and managers trigger the charge. Processes and materials provide the grip. This chapter examines the fingerprints, observing the impression of workers, managers, processes, and materials on an organization's quest for quality.

INDISPENSABLE QUALITY

No one takes pride in producing shoddy goods and services. But the opposite is not necessarily true. A disturbing number of lackadaisical employees just put in their time, carefully watching the clock for start and stop times, concerned with quality only to the extent that their per-formance meets minimum standards, and convinced that their paycheck is earned by enduring forty hours per week. They are probably not even aware of the damage they are doing to the organization's reputation, or the frantic effort of fellow workers to rectify the shoddiness of their work. Quality has to be designed and built into a product or service, reigning preeminent in everyone's activities.

Experts point out that "quality is free," being just a matter of getting people to do the things they ought to be doing anyway. None-theless, reminding people of what they ought to be doing, providing them with the time, skills, and equipment to do it, and verifying that it has indeed been done, is costly. All the pieces have to fit together to avoid spasms of corrections in response to complaints from internal inspectors or disgruntled customers, as evidenced by all the components of quality assurance found in an industrial enterprise (see Exhibit 28).

Two aspects of quality are implied by the display of functions in the exhibit. *Objective quality* is a measurable property of the product or service. It is the property of statistical quality control, a well-developed discipline with roots in American industry that stretch back to the 1930's. *Subjective quality* is a perceived value that influences customer purchases and worker attitudes. Customers with faith in a product con-sistently choose that product rather than one offered by a competitor and may even be willing to pay a premium price for it. Equivalently, workers who believe that the quality of their output is respected have pride in

EXHIBIT 28   *BROAD-BASED INPUT MOBILIZED FOR HIGH-QUALITY OUTPUT*

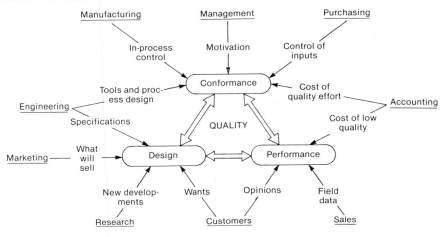

their work and greater motivation to maintain or improve their superiority. Quality breeds quality.

EXHIBIT 29   *THE VOYAGES OF DOCTOR DEMING*

The modern guru of quality is Dr. W. Edwards Deming, an American expert with an important message that was first heard across the Pacific. Dr. Deming took his expertise on statistical analysis of quality to Japan in 1950, gained fame as the father of the Deming prize for quality control, and returned to the United States as an acclaimed consultant. His sobering message for his homeland is: "American management has no idea what quality control is and how to achieve it."[2]

Deming aims his sharpest barbs at top management for not paying attention to quality, especially statistical methods for quality assurance. His recipe for quality control is deceptively simple: tally defects, examine them to find their source, correct the cause, and then keep a record of what happens afterward. He preaches that statistical analysis, not investments in equipment and automation, is the way for America to garner the gains the Japanese have enjoyed, offering the following advice to do so:

- Rely on statistical evidence of quality *during* the process, not at the end of the process. The earlier an error is caught, the less it costs to correct it.
- Rely on suppliers that have historically provided quality, not on sampling inspections to determine the quality of each delivery. Instead of a number of vendors, select and stick with a few sources that furnish consistently satisfactory quality.
- Rely on training and retraining to give employees the skills to use statistical methods in their jobs, not on slogans to improve quality.

Employees should feel free to report any conditions that detract from quality.

- Rely on supervision guided by statistical methods to help people do their work better, not on production work standards. Statistical techniques detect the sources of waste and teams of designers, supervisors, and workers eliminate the sources.
- Rely on the doctrine that poor quality is flatly unacceptable. Defective materials, workmanship, products and service will not be tolerated.

YOU CAN FOOL
SOME OF THE PEOPLE
SOME OF THE TIME

A knowledgeable purchaser of industrial goods, armed with performance specifications and expertise about exact needs, can make astute quality judgments. Typical consumers are hopelessly confused. They kick tires, slam doors, feel the texture, and study the carton. Such superficial indicators supplant true quality judgments. Professionals rate the quality of a product by its fitness for use—how well it performs a task and how long it will continue to perform it. Consumers tend to rely on "fit and finish" and other cosmetic features.

Frustrating experiences with machines that refuse to run, utensils that break, gadgets that are unsafe, and clothes that lack stitching, can breed wary consumers. Such tribulations have eroded the time-honored advantage of "made in America." According to the results of a poll of ten thousand households that was sponsored by the American Society of Quality Control (ASQC), 75 percent think that foreign-made products are equal to or better than U.S. goods.[3] Of the more than seven thousand respondents to a National Family Opinion Survey, 49 percent felt that the quality of American products had slipped in the previous five years, and over 53 percent expected it to remain at the same low level or decline further during the next five years.

Some quality experts say the criticism of American products is unjustified. They claim that the reliability of U.S. goods is actually increasing, rather than decreasing, but foreign competitors are upgrading theirs faster. They also point out that quality expectations have risen even faster, reasoning that

- New products are more complex, so there are more things that can go wrong, but consumers forget the extra attributes while remembering "old-fashioned reliability."
- The public is more aware of product failures; older products may have had

as many defects, but there was no mechanism for mass recalls of unsafe items as there is today.

- A shortage of skilled repair workers has aggravated whatever quality problems exist, causing minor repairs to become major annoyances when they are not fixed the first time.

Whether consumers' perception of poor quality is true or not, it places conventional quality assurance practices in jeopardy. Are they sufficient? If they are, why has quality deteriorated?

Amost two-thirds of the respondents to the ASQC survey doubted that U.S. workers are concerned about quality. In contrast, stories are told about the inbred diligence of German workers and the authority of every Japanese assembler to halt the production line if a defective product appears to be slipping through. Yet German and Japanese companies seem to be able to maintain their customary level of quality when they operate on U.S. soil with U.S. workers. Dr. Norbert Kaesling, quality control manager at the Westmoreland, Pennsylvania, plant of Volkswagen, says, "The American worker can do a good job if he is given proper tools and training."

There are too many examples of high-quality American-made products to even question the basal caliber of American abilities. Yet the examples of shoddy quality cited by consumers show that improvement is needed in certain areas. The only possible conclusion in these cases is clumsy management—managers who lack either concern for quality or competence to attain it. An abiding quality (alias productivity) emphasis by management is evident in the techniques described in Exhibit 30.

EXHIBIT 30   *ALL OUT FOR QUALITY*

In 1974 a division of Motorola was acquired by Matsushita Electric Industrial Company. It employs twelve hundred people in Franklin Park to produce color television receivers and microwave ovens. Five years after the changeover, in-process defects had dropped from 1.4 to 0.07 defects per set and productivity had jumped almost 30 percent. The labor required to produce a color television receiver was cut in half. These gains were achieved by blending new equipment, technology, training, and managerial practices to revitalize an already skilled labor force.[4]

Equipment. Automatic equipment developed in Japan for chassis assembly was utilized. Design changes reduced the number of required workers by 26 percent. Equipment and design engineers worked together to improve "producibility," making quality products easier to manufacture.

Technology. New assembly lines allowed workers to control their work flow individually. In place of a continuous, conveyor-paced line, operators were given foot levers to detour work to their station and to forward finished pieces to the next work stations. Closed-circuit television systems were installed to broadcast quality information to workers on the production line.

Training. The importance of quality was continually emphasized, placing responsibility on production workers, not inspectors. End-product inspection teams were replaced by a few in-process auditors who moved from one assembly line to another sampling quality. New employees receive both classroom and on-the-job training, up to five days of each, during which they learn about quality expectations, are judged on whether they can do the work adequately, and see if they like the work conditions.

Managerial Practices. Once a week all operations cease for ten to fifteen minutes while supervisors communicate with their crews. A supervisor typically talks with forty-five workers about quality, productivity, absenteeism, scrap, and any other subjects that might come up. If the supervisors cannot answer a question, they make a note of it and come prepared with an answer at the next meeting.

Every six months manufacturing and quality control people meet to set quality goals for different areas. Bar charts are kept to signal which areas are above, near, or below their targets. Special effort is concentrated on a particular production line, called the "model line," to improve its performance. Workers on that line and support groups meet once a week to explore progress. Reasons for successes in the model line are identified and adapted to fit other lines.

A quality emphasis month is declared twice a year. Awareness is aroused by slogan and poster competitions, crossword puzzles with quality terms, and suggestion contests. Winners are entertained at a restaurant and given a modest award.

The underlying purpose of all activities is to create an environment that will be conducive to co-operation and encourage people to work together to identify problems and offer suggestions to solve them.

MANUFACTURING QUALITY

Prescribing general cures for poor quality is easy. Books are full of dos and don'ts. The technical properties of statistical quality control are well known, albeit mathematically demanding. But the transition from theory to practice is a bumpy trip over many little frustrations, individually inconspicious, but collectively a barrier that cannot be smashed in one mighty drive. Small gains are secured from simple accomplishments such as

- Fitting workers with new glasses that allow them to see why errors are occurring
- Providing sorters with footrails that allow them to shift positions easier, thereby reducing fatigue and improving grading

Larger gains are delivered by getting people to stop trying to fool each other about quality. Managers are occasionally guilty of false assurances to quality planners:

- Don't worry about the new quality tester. It will be in the next budget.
- This is an absolutely reliable forecast you can count on.
- That was just a natural dip that will correct itself.
- We want top quality and are willing to pay top dollar to get it.

Meanwhile, quality planners may resort to a few alibis too:

- Don't worry about that rejected order. It can never happen again.
- What you see can't be. I have statistics to prove it.
- Unless you give us authority and money, we can't be held responsible.
- Oh, *that* estimate. Well, there's nothing wrong with the system itself. People just won't cooperate. It's their fault.

Most manufacturing quality problems stem from three basic roots: product design, process control, and management commitment. Each of these factors hosts a huge number of operational implications that have to be integrated, but the implications vary from one unit to another, imposing special constraints that forbid uniform solutions. Currently fashionable considerations for each factor are largely drawn from the quality assurance practices of foreign manufacturers.

Designing Quality into the Product

Quality not incorporated into the design and manufacturing planning phase is difficult to add later. Step one is to ascertain whether there is a market for the product. From customer expectations and estimates of sales quantity, engineers determine product specifications and manufacturing processes. Frequent design reviews are usually required to select materials and components, ensure safety, and schedule production resource development. Where product specifications cannot be met with existing machines and processes, better manufacturing capabilities must be developed or the design modified to accommodate available capabilities.[5]

Product designers are often seduced by architecture and dollar signs. Their quality morals can be protected by having quality experts involved from the beginning, not brought in after the design is finished. An aesthetic triumph on the drawing board can lead to production disasters hidden by euphoric dreams of market conquests. Besides avoiding manufacturing cost overruns, products that are easy to make are more likely to be made more reliably, and the resulting reliability may in the long run do more for sales than a clever but tediously producible shape.

Suppliers should also be brought into the design phase if they are expected to provide special services. Major manufacturers are increasingly insisting that vendors have the tools, labor force, and expertise to meet tougher standards, and they are willing to cooperate to ensure that components are available on time at the specified level of quality and volume. Vendor reliability is often rewarded by longer contracts, especially for high-technology goods.

Building Quality into the Product

An old quality control adage alleges that you cannot inspect quality into a product. Inspection, however, can at least furnish evidence that a certain quality level exists, or if not, where to look for it. A casual acquaintance with quality inspection may evoke the image of a white-coated operator hunched over a magnifying glass to scrutinize passing products. Inspections predominantly take other forms: engineers measuring the grade of a roadbed in foul weather, technicians testing samples in the comfort of a lab, workers using calipers and gauges to determine the acceptability of their work, and purchased parts or produce being graded for acceptance. In some situations, inspections are completely mechanized. In all situations, the intent is to distinguish a level of accomplishment.

Deciding *when* to inspect during a production process is reasonably uncomplicated. Logical choices include the beginning and end of a production cycle where acceptance sampling maintains the quality of incoming materials and finished product inspections ensure outgoing quality; in-process inspections should precede costly, irreversible, or masking operations. Deciding *who* inspects is less apparent.

Inspection policies range from frequent and rigorous inspections by a large quality control staff to complete reliance on operators to inspect their own work as they do it. German manufacturers are known for their elaborate product inspections.[6] Japanese manufacturers, however, tend to employ few inspection teams, relying instead on their workers to measure and continually assess quality. What both policies have in common is an extensive record-keeping system. Data are collected on the number of rejects, name and location of defects, source of fault, and degree of seriousness. Computers grind out cumulative records to pinpoint trouble areas and predict incipient quality problems. The information is fed back to inspection teams and disseminated to workers, often in the form of artistic bar charts that increase quality awareness.

Other characteristics of inferior quality are time overruns on contracts for large projects, delivery delays, slow repairs, and excessive downtime in machine centers and production lines. These *timing* problems can often be traced to the poor quality of purchasing procedures, material-handling systems, maintenance, and safety programs, all of which proclaim again the multidimensionality of the quest for quality.

Inventories are accumulated to protect production operations from time delays. A stockpile of anything serves as an insurance policy against disturbances that could disrupt ongoing shipments or production, but it is an idle resource, consuming space and investment funds. Attempts to minimize inventory and still protect operations and deliveries have led to computerized balancing systems such as MRP—material requirements planning.[7] Like most evolving technologies, implementation of MRP is seldom hitchless and occasionally formidable, but the potential rewards to productivity from improved material management, as enlarged upon in Exhibit 31, ensure its continued cultivation.

EXHIBIT 31   *JUST-IN-TIME PRODUCTION*

An ideal inventory system would have a single unit enter the production process exactly when it is needed. Irregular production requirements forbid such exact scheduling, but the Japanese keep their inventories lean by a system appropriately called "just-in-time," or *Kanban*. This system relies on fixed production schedules and careful planning to have small batches of materials and parts arrive at work stations only as they are needed.

A Kanban is actually a small card on which directions are given to produce or deliver a certain item. A Kanban is thus a tool that triggers production or delivery of necessary products in the appropriate quantities at the precise time.[8] The simplicity of Kanban is refreshing—no elaborate computer programs or multisheet ordering forms. Kanban convenience, however, comes at the expense of flexibility. Production schedules must be set well in advance, products must be standardized wherever possible, and workers must exercise extreme conscientiousness in handling Kanbans. Substantial cost savings make the effort worthwhile.

Direct savings from reducing the amount of inventory on hand include lower interest expenses owed for stored stock, less warehouse and factory space to heat and maintain, and reduced handling. A not so apparent advantage is the way that the removal of buffer stocks exposes operations to closer scrutiny. A machine breakdown is more consequential, and defective work practices cannot be ignored when parts are needed quickly.

Just-in-time production requires nearly perfect delivered quality and complete trust in vendors when parts are subcontracted. It explains the close partnership between a company and one, or perhaps a select few, reliable parts-vendors, and it reaffirms the rationale for preventing defects rather than detecting them. In effect, the Japanese have capitalized on high quality at each stage of production to cut production costs—a remarkable twist to conventional reasoning that better quality must be bought by higher manufacturing cost.

Managing for Quality

A call for management commitment is a standard issue in all drives to improve operating efficiency. Calls are typically answered if managers can clearly see economic gain and a straightforward program to achieve the gains. Quality improvement does not have the immediate attraction of a cost-reduction proposal because the gains are generally not instantaneous or assured. Quality is therefore likely to be given lip service rather than a budget. What has to be recognized is that quality and productivity are two sides of the same coin. If productivity is worth pursuing, then quality must share the attention. Consistently higher levels of quality and productivity cannot be attained by a big-bang campaign, and quick profits are not automatically registered, but long-term prospects should be sufficient to attract unreserved management commitment.

Quality assurance and safety interests have a lot in common. They share a wholesome thrust: protection of workers and consumers. And better records in either one contribute to higher productivity. It is natural, therefore, to weave the three concerns together. Many plants have well-established safety programs and less well developed quality and productivity activities. In such cases it may be possible to build on the safety-oriented organization to direct the attention of workers and supervisors toward related quality and productivity considerations. In this way, management commitment is not diluted by independent activities that have the same overall objectives.

Some tactics to consider:

- **Give greater visibility to concern for quality by utilizing both proven and innovative techniques.** Post flashy statistical control charts in areas responsible for the graphed data, have a regular column on quality in the company news organ that reports customer opinions as well as internal accomplishments, and so forth.
- **If a productivity push is being planned, give quality and safety efforts a prominent role.** Assign representatives to a Productivity Council who are agents for both quality and safety. If a productivity program is still a future objective, get the quality and safety leaders together to launch mutually supportive activities; then roll these over into a coordinated productivity drive.
- **Start a Quality College, or invigorate existing training to focus on quality.** Do not be content with motivation lessons. Teach principles and statistical techniques of quality control: cause-and-effect diagraming, basic statistical relationships, graphical correlation analysis, and control charting. Results can be gratifying. We have found that line employees welcome the opportunity to learn about quality control and put the acquired skills to work on their jobs. By spreading the training sessions over several months, attention to quality performance is maintained over an extended period during which substantial progress can be recorded.
- **Delegate partial responsibility for inspection to individual workers in offices as well as the factory.** After the operators have been trained, they

can either augment or replace some of the duties of regular quality inspectors. This delegation is confirmation of trust in employees and builds company loyalty.

- **Keep banging away at the importance of quality.** When activities begin to get as spontaneous as a metronome, spice them with contests, a "QC Day," or special programs. Although banner waving has only a brief impact, one-time spectaculars can rejuvenate a tired routine. Some ideas are available from classic Zero Defect campaigns.

EXHIBIT 32   *OBJECTIVE: ZERO, THAT IS,* NO *DEFECTS*

Everyone surely agrees that the objective of attaining zero defects is noble, maybe not possible, but idealistically sound. From its introduction in aerospace-defense industries in 1962, the Zero Defect (ZD) concept has spread over the world. To some users it is a motivational approach in which posters and speeches are aimed at employees to get them to sign a pledge for better quality. In other applications, generally more successful, ZD is used to change attitudes by emphasizing prevention instead of cure, to get a job done correctly the first time, every time.

According to ZD philosophy, the two main causes of mistakes are lack of knowledge and lack of attention. The easier of the two to correct is knowledge. Training, follow-up, and feedback can develop the needed quality skills.

Lack of attention is more serious and more difficult to combat. In some situations an altered work environment can compensate for inattention through better communicatons, easier material identifications, and simpler procedures. Of at least equal importance to physical conditions is mental indoctrination to convince workers they *can* produce zero defects. The people-are-human-and-humans-make-errors attitude has to be replaced by a belief that mistakes are not normal; they do not *have* to happen.

"Error Cause Removal" is a key feature of a ZD program. Each worker is encouraged to identify and concentrate on all causes of errors on the job. "Error Cause Identification" forms are filled out to describe each error situation and are submitted to supervisors; if a solution to the situation is known, it too is recorded. As in any suggestion plan, rapid response by supervisors is vital. The dispatch with which suggestions are acted upon largely determines the integrity of the campaign.

The following administrative features are typically included in the planning, initiation, and follow-through of a ZD program:

Planning. After an administrator has been selected, a ZD committee is organized with a representative from all departments included in its horizontal makeup. Once planning has been completed, the committee acts as a liaison team to launch the program. Orientation and indoctrination sessions are conducted for managers and supervisors before the program kickoff. Support is also sought from union officials.

Promotion. Interest in the program is stirred by publicity. A "teaser" approach uses posters, bulletin-board notices, and announcements in company papers or over the address system to build enthusiasm for a climactic kickoff. The inaugural should be impressive. Mass meetings followed by individual department confabs are common. Top managers speak at the large gatherings, and supervisors explain details at group get-togethers. Banners, posters, pennants, and wandering visitations remind employees throughout the kickoff day that the program is not a one-shot promotion.

Continuance. All employees are encouraged to sign pledge cards signifying their intent to reduce mistakes. Employees' contributions are further emphasized by Error Cause Removal reporting. Individual achievements are recognized by pins, plaques, dinners, and announcements. Departments also receive recognition for meeting goals. "Days without Errors" scorecards are posted. Particularly good ideas are exchanged between departments, with credit given to originators.

Whether the ZD concept for quality improvement and maintenance is a guide or gimmick, momentary or momentous, is resolved by management's commitment and talent to implement it. If workers really understand that *zero defects* is an actual statement of the quality objective, and if management has enough conviction to keep chasing the objective, quality climbs—as does productivity.

SERVICE AND GOVERNMENT QUALITY

Quality is quality, be it in industrial products or in services produced in the public or private sectors. The most common discrepancy is that quality and productivity are far more difficult to measure for services, making it impossible to get a handle on current performance in order to know what to improve. Difficult to measure, yes, but impossible to improve, no. Service activities are coming under closer scrutiny, being exposed to the same objective analysis techniques that industrial engineers have used for half a century to study manufacturing, and solid measurements are evolving. Improvement methods that work in manufacturing are usually applicable not only in service industries but also in government—methods improvement, automation, and worker participation.

Inferior service quality is criticized just as vehemently, or perhaps more so, than defective products. Clues for correction are embodied in the criticism:

- Volume has prompted mail-order companies to install automatic equipment to dial customers and inform them that the merchandise they ordered is ready. The cheery monologue was not well received in one city where the calls were made from midnight to 5:00 a.m. It seems that someone unplugged and moved the equipment that day and then forgot to reset the clock. **Objective:** Pay attention (à la ZD).

- Nearly half the buyer complaints reported to Better Business Bureaus are about mail-order companies. One complaint told of sending $10 to a mail-order house for a "valuable engraved picture of Abraham Lincoln." A Lincoln penny was sent by return mail. This near fraud still beats no reply at all to paid-for orders, as often reported. **Objective:** Have a legitimate product before worrying about quality.
- A dress was returned to a department store for a larger size. Bills sent for both dresses were excused due to "computer error." **Objective:** Build in quality checks for automated procedures (and people procedures, too).
- Taxpayers complain about the cost of schools. During the past decade the student population in Boston schools declined by 33 percent while the teaching staff increased by 13 percent and the nonteaching staff by 150 percent. **Objective:** If quality is up, be sure customers know it (and taxpayers, too).

Designing Quality Services

Service is a commodity. Just as a product's quality can be evaluated by its reliability, finish, and conformance to specifications, so too can a service be measured by timeliness, accuracy, and completeness. Some dimensions are obvious. A new roof should not leak, a cashier should give the correct change, and deliveries should be delivered to the right address. Other aspects of service are less distinct. How thoroughly should the roofer clean up after the job? Should a cashier be a lookout for shoplifters? What is the value of special effort made to deliver, safely, an incorrectly addressed parcel?

After finding out what customers want, the next step is to decide to what degree each want can be satisfied within resource constraints. Should a fast-food chain staff its shop to serve every customer within two minutes from the time an order is placed? How vital is it to have reservation phones answered within twenty seconds? Is a 5 percent error rate for medication doses meted out in nursing homes too high? How important is it to have 95 percent of all airline flights leave on time and have the baggage delivered to the terminal claims area within fifteen minutes of the flight's arrival? Answers to these types of questions put dimensions on service and provide needed reference points for assessing quality.

When there is direct competition, companies can compare their service levels with those of the competitors to establish base lines for quality control. Airlines regularly compare their offerings with those of competitors to keep their passengers satisfied *and* to keep costs under control by not offering excessive service. Lack of competition forces many government agencies to set standards according to internally determined objectives; for example, it is almost impossible to rate the quality of a military unit without a war. A few government services have counterparts in the private sector; for example, the General Accounting Office found that federally owned power stations are more labor intensive

(98 percent) and cost more (20 percent) per kilowatt-hour than private utilities.

Historical performance records are a reasonable base for quality assessment if no other references are available, but they are suspect if technological improvements have upgraded service functions in recent years. Expecting the same quality of work from a modern automated office as from a 1965 office is as absurd as concluding that a slide rule is equal to a hand-held calculator. Health care is a good example. It is a labor-intensive industry that has benefited from massive research expenditures and has grown until it is now the third largest industry in the nation. Elaborate life-sustaining mechanisms, new drugs, and better-educated workers provide services undreamt of just a few years ago. The resulting elevation of patients' expectations has altered service standards, other than the timeless esteem for tender loving care.

EXHIBIT 33   *NURSING QUALITY*

Nursing activities in hospitals illustrate most of the considerations required in quality control of services. Design of the procedure starts with the identification of nursing specialties: medical, pediatrics, intensive care, etc. Specific characteristics are determined within each specialty and are collected under responsibility categories such as patient care, patient environment, nursing care plan, and record keeping.

A checksheet is then prepared which contains questions about all the characteristics; answered sheets reveal the level of performance. Following are typical questions to be answered yes, no, or not applicable:

- Have adequate measures been taken to make the patient with no need for immediate attention as comfortable as possible?
- Is the patient clean and dry?
- Is the bed neatly made and in proper position?
- Are the bedside stand and personal effects within easy reach?
- Is the appropriate armband identification being worn?
- Have discontinued drugs been returned to the pharmacy?
- Are progress notes complete and current?

About ten to fifteen questions are included in four to eight categories. A nursing supervisor makes unannounced observation visits to each unit on each shift. She marks answers and comments on the checksheet. Feedback occurs when reports are returned to the nursing units.

Composite quality ratings are obtained by weighting scores in each category. For instance, an inspection could reveal ninety yes and twelve no (88 percent yes) answers for "patient care" and fifty-eight yes and fifteen no (79 percent yes) for "patient environment," which converts to a weighted score of 35 (when 40 is perfect) for patient care and 16 (20 is perfect) for patient environment. This weighting puts more importance on patient care than environment. The *quality index* is the sum of the weighted scores. The result from each inspection is recorded on a chart to show quality trends.

Maintaining Service Quality

Maintenance of satisfactory service is complicated by the relationship of quality to productivity. Since the service sector is labor intensive, gains in productivity are mostly obtained by reducing labor-hours, but such improvements have full effect only if the existing quality level is maintained with the reduced work force. In most cases this means that the quality of performance by retained employees has to increase to perpetuate the quality of the organization's output. The end result is a quality treadmill where belt speed is the productivity rate; as the quality increases, it is necessary to run faster just to stay in place.

Time is a critical parameter in service, just as in manufacturing. Since time cannot be stored on a shelf to be pulled off when needed, the inventory practices used in manufacturing are not directly adaptable to most services. However, time can occasionally be "bankrolled" by reserving resources that can be tapped during busy periods. An information bureau, for instance, bought time by developing an electronic reference system to expedite answers for routine questions; quality went up and so did capacity. Tickle files and oft-used paragraphs held in computer memory serve the same function for executives, as does any advance work done during slow periods. Consultants or skilled part-time workers who can be called in during rush periods are also time buffers.

The systematic way to uncover time-wasting operations is by applying industrial-engineering techniques traditionally associated with manufacturing. Elimination of unneeded acts and unnecessary movements frees operators to spend time on activities that contribute to quality. Intel Corporation has vigorously analyzed its administrative procedures by using conventional work simplification techniques to correct such situations as requiring twelve pieces of paper and ninety-five administrative steps to order a $2.79 mechanical pencil; after simplification the process took only one form and eight steps.[9]

EXHIBIT 34   *MAPPING MOVES TO IMPROVE SERVICE*

Methods analysis is a favorite technique of management analysts for studying service functions. It relies on charting to portray the present method of doing things as the first step in designing an improved way of operating. A flow process chart, as displayed in the accompanying diagram, employs five symbols to represent what is happening: A circle is

Type and Purpose	Characteristics	Illustration	
		Symbols	Description
Single column— to study the detailed steps in a relatively simple process	Charts are often drawn on printed forms; processes are shown by connecting appropriate symbols; space is provided for additional data	○ □ ⇨ D ▽	Invoice in mail room
		○ □ ⇨ D ▽	Determine addressee
		○ □ ⇨ D ▽	To addressee's secretary
		○ □ ⇨ D ▽	Placed in action tray

		Operator	Activities
Multicolumn— to analyze detailed steps in the flow of work that is quite complex	Horizontal lines show operational areas; symbols are entered to show activities of the process	Mail clerk	[1] ⇨
		Secretary	② ⇨ ④
		Manager	③

		Mail room		Manager
Layout diagram— to improve the layout by avoiding unnecessary steps	Lines indicate the travel and symbols show the activities on a layout often drawn to scale			File
				Secretary

Source: James L. Riggs, *Production Systems: Planning, Analysis and Control,* 3rd ed. (New York: John Wiley, 1981), p. 311.

an operation, an arrow means movement, a square means an inspection, a *D* stands for delay, and a triangle indicates storage. Nearly all work procedures can be mapped with these symbols, supplemented when necessary by brief descriptions. Lines connecting the symbols indicate the sequence of operations, who does them, and where they are done.

An analyst mentally tears the chart of current procedures apart with the intent of eliminating, combining, or rearranging operations. If a better method results from the mental gymnastics, it is committed to an "after" chart of the revised process. This new version is a picture of proposed improvements, ready for review, or available as a blueprint for installing the improved arrangements.

Physical conditions at the place of work have an overriding effect on the quality of output. Attempts to make this environment safer, more comfortable, and conducive to quality are based on principles of *human factor engineering,* also known as *ergonomics.* Extremes of hot and cold temperatures, low illumination, and high noise levels have mostly been eliminated in modern plants and offices. Less attention has been given to such irritations as uncomfortable chairs, annoying glare, hard-to-reach files, and exasperating equipment arrangements. Experts argue that more attention to the relationship between humans and machines will reduce resistance to new technology in the service sector and hasten acceptance of the "office of the future."[10]

The obvious importance of operators' skills in providing high-quality service should make the importance of training equally obvious. Yet some managers apparently assume that employees naturally possess the ability to "get along" and the skills to do familiar operations without special training. If anyone can be a salesperson, attendant, or janitor, why do some people do the job so much better than others?

McDonald's runs its Hamburger College to teach its graduates more than how to cook Big Macs (turn, never flip, a patty, and do only one at a time). Disney University indoctrinates new employees (three days for dishwashers) and teaches all kinds of "get-ahead" courses for the citizens of Disney World. Just facing customers with a smile and eye contact is a learned talent. Dealing with complaints takes still more talent, and as the variety of needed talents increases, the expediency of training increases commensurately.

Once a service is functioning as intended, furnishing the quality and quantity expected by customers, the final phase of maintenance is monitoring. Performance measures were discussed in Chapter 4. Characteristics of acceptable quality can be developed for every type of service there is. Whether the service originates in a bank or a brothel, is dispensed by a bookie or a bureaucrat, there exist measurable criteria by which quality can be tracked. AT&T, for example, rates 130 criteria each month to check its internal operations and surveys its customers to determine how service sounds at the other end of the phone line. Fast-food chains employ traveling inspectors who taste the quality and then go behind the counter to rate a long list of factors.

Essentially the same statistical techniques used to inspect manufactured products are applicable to services. Only the setting and the gauges differ. In a service setting an inspector counts the number of errors on a page, asks customers whether they are satisfied, and collects performance data that indicate the consistency and level of output. As in manufacturing, the service dispensers themselves are often the best data collectors. Counting errors and tallying complaints are sobering motivators for service improvement. Statistical-sampling methods and how to interpret the results should be part of all employees' training if they are going to police their own performance. Employees who know what is expected of them, how to provide it, how to measure results and why, are the vanguard for quality assurance.

Managing Quality Service

The tone of an organization's quality originates at the top and then drips or gushes to the levels below. Without strong top-down direction, each level assumes its own posture toward quality, almost guaranteeing uneven performance, with irregularities going unnoticed through lack of concern. There are always going to be variances in the quality of services rendered by different units, but they should be premeditated, not left to chance.

With the exception of posh establishments, service today tends to be less deferential and personal than in the past. Prices are held in check by stressing fast and efficient operations, usually at the expense of extra refinements and courtesies. Where prices dip with quality, the trade-off is genuine, often being part of the marketing strategy. It is higher prices for less quality that has aroused censure of the postal service, railroads, and nursing homes. Such examples are fodder for the perception that management either is not aware of declining quality or does not care.

Quality is particularly perplexing in government activities. The public perception of the quality of government services has never been very high, and the extravagant episodes cited in news reports hasten the deterioration. Whether expectations are too high or reports are exaggerated, it is as senseless to blame civil servants as it is to blame blue-collar workers for purported quality deficiencies. The problem is the system. While tax revolts and slashed budgets put more pressure on management to protect the quality and quantity of services, the system's bureaucracy exhibits an extraordinary capacity to resist reform:

- A typical response to a budget cut is to eliminate investments in labor-saving electronics, delay maintenance, and scale back training that would boost quality performance.
- Attempts to avert a budget cut by threatening to cancel a popular service, and then being forced to carry out the threat when the bluff is called, causes public opinion to drop another notch, reflecting disapproval of both the political maneuvering and the end result.
- The traditional practice of rewarding managers who expand their staffs and balloon their expenditures, usually generating more show than service, ignores and frustrates managers who raise quality within their regular appropriations.

With no unambiguous bottom line to discourage such practices, the most-promising reversal strategy is to encourage bureaucrats to award recognition to agencies that solicit public input to define objectives, lay out clear resource commitments to achieve the objectives, and establish a measuring system by which progress can be judged objectively.

No one claims that it will be easy.

Managers in the private sector, laboring under their profit burden, do not have it easy either. Their options are broader than those of their government counterparts, especially in their capacity to make use of financial incentives. But they still have to focus on quality, not cosmetic enhancement but basic tangible advances.

SECURITY OF QUALITY

Management's posture toward internal theft is a revealing indicator of concern for both quality and productivity. A managerial stance on thievery by employees is uncomfortable to assume and delicate to hold. As such, it is a test of mettle for managers in either manufacturing or service industries, private or public. Every organization is subject to four primary types of theft and many ingenious variations:

1. Money.   In 1981 an executive in the Beverly Hills branch of the Wells Fargo Bank nearly got away with $21 million by using the bank's computer to conduct false interbranch transactions. In a stranger case at J. Walter Thompson Company, a $100,000-plus-a-year executive reported fictitious revenue of $24.5 million from her unit of the company, creating a scandal and lots of accounting problems, but no cash loss. Money drained via cash registers and petty thefts saps an organization's funds less dramatically than computer fraud, but just as damagingly. There is no substitute for strict auditing to uncover paper swindles and plug cash drains.

2. Information.   Back in the old days before every company had a computer, important papers were secured in fireproof safes or bank vaults. Sensitive information is now being stored in computer files where an unauthorized operator can gain access to it by pressing a few keys on a computer terminal. Computer security experts admit that there is no foolproof method of protecting access by using secret codes or hiring data security specialists. Guarding against data theft has the collateral advantages of lessening the threat of vandalism and destruction by natural disaster.

3. Property.   Raw materials, parts in process, finished products, and tools and supplies are all targets for pilferage, and occasionally for big-time burglary. Containerized shipping owes its development as much to theft prevention as to transportation convenience. To counteract stealing, companies are instituting more elaborate checkout systems, internal detective forces, surveillance devices, and tattler rewards.

4. Time.   Perhaps the most insidious and certainly the most prevalent form of thievery is time theft. Most incidents seem trivial: arriving at work a few minutes late or leaving early, spending prolonged moments in socializing with co-workers, reading magazines on company time, taking extended coffee breaks, deliberately slowing down in order to create higher-paying overtime work, operating another business on the side, and so forth. Management's challenge is to distinguish between what is a reasonable respite from work, because even the most conscientious employee deserves to goof-off occasionally, and what is deliberate, planned, and continual time theft.

No solid statistics are available on the extent of stealing because few organizations other than the smallest ones keep exhaustively accurate accounts. Consensus says it is substantial, maybe massive. But there is no consensus about how to correct it. Productivity-minded managers realize how punishing in-house thievery is to the productivity ratio; it lowers the quantity and quality of output and increases the paid-for input—a double whammy.

EXHIBIT 35   *A POLICY TO SHRINK SHRINKAGE*

The discrepancy between the amount produced and the amount available for sale, or how much is purchased and how much is utilized, is *shrinkage,* and it is just as damaging to productivity as sloppy work. In practice, it may be more damaging because it is a direct drain on cash flow.

There are two types of shrinkage.

The purchase price of most commodities includes a buffer to compensate for a certain percentage of inferior or defective material. These deficiencies are expected and are worked into the cost calculations. Clever handling can reduce the negative impact of *expected* shrinkage on the production system.

The other type of shrinkage is an unanticipated decrease in value caused by negligent damage, theft, careless accounting, and general inattention. All can theoretically be corrected except for rare acts of nature. Most foreboding for future productivity is the trend toward converting *unexpected* shrinkage into *expected* shrinkage.

Instead of fighting petty theft, pilferage is accommodated in the selling price. Instead of controlling wreckage in the warehouse, a damage allowance is accepted. Whenever a penalty is considered inevitable rather than preventable, the forfeit is institutionalized. And the institute suffers.

Goods can be ruined at both ends of a process that yields a service or a product. Raw materials or supplies, which are inputs to the refinement process, are eroded by careless uncrating, misassignments, tardy delivery, and negligent record keeping. Finished goods or services are also subject to damage, deterioration, and misplacement. Such losses are especially cruel because they destroy quality at the final output stage after it has been painstakenly created within the production system.

Blames radiate in all directions: irresponsible operators, incompetent supervisors, negligent managers, malfunctioning machines, and inadequate facilities. Any or all could be guilty. Who is at fault when a crate of perishable produce gets lost in a corner until it spoils? Or a stack of collated papers is scattered? Or the glossy finish of a product gets scratched? It is easy to blame the direct perpetrator, the last operator to touch the item, but guilt seldom ends there. Facilities should be provided to safely accommodate movement, storage, and security of goods. Better supervision inhibits horseplay, careless acts, and malicious mischief. Improved planning avoids overcrowding and overwork. Close control of stock records minimizes spoilage and "lost" supplies.

Time shrinkage occurs when someone is paid while not on the job. This differs from wasting time while at work, although both have the same eventual effect on productivity. A disguised no-show or a sneak-out-early is a premeditated act. It is likely to be a more serious symptom of trouble than time wasting, owing to the need for conspirators. Someone has to check in or cover for an undetected absentee.

Obvious preventive measures are rigid procedures for checking in and out, assigned work areas, random headcounts, and work sampling. The underlying cause is difficult to confront. Like malicious mischief, disguised absences indicate poor morale and weak supervision. White-collar time thieves are more numerous because they are not as closely regulated as their blue-collar counterparts, and there is managerial reluctance to blow the whistle on peers and office mates.

The general cure for shrinkage is, of course, good management. As in all management cures, it is first necessary to recognize that a problem exists. Next comes the commitment to do something. Then come objectives. Since shrinkage is a physical manifestation of weak organizational pride, the overall objective is to instill trust and allegiance in the whole work force. Loyal employees do not steal; they realize their personal gain is at the expense of their co-workers. Damage is avoided by faithful operators who are well trained and conscientious. Time thefts are discouraged by peer pressure.

Shrinkage is just a small part of productivity, but a very sensitive one. Its control depends far more on management skill and employee involvement than on technological tricks. Skill and involvement require a personal touch.

EMPLOYEE POWER: Worker Involvement

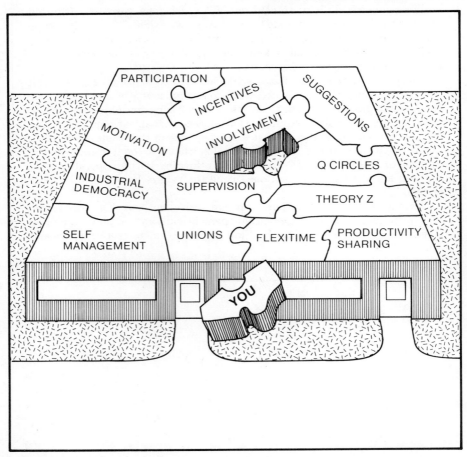

8

The "YOU" in the facing diagram is an employee, a hired hand, a borrowed brain. An employee is also a person with feelings, abilities, and ambitions. Employees bring personal characteristics to work where they merge with the social texture of the rest of the work force to shape an organization. When the characteristics blend smoothly, the organization is well regarded by its members and is usually productive. A growing awareness of employees' work-life expectations and the productivity gains that can be achieved by fulfilling them is gradually complementing traditional managerial lore.

While the rapid deployment of robots and computers can aptly be called revolutionary, the trend toward recognition of employee power is strictly evolutionary. Management theorists have been expounding on the merits of a "motivated" work force ever since the word was coined and have sundered the mechanics of motivation to compile a bewildering mixture of explanations and suggestions. Bits and pieces of behavioral methodology have steadily found their way into employee-relation practices, sometimes building trust that produced lasting results, but more often arousing grand prospects that soon clashed with the realities of entrenched beliefs that equated worker participation with management giveaways. Isolated successes were extolled in the literature, but the behavioral movement remained more faddish than fervent—until now.

The sudden spurt of interest in worker-oriented programs hit the United States in the late 1960s. Whether it was born of desperation or enlightenment, the concern for greater employee involvement now rates top billing in business journals, convention proceedings, and management meeting agendas. This interest may yet fade as it washes against resisting management styles and the prevailing "quick-fix mentality," but it is conceivably the first manifestation of a basic structural upheaval in the relationship between the managers and the managed.

This movement has no accepted name nor clearly defined principles and conceptual underpinnings. Its most recognizable U.S. examples are *quality circles* and *quality of work life* programs. In other countries where the movement started earlier, names associated with it include *industrial democracy* and *self-management*. Whatever it is called, this rationale expands the responsibilities and influence of employees by delegating authority downward to allow wider participation in planning and decision making. It assumes that people want to participate in work-related activities, are willing to work toward common objectives, and will improve productivity as they do so.

QUALITY OF WORK LIFE CONCEPTIONS

Ted Mills, the eloquent president of the American Center for the Quality of Work Life, defines *quality of work life* (QWL) as "a cost-effective, value-based, process-based, problem-solving technology for making work organizations more contemporary, productive, and effective."[1] He expands the definition by adding "and profitable" when it is applied to private-sector industry.

This pithy recital is wealthy in implications. "Value-based" refers to the foundation of respect for human needs, abilities, and dignity that supports QWL. "Process-based" indicates a flexible approach that emphasizes development of individual skills and an organizational structure to provide opportunities for exercising personal abilities in solving operational problems. These bases nourish participation in decision forming that draws on the skills of an educated work force to enhance productivity and simultaneously improve work-life satisfaction.

The nebulosity of the QWL depiction has fostered a broad variety of applications, all sharing essentially the same intent but inevitably differing in content and substance. And differ they should, to conform to each organization's composition. QWL efforts flop when they are imposed in a hostile environment or initiated without adequate preparation and commitment. Before an organization jumps into QWL, an audit should be conducted to determine management's commitment, workers' attitudes, and what types of QWL activities are most appropriate.

Managers' reservations about QWL generally stem from hearsay about bad experiences with participatory schemes or a deep-seated feeling that QWL threatens their right to manage. Until the misconceptions and apprehensions are overcome, there is no way that the necessary commitment can be obtained. To gain accord, they should recognize that

> QWL is more than happiness therapy—interpersonal concerns are important, but it is well known that contented and adjusted employees are not necessarily productive workers.
>
> QWL is not a replacement for the grievance system or the established communications network—complaints may be taken care of informally and the work atmosphere may be a bit less formal, but traditional information channels are still necessary.
>
> QWL is adaptable—not having a rigid structure means that there is no canned program for automatic application; instead each organization designs activities to counter particular weaknesses while advancing desired strengths.
>
> QWL is not planned permissiveness—although time off may be granted for QWL activities and new operational relationships may evolve, output expectations are not lowered, nor is the management function abridged.
>
> QWL is for anyone—comparable advantages from employee participation can be found in offices and service agencies as well as in factories, and participants can wear white or blue collars and can be union or nonunion.

Many companies already have QWL, though it might not be a formally instituted regimen. Where people management is an effective cornerstone of corporate culture, and the people realize its preeminence, a special QWL effort is redundant. Conversely, where people concern has been neglected, as evidenced by union friction, low morale, and shoddy performance, QWL effort *might* alleviate the deficiencies. "Maybeness" arises from the reality that an organization that previously placed a low priority on people management will assuredly encounter turnaround difficulties in starting QWL.

EXHIBIT 36   *PRODUCTIVITY AUDIT*

A QWL or productivity audit is an advisable exercise before plunging into a major people-oriented program. The purpose of the audit is to identify the inadequacies of current operations, attitudes of employees, and sentiments of management. Among the questions to answer are the following:

What is the nature of grievances or gripes heard from the work force?

What is behind disturbances that affect employee and/or union relationships?

What are the most serious problems that inhibit production—absenteeism, turnover, accidents, downtime, reject rates, etc.?

What characteristics of operations contribute to lower than expected performance—inattention, horseplay, lack of enthusiasm, make-work, no respect for quality, etc.?

What opinions do employees have about working conditions—adequacy of facilities (crowding, lighting, ventilation, noise, etc.), condition of equipment, and conveniences (cafeteria, parking, in-plant transportation, etc.)?

What apprehensions do employees have about the organization—paternalism, misemployment, restrictive procedures, too much paperwork, unfair performance appraisals and promotion policies, provincialism, weak internal communication, etc.?

What is the prevailing perception of management—not willing to listen, ineffective structuring of assignments, weak supervision, lack of interest in employees' concerns, unkept promises, unwilling to share information about future plans, etc.?

What are the attitudes of individual managers toward employee participation in operations and planning?

What is the extent of management's commitment to QWL—willingness to share responsibilities and revise operating procedures, dedication to the concept of deeper involvement, provisions for financial backing, ability to react to suggested changes, etc.?

What are the long-range plans for the organization?

Based upon the answers to such questions, an organization should comprehend current strengths and weaknesses, be able to set reasonable objectives, and be in a position to decide how to move from here to there, aware of restrictions and the value of improvement. From the lengthy list of fashionable tactics that can be initiated to implement QWL, each

> organization can then select the tactical options that best suit its employees, workplace, and strategic objectives.

SMORGASBORD
OF PARTICIPATION
STRATEGIES

Why get involved? Many barnacled bosses view the parade of participation schemes as recycled theories and one-night stands. They scoff at the possibility of lasting good, pointing out that faddish programs tend to be superficial, temporary, and unappreciated after the introductory passion has subsided, leaving in their wake a cynical work force, whetted appetites for more freebies, and a larger human relations department that thrives on make-work activity. To them, involvement equates to frustration. To the "enlightened" breed, involvement is a modern necessity.

A quick scan of any firm's financial data shows why people planning is worth thinking about. A typical manufacturing firm finds each dollar of its revenue roughly distributed in the following pattern:

Compensation to employees	43¢
Paid to suppliers of material and services	45
Debt retirement and asset replacement	7
Federal, state, and local taxes	3
Return to shareholders	2

The spotlight centers on employee compensation, revealing what a large chunk of income is parceled out within the walls of the company as wages and fringes. Less attention is often given to the validity of these pay-rolled outlays than to bills from outside suppliers. More attention to returns from payroll dollars may disclose how active employee involvement generates more income dollars.

Crusty managers with long memories of flawed employee programs may not appreciate the difference between today's employees and those who participated in past years, nor may they be aware of younger managers' concerns about employee satisfaction. The latest generation looks askance at the venerable contract of "a day's work for a day's pay." Young, educated, and ambitious employees tend to expect generous pay *and* significant, personally satisfying work. Being more mobile and attuned to leisure-time glorification, they put less value on a good attendance record and employer loyalty. The combination of upraised work-life expectations and indifference to many conventional precepts of employment is straining industrial mores, but it also presents an opportunity to harness willing energy in reshaping the work environment to counter typical anxieties; that is, getting youthful workers more involved to satisfy their own ambitions and, coincidentally, the organization's objectives.

Productivity is assuredly one of the objectives. It is one "win" in the twin criteria for contemporary employee involvement: *win-win*. A better work life won by employees enables the organization to win productivity *if* the involvement strategy is well conceived. Diverse practices for the motivation and participation of workers have evolved over time and in different lands. Prominent features of a few participative strategies are reviewed in the following paragraphs:

United States.   Theories about the relationship of workers to their work during this century have swung from mechanistic to humanistic in response to changes in the work force and work setting. In the early "scientific management" era led by Frederick W. Taylor, efficiency was promoted by reducing and simplifying the content of individual jobs. The influence of workers' attitudes on the output from their jobs became apparent in the celebrated Hawthorne studies of the 1930s. During the 1950s and 1960s, behavioral science was in vogue, with such thinkers as Abraham Maslow, Douglas McGregor, Rensis Likert, and Frederick Herzberg exploring relationships between employee motivation and management styles. Recent emphasis on "organizational behavior" has focused on interactions among workers and managers in work situations impacted by technology and societal aspirations.[2]

Trends are more revealing than results of individual studies. Most theories are tested in small-scale experiments conducted in real-world workplaces but guided lovingly by the theorists who originated the methodology. It is therefore not surprising that the majority of methods win local success, spurred by the enthusiasm of the experimenters, who award individual attention to the participants—Hawthorne rediscovered. Not all of the reported successes could be replicated outside the experimental setting, creating considerable skepticism in workaday managerial ranks, but the collective evidence from the studies and their extensions clearly confirms that greater employee involvement will benefit most U.S. organizations.

Europe.   The shift of politics toward more social democratic, or at least more labor-oriented, governments in most European countries has fostered the spread of "industrial democracy" over the past twenty-five years. Unrestricted collective bargaining in Sweden has carried power sharing to the point where almost all operational and strategic decisions are made jointly by union and industry. Workers won directorships on the boards of German coal and steel companies in 1952, and the concept of "co-determination" spread around the European continent. In France the concept takes shape as more rights for "work councils" to consult and act with management, while in Italy the direction is toward changing the social infrastructure to force industry to help solve society-oriented problems. Novel "self-management" is instituted in Yugoslavia where employees own all but the smallest companies or government-controlled organizations; managers are elected, worker councils make all significant decisions, and pay for everyone is linked to profits.

The rapid transfer of industrial decision-making powers from the few to the many in Europe was influenced by a lingering sense of class distinction and a penchant for political solutions. This trend is not Communist inspired; the extreme European left deplores industrial democracy. It is a sweeping belief that working men and women should have greater say in all affairs that affect their occupations. It has altered social expectations, serving as a social safety valve for restive workers. But it has also placed heavy tax burdens on the populace and strangling regulatory restrictions on business. With all its ups and downs, especially apparent during a recessionary period as in 1981–82, the system of industrial democracy and codetermination deserves close attention because it represents a massive experiment in ways to make the work environment more responsive to input from its inhabitants.

The message emerging from employee participation trends in the industrial world is one of workplace democratization.[3] In the United States the movement appears to be toward general involvement by individual workers or small groups in day-to-day operations and voluntary union-management cooperation in strategic actions, as opposed to the European version of collective group participation by formalized procedures and government-legislated union-industry power sharing.

A pragmatic consideration of the involvement question suggests that greater employee participation may be the most cost-effective way to secure productivity gains; it relies more on an investment of management dedication than dollar investments in technology. It also offers a humanitarian bonus of improvements for the work lives of all the contributors to productivity.

QUALITY CIRCLES

By far the most celebrated new form of involvement is *quality circles*. Based on glowing accounts of their impact on quality and productivity in Japan, circles are springing up around the world—Korea, Australia, China, Mexico, Brazil, United States, and Europe. They do not always lead to the apparent harvests reaped in Japan, but they do demonstrate concern for employee interest and promote cooperation.

The academic origin of the quality circle (QC) concept is in doubt, but the fame assuredly came from the reputation gained by quality circles in Japan. The QC principles were postulated in the United States long before taking hold in Japan, as were the statistical quality control techniques that are emphasized in circle activities. Nonetheless, it was the work of Dr. Ishikawa and the Union of Japanese Scientists and Engineers (JUSE) that sparked growth from a single quality circle registered in 1962 to over one hundred thousand now registered in Japan. The worldwide surge of interest is a direct result of Japan's enormous economic success.

The first major U.S. implementation was the 1974 introduction of circles into Lockheed's missile works in Sunnyvale, California. From there, circles have been spread by consultants, literature, and professional societies to organizations big and small in both the public and private sectors.[4] With growth came mutations. The Japanese prototype has been augmented in some cases by more training and rewards, and in other cases has been restructured to fit American management styles and to stress particular production functions. In effect, quality circles are the latest vehicles to bear the banner of employee involvement in the long caravan of participation strategies.

Structure and Operation of Quality Circles

Membership in a quality circle is typically made up of six to ten people who are engaged in similar work. The group is guided by an appointed or elected leader to identify, analyze, and solve quality problems. They usually meet during normal working hours for about one hour in an appropriate meeting room near the work area. Circles can be formed in any unit or at any level of an organization, with participation normally on a voluntary basis.

Behind individual circles is a shadow organization that supports their activities. A "facilitator" may be assigned to several circles to help them plan meetings, conduct training, and make arrangements for special activities. A steering committee of middle-level managers is sometimes formed to hear suggestions from the circles and to award recognition for certain accomplishments.

Most circles operate informally. Members are encouraged to exchange ideas freely but to keep the quality or productivity subjects in mind. As circles mature they are expected to not only discover troubled areas but design ways to overcome the difficulties. A successful quality-circle implementation should provide most of the following benefits:

- Develop individual abilities and confidence
- Enhance employee communication and work attitudes

- Raise the quality of output and reduce waste
- Improve safety and reduce production costs
- Decrease absenteeism and grievances
- Increase job satisfaction and involvement

The organization of a quality-circle program and the way it is run should reflect the company's objectives. If product quality is the key issue, quality control techniques are featured. Developing better communications between workers and supervisors will be emphasized if the intent is to reduce grievances. Productivity awareness may be the main message for a company that simply wants its employees to associate more closely with its production objectives. A detailed plan for establishing a modified quality-circle program is described in Chapters 9, 10, and 11.

Participation Pratfalls

The benefits listed previously do not automatically accrue from starting a circle program. There have been impressive successes. Lockheed Corporation claims that its investment of about $700,000 to establish quality circles has returned more than $5 million over a four-year period. Johnson and Johnson believes that its program led to savings of $480,000 by just reducing material-handling time. Westinghouse says that its quality circles are living up to expectations. But according to Dr. Matthew Goodfellow, not all companies have enjoyed comparable triumphs: "While success has a thousand fathers, failure is an orphan. Nobody boasts of a QCC [quality control circle] which failed to achieve its objective. In studying 29 companies with QCC programs, we found only eight that were unquestionably successful."[5]

Quality circles are a mixed blessing, even in Japan. A consultant who returned from a five-year stint in Tokyo says, "The Japanese don't expect a quality circle to cut costs. Introduction of one actually reduces productivity by 2.5 percent, which is typically the amount of extra time workers spend conducting the business of the circle."[6] The major factors hampering Japanese quality control circles, according to Professor Rintaro Muramatsu's survey of 276 plants, are rated as follows:[7]

1. Lack of understanding on the part of superiors or top management (30.1 percent)
2. Difficult conditions for QC circle activities (28.4 percent)
3. Apathy on the part of members (14.9 percent)
4. Lack of efforts for training and promotion (11.9 percent)
5. Incompetence of leaders (6.5 percent)
6. Weak constitution of promoting body (5.2 percent)

It is also intriguing to note that not all of the Japanese firms famous for their quality control circles in Japan have attempted to operate such programs in their U.S. facilities.

There are innumerable reasons why any employee participation program can fail. The most common are lack of preparation before starting one, selection of weak leaders, insufficient backing from managers, lack of cooperation from unions, and expecting good results too soon. Quality circles are particularly susceptible to pressure from unions and lack of pressure from middle management.

Both unions and middle managers need to have a sense of ownership in the circle program. If union leaders are opposed, they can easily destroy the atmosphere of cooperation needed for viable circles. A union committeeman, committeewoman, or steward should be involved in the planning stage to make sure that circles are not just another attempt to extract productivity without rewarding workers and to be in a position where the union can share in successes. In a rather strange twist, middle managers have sometimes been left exposed just like unions by the fervor with which top management has adopted quality circles; they have been bypassed in a hasty effort to install circles by direct involvement of top executives. Besides the initial resistance generated by not being included in the implementation of the program, middle managers may feel threatened by circle successes that could be interpreted as corrections for poor management.

The circle members themselves may lose interest in the program if they perceive it as strictly a productivity push rather than a mutually beneficial endeavor. They also get bored when circle activities become routine and ritualistic. One way to maintain the spontaneity is to vary the emphasis, have joint meetings, and provide different forms of recognition. Genuine enthusiasm is more likely to be attained and maintained when participants can clearly observe that their involvement is appreciated and they are regularly reminded of it.

EXHIBIT 37   *GOVERNMENT GETS GOING IN CIRCLES*

The quality-circle movement has pranced gracefully into city, state, and federal governments. Its emphasis on communications and participative planning is ideal for providers of labor-intensive services. In an era of belt tightening, circles have been particularly effective in attaining consensus for budget cutting, and in maintaining morale while enduring the cuts.

Circle successes have been reported from cities as small as Champlin, Minnesota (population 9,006), to agencies as large as the Norfolk Naval Shipyard. After the 1979 introduction of quality circles at Norfolk, the program grew to fifty active circles with five full-time facilitators by December 1981. During that period the cumulative cost of the program added up to $332,612, but total savings realized from circle-originated proposals amounted to $1,133,759, a return of $3.41 for each dollar invested. Moreover, the progress report issued by the shipyard stressed that "the real value of the program lies in improving the quality of work life and the employee's self image."

The same circle structure fits the private and public sectors, as do most of the operating procedures. It is usually wise to start a few pilot teams even when a large department has decided that it wants to go all the way with circles. Centralized facilitator training has been effective when several departments within an agency are involved with circles; customized training for individual circles can also be developed by the agency's training specialists. After the circles have become well established, members or whole teams can visit similar circles in other areas to share experiences, thereby spreading good ideas and becoming familiar with related operations. Additional attributes of circles in government include opportunities to

> Discuss problems in a nonthreatening atmosphere
> Call on technical expertise in other parts of the organization
> Form teams that cross normal organizational boundaries to work on problem areas such as energy conservation, form simplification, development of administrative manuals, and community relations
> Influence decisions that were previously made without consultation
> Rally support for innovations
> Reduce conflicts in the work environment
> Improve visibility and be recognized accordingly

SHARING TACTICS

Sharing means giving and getting. When employees are given an extra share of money, conveniences, or decision-making rights, they are expected to share their knowledge, skills, and interests to improve productivity. Without a clear cause-and-effect understanding, a sharing program is a superficial exercise. Employer commitment is sustained by measurable gains in quality and quantity of output, just as employees need physical evidence of improved work life to nourish their continued cooperation. Expectations of both parties should be defined early in the sharing process.

EXHIBIT 38   *SHARING ADVICE FROM ABROAD*

In a presentation to a visiting contingent of the U.S. House Ways and Means Committee, Ryuji Fukada, general manager of a Sumitomo division, listed three conditions of successful Japanese businesses that lead to superior worker performance:

1. Positive attitude on the part of top management concerning management techniques
2. Understanding and cooperation of the union
3. Interest of employees in creative work and their finding satisfaction in it

These conditions are held responsible for the "Japanese system in which the world-renowned small groups at factories strive, without being instructed by management, to achieve major improvements in production which management never dreamed of."[8]

Shared concern for production is a worldwide management objective. Werner Freiesleben, a chief executive of Wacker Chemie, who manages plants in Portland, Oregon, and in Burghausen, Bavaria, notes a difference between worker attitudes in the two plants: "The average American worker doesn't identify with his company to the extent other workers do. If you ask an American what he does, he'll tell you his occupation. It's a job. He could be working for any company."[9] To build company loyalty, Freiesleben believes that a company must first prove its loyalty to employees.

Innovative sharing plans are most evident in "green pasture" plants designed from scratch to accommodate nontraditional work practices and relationships. New plants have advantages of the latest technology and fewer we've-always-done-it-this-way obstacles to overcome. Reportedly successful innovations often include self-management procedures such as the following:

*   Organization of teams to self-manage performance of a distinct function. Team members have no specified jobs, usually developing all the necessary skills to handle any team duty. Menial tasks are prorated to everyone as a small part of each day's duties.
*   Workers who handle a certain process or work in one department are assigned output goals and given the freedom to achieve the goals by their own methods. They set their own schedules, select and train new employees in their area, recommend who gets pay raises, and even initiate discharges if necessary.
*   Pay schedules that vary from everyone being on salary to everyone, including engineers, accountants, and managers, being paid at hourly rates. Where workers are expected to be able to do several different types of jobs, pay may be based on the number of jobs they master, regardless of seniority.[10]
*   Production workers rotating to "outside" jobs such as sales and customer relations to see how their products are esteemed in the market. Upon returning, they are likely to be more quality conscious and prepared to seek product improvement.

Many of the fresh approaches to worker participation are labeled "collaboration" by organized labor and are condemned accordingly. In cases where procedural changes refute such cherished union precepts as seniority, they are scorched by accusations of despotism and iniquity. Milder forms of participation may be smeared as being exploitive or simply another brand of paternalism. Yet most union leaders are aware of a restlessness in the rank and file, especially among young workers, about wanting more from their jobs than just wages and benefits. The Communication Workers expressed their discontent by marching with signs saying, "We are people, not machines" in a campaign to reduce job stress. Several unions have cooperated with, or at least not actively opposed, the initiation of quality circles and QWL programs. At contract time, issues other than wages are receiving more attention.

EXHIBIT 39   *UNION/MANAGEMENT—QWL CONTRACT*

As part of negotiations between AT&T and the Communication Workers of America, joint National Union/Management Committees on the Quality of Work Life (QWL) agreed on nine principles as a framework for joint union/management activities. In doing so, they

recognized the desirability of mutual efforts to improve the work life of employees and enhance the effectiveness of the organization. The company and union also expressed their mutual belief that activities and *experiments* initiated and sponsored jointly by management *and* the unions can prove beneficial to all employees and the company, and that by encouraging greater employee participation, work can be made more satisfying and organizational performance and service quality can be improved.

The following principles were agreed on and are presented here to inform readers of language they might wish to consider if and when they undertake an employee involvement or other QWL approach to long-term organizational productivity improvement. Even nonunionized organizations should consider many of these points.

1.   The essential component of a Quality of Work Life (QWL) effort is a process which increases employee participation in the decisions which *affect their daily work and the quality of their work life.* Specific local concerns and local problem-solving should be the basis of QWL efforts.
2.   The goals of QWL efforts are:
    a.   To employ people in a profitable and efficient enterprise.
    b.   *To create working conditions which are fulfilling,* by providing opportunities for employees and groups at all levels to influence their working environment.
    The pursuit of these goals is guided by the basic human values of *security, fairness, participation and individual development.*
3.   QWL holds as a basic tenet that employees are responsible, trustworthy and capable of making contributions when equipped with the necessary information and training. Management and the unions seek

to better acknowledge, employ and develop the potential of all employees and are committed to providing the necessary information and training to encourage maximum contribution to the success of QWL.

4.   QWL efforts must be viewed as a supplement to the collective-bargaining process. The integrity of the collective-bargaining process, the contractual rights of the parties and the workings of the grievance procedure must be upheld and maintained. *The process of implementing an improved quality of life at work shall not infringe upon existing employee, union or management rights.*

5.   Authorized representatives of the unions shall participate in the planning, development, implementation and evaluation of specific QWL activities which involve union-represented employees.

6.   Voluntary involvement by management, the unions and employees is essential to the success of mutual efforts. Participation in specific QWL activities shall be voluntary. Individuals shall have the right to participate in or to withdraw from such activities without penalty.

7.   Innovations which result from the QWL process will not result in the layoff of any regular employee or negatively affect the pay or seniority status of any union eligible employee, whether he or she is a participant in the process or not.

8.   The success of QWL efforts requires a spirit of mutual respect and trust among the employees, management and the union. Each party must give serious attention and consideration to the needs and values of the other parties. Management, the unions and employees must respect one another's legitimate needs and constraints. The success and maintenance of Quality of Work Life requires flexibility and continuing support and leadership from management, the unions and employees, at all levels.

9.   *Quality of Work Life is not a 'program': there is no universal or one best approach.* It is a process which has great potential, but it can't be the answer to all the problems of employees, the union or the company.

Sharing programs will continue to expand without organized labor's backing, but its endorsement would help immeasurably. Since the movement is still in a formative stage, union leadership has an ideal opportunity to guide development along lines that protect workers' rights of free speech, privacy, and fairness. Where management is reluctant, union advocacy could power the movement. The challenge to both union and management is to seek out the sharing options preferred by the work force and implement those that simultaneously strengthen productivity and work satisfaction.

EXHIBIT 40   *THE MUDDLE IN THE MIDDLE*

Every new turn in the progression of labor-management tactics twists the blue-white collar worn by supervisors. The critical position of the first-line supervisor, between hourly workers below and mid-level managers above, is acknowledged by sterling epithets: the link between management and labor, deacon of the doers, and management's voice in the shop. But such concessions of indispensability are too seldom accompanied by efforts to bolster the position. Rather, the supervisor's position is often made untenable.

Events in the workplace have conspired to erode the respect once given to supervisors. No longer can they hire, fire, and promote on their own judgment. Hourly workers tend to view a supervisor as a disciplinarian unattuned to their wants and at odds with their desires to make work more significant. Most supervisors have neither the time nor the tools to fulfill all of their assigned roles: recordkeeping, scheduling, training, expediting, motivating, coordinating, and communicating between labor and management. It is no wonder that managers moan that the people they want to promote to supervisors are too shrewd to take the job.

Three issues need to be resolved to revitalize front-line supervision:

1. Selection and Training   Picking out workers to be supervisors on the basis of their craft skills is no longer a sufficient criterion. They must also have interpersonal skills to handle people problems. A voluntary testing procedure can disclose promising candidates, and selected individuals can fill in temporarily for regular supervisors when they are absent. The experience gained as a replacement provides training for the apprentice supervisors and also gives them a chance to see if they like the job before ties are cut with their blue-collar peers.

Regular training sessions should be provided to upgrade supervisors' communication skills, grievance-handling capabilities, technical competence, and awareness of company policies. Including supervisors in all the planning stages of any program that affects their crews serves the dual purpose of designing a sturdier program and preparing them to administer it.

2. Adequate Compensation.   Stock options, bonuses, and travel perks are rarely offered to those who occupy the first rung on the management ladder. Often they are paid barely more than the workers they supervise and may even have to supervise overtime work without overtime pay. Such wages dissolve self-esteem. Allowing extra pay for extra work, topping the highest hourly earner by a certain percentage, and other salary alternatives can give recognition to the pressure-packed responsibilities of supervisors.

3. Responsibilities and Authority.   Supervisors usually have responsibilities for production, quality control, safety, and cost control, yet they may have no say in developing the respective policies and procedures. Staff experts in each of the responsibility areas drain away part of the supervisor's authority, creating a power vacuum in which supervisors flounder to control output. Each supervisor's boss should stay abreast of what is happening to be able to step in with the support needed when difficulties arise.

Involvement programs can severely complicate the dealings in the middle. When teams fired up with participative spirit bump into nonparticipating supervisors, both sides get bruised. If a team is driving along a path the supervisor knows is faulty, he or she is caught between halting the drive to the detriment of the participative compact or letting it go on to an ignominious end that ruins future initiative. One way to ease the mess in the middle is to designate supervisors as team leaders. This tactic reinforces the supervisor's position and channels information along lines less likely to be corrupted by confusing noise.

Resource Sharing

Nearly every organization shares some of its resources with its employees. Sharing may be as modest as tool loans for personal use, and lenient time accounting when a worker is beset with a private problem. Even limited sharing can be an effective motivator when employees appreciate that they are being awarded extra privileges and realize that resources are insufficient to provide more. This condition is characteristic of government services where long-established rules forbid most forms of monetary work incentives.

Resource sharing should be perceived by the recipients as productivity-related rather than catch-up permissiveness. There is a limit to the amount of things to share. When a rule is relaxed, it soon becomes a new rule. A bonus that is given consistently without reference to performance is soon taken for granted and is no longer a productivity booster.

Although productivity gains may be difficult to pin down for many forms of sharing, their effect on productivity should be scrutinized in any evaluation. Removal of minor irritations in the work environment, as often identified by employee-involvement groups, can easily be justified from a perspective that any dip in the nuisance level benefits productivity. However, changes proposed to erase major annoyances have to be inspected closely because they may have downstream effects on productivity that are not apparent in the initial complaints.

Any resource associated with the operation of an organization is a candidate for sharing—information, time, facilities, work activity, decision making, money, and so forth. Some nonmonetary examples follow.

Variable working hours, Flexitime, and *4/40 workweek* are popular time-sharing programs. Flexible scheduling allows a degree of employee control over work requirements. When it does not conflict seriously with production objectives, Flexitime can contribute to productivity by relieving worries about personal affairs such as when to make doctor appointments and how to avoid traffic congestion in getting to and from work. A workweek shortened to four ten-hour days can also help productivity through overlapping schedules that double-shift periods of high activity.

Police and fire departments have used four-day workweeks effectively to meet protection requirements and concurrently provide employee-pleasing three-day vacations. *Compressed scheduling* in an extreme form gives employees thirty-six hours of wages for working two twelve-hour days over a weekend; then they get five days off.

Gearing working hours to output, called *earned* time, is possible when reliable production standards are in place. A crew is given a specific output assignment each day. When it has been completed, everyone can leave and still receive a full day's pay. Close cooperation and comradery result when production demands are stable and the supply system runs smoothly. High morale sometimes leads to amazing accomplishments even under adverse conditions. Lacking is any incentive to increase productivity that can be passed to the organization; all improvements are consumed by additional minutes of off-time unless a sliding scale of shared gain is agreed upon.

Recreational facilities are provided by many organizations. A company-maintained athletic complex may offer swimming, tennis, indoor sports, and even golf. Local outings are organized and vacation trips planned by a company-run "relaxation center." Whether relaxation actually leads to later work effectiveness is debatable, but a better attitude surely increases work enjoyment.

Job sharing is increasingly being used as an alternative to layoffs. Under this arrangement, two people voluntarily share one full-time position, both being part-time employees. Occasionally firms engage in job sharing to gain the use of two different sets of skills for the price of one. However, job sharing causes additional training and supervising difficulties.

Flexible benefits are offered by the American Can Company under the rationale that employees are not told how to spend their paychecks, so they should not be told what benefits they need. Employees can spend credits, allocated according to age, salary, length of service, and family status, to buy extra vacation days, more savings for retirement, and additional medical, dental, life, and disability coverage. This smorgasbord of options allows them to customize benefits to their personal needs, a privilege especially appropriate for families with more than one jobholder. Higher administrative costs of so-called cafeteria-style benefits are partially offset by not having to provide identical full benefits to every employee and by the goodwill from employees' greater appreciation of how much their benefits mean to them.

Employee Assistance Programs. The gamut of assistance programs extends from subsidized education to maternity leaves for fathers, and the potential for additional requests for "rightful" services is endless. Emotions should be set aside in assessing the worth of attractive fringe services to determine their bottom-line effect on productivity. If the credit union is a convenience that supports the quality and quantity of output, great, keep it! If the company plane is a frill, sell it.

Many assistance programs are difficult to assess. Their value to employees is often obvious, but traces of that value in organizational productivity are usually tenuous. For instance, some companies have set up or joined a network of hot lines that provide twenty-four-hour counseling for employees who are troubled by alcohol, drug, financial, mental, or legal problems. Callers are promised confidentiality. According to William C. Norris, the chief executive at Control Data where counseling services have been offered since 1974, the program saves ten times its cost through increased productivity.[11] The humanitarian benefits of such counseling are unquestionable, but obtaining solid proof of productivity gains is a formidable task. Yet it apparently can be done.

Awareness Breaks.   Information sharing is the reason behind regular group meetings held during working hours. A typical pattern is a gathering of department or crew members to discuss recent happenings. Meetings are scheduled weekly for fifteen to thirty minutes during the regular shift at times convenient for the group. A supervisor or manager leads the discussion, sometimes guided by a packet of subjects prepared by headquarters, about the status of orders, work progress, company policies, regional politics, and local events. The leader jots down notes on the topics discussed for a record of questions raised and responses given. If a question cannot be answered when asked, feedback is promised within two weeks.

Awareness sessions are less intense than quality-circle-type involvement, but they serve a comparable communication-improvement function. In some companies the sessions are also directed at specific problems to impart management's concern and to solicit solutions, which is known in one firm as the PITS—problem involvement therapy sessions.

Labor-Management Committees.   The concept of labor-management committees is not new. It dates back to World War II when plant committees dealt with material conservation, work performance, and morale. Emphasis has now switched more to social problems of alcoholism, drug abuse, education, retirement, and health, although attention is also devoted to productivity considerations of safety, job security, and work practices. Committees typically operate within the collective-bargaining environment but do not directly deal with grievances or contract matters. They instead look into problems that underlie grievances and strikes in order to detour future conflicts and to promote mutually beneficial activities for long-term survival.

Start-up can be facilitated by the Federal Mediation and Conciliation Service if local efforts are thwarted. Service staff members meet separately with labor and management representatives to prepare two lists of what can and should be done to improve relations. Joint meetings of labor and management are then held to clarify issues and explore mutual objectives, resulting in a consolidated list of common goals. Finally, responsibilities are assigned for actions to initiate local committees.

> A very formal procedure used in a steel company went as follows: To bring both union and management together, classroom attendance was required by first, the executive committee of the local union, and second, management personnel at the general manager level. Separate classes were held for superintendents and shop stewards. After indoctrination about the principles involved, local stewards and superintendents attended classroom sessions together. From these sessions it became apparent that people wanted to participate with management in correcting problems they thought existed. Finally, teams composed of supervisors and hourly personnel were developed in specific areas.

A spokesperson for management summarized team results as "Some were successful; some were not."[12]

Although there is no standard pattern for labor-management committees, the following structures and conventions are representative:

- Equal number of representatives from labor and management, with equal voice.
- Top local union and management officials are members.
- Two co-chairpersons, one from each side, are appointed.
- An agenda is submitted to committee members in advance of meetings.
- Priority is given to subject areas in which both parties can reach agreement, and immunity is ensured to encourage the expression of personal views.
- Subcommittees may be appointed in investigating shop-floor problems.
- Membership is rotated to involve more people.
- A secretary keeps minutes of the meetings, which are posted on bulletin boards to keep everyone informed.
- Meetings are held regularly—monthly for larger units and more often, or as needed, at subsidiary levels.

Formalized joint consultation is often brought about by a threat perceived by both parties as affecting their mutual security: loss of markets to competitors, excessive grievances and/or strikes, and pervasive workforce dissatisfaction as evidenced by high absenteeism and work spoilage. Beyond crisis control, continuing participation programs are sometimes formalized by letters of agreement between the union and the company. Two key paragraphs from the agreement between the United Auto Workers of America and the General Motors Corporation about recognition for a quality of work-life program are quoted below:[13]

The Corporation agrees to request and encourage its plant managements to cooperate in the conduct of such experiments and projects, and recognizes that cooperation by its plant floor supervision is essential to success of this program.

The Union agrees to request and encourage its members and their local union representatives to cooperate in such experiments and projects, and recognizes that the benefits which can flow to employees as a result of successful experimentation is dependent on the cooperation and participation of those employees and the local union representatives.

Productivity Sharing

A sure way to attract the attention of the troops is to wave dollar bills. Attaching cash payments to productivity gains is a powerful inducement for active productivity promotion. It is the most obvious possible way to show the people who create productivity that they have a personal stake in its creation; they unmistakably gain as the organization gains. But the linkage between pay and productivity is not easily connected. There are barriers of distrust to break through, administrative tangles to unravel, and touchy decisions to make about the nature of sharing—who shares for what, and how much?

The first and simplest version of productivity sharing is straight piece-rate compensation—direct payment for the amount of work done. Many mutations have evolved in response to criticism and to fit new situations. A base pay level with incentive premiums paid for above-normal output ensures a minimum wage. "Measured daywork" is a widely used version that gives a worker a standard hourly base rate, which is bumped up or down when actual performance is compared with the established standards.

Wage incentive plans for individuals and small groups are generally opposed by unions for pitting employees against each other and having standards of questionable accuracy. From the standpoint of productivity, workers often resist the introduction of new equipment and work methods because of possible impact on their earnings, and because incentives that reward only greater output provoke workers to waste materials, squander energy, and abuse machines. Other incentive plans are more suitable for indirect workers, employees in service agencies, and highly automated processes.

Suggestion Systems.   The suggestion box is chided for its ubiquity and quaintness. Yet its deposits have generated untold millions of dollars in cost reductions. Rewards for accepted suggestions, normally a percentage of the first year's savings up to a maximum amount, have enriched the wallets of a multitude of innovative workers. Declining respect for broadcast suggestion systems has accumulated from the perceived unfairness of rewards and laxity in feedback. No matter how large the rewards are, suggestions secured from employees are invaluable to productivity, and better ways to tap and reward work-force innovations are continually being sought.

- The magnitude of suggestions submitted in Japan is legendary. Employees of Toyota wrote 1.3 million suggestions in 1981, an average of twenty-seven per person. Ninety percent were adopted in one form or another. Rewards ranged from $2 to over $800, depending on the promised savings. Cost reductions from suggestions accepted in the last six months of 1981 exceeded $45 million. The tight identification of Japanese workers with their employers gets credit for the rousing success of the suggestion system.
- In some quality-circle programs the conventional suggestion system has been revamped to provide an avenue for rewarding circles that discover major cost savings. Most projects to improve quality or productivity are carried out as normal circle activities and receive the usual recognition, but a mechanism should be available to give a substantial award to the circle members when they develop a significant improvement.
- The U.S. Navy, in conjunction with the FMC Corporation, designed an incentive program that distributed $865,000 to all employees. It was based on reliability tests conducted by the navy on ordnance produced by FMC. Employees, informed that they would be rewarded for each successful test, submitted hundreds of suggestions to improve quality, productivity, and safety. Over a three-year period, every employee received about $80 in the form of a jacket, $25 Savings Bond, Christmas package, and calculator. Drawings for big prizes were held (cars, boats, mopeds, microwave ovens, cash in amounts from $100 to $2,500, etc.), which awarded more than one thousand out of thirty-six hundred employees with at least one winning ticket.
- Cash awards for superior service are relatively rare but are not unknown in the public sector. The Federal Personnel Manual System (*Blue Bulletin*, No. 87, dated June 17, 1980) states: "The Incentive Awards Program provides a means for establishing a positive relationship with employees and for developing a work force highly motivated toward achieving organizational goals and objectives." A guideline of one percent of the salary budget is recommended. In fiscal 1980, $44 million in cash awards was given out in the federal government, less than 0.1 percent of the federal civilian payroll.

Lump-Sum Bonuses.   Annual bonuses are usually associated with executive compensation packages, but similar bonus arrangements have been tried for special groups. An award of a known size is won when a predetermined objective is achieved, or the bonus may vary in size as a function of how close performance comes to targeted goals. When productivity improvement is the target, bonuses may improve the aim.

A bonus based on profit is the oldest type of gain sharing. It aligns employee performance with the base line of organizational prosperity, but it lacks a comparable relationship with productivity. Employees cannot readily observe how their individual activities influence their profit share, partly because management is often unwilling to reveal full information about financial transactions that also affect profit. If payments to employees are delayed until the end of an accounting period, it further isolates reward from performance.

Formula Bonus Plans.   A precise relationship between productivity gains and worker performance can be obtained by mathematically defining the size of the gain and proportionate shares. Although formulas vary considerably, their similarities include provisions for frequent bonus payments, production rather than sales-based measurement of gains, and emphasis on employee involvement. The three most frequently cited plans are described in Exhibit 41.

EXHIBIT 41   *SCANLON, RUCKER, AND IMPROSHARE PLANS*

Since Joseph *Scanlon* conceived his plan in the 1930s, it has undergone numerous modifications, but its basic concepts of employee involvement and recognition have remained intact. Employees participate through a formalized suggestion system that operates at two levels: (1) monthly meetings of a production committee composed of elected employee representatives to review suggestions, and (2) a higher-level screening committee composed of representatives from the production committee and management, meeting monthly to discuss company operations.

Recognition for increased productivity comes from a monthly bonus based on a single ratio:

$$\text{Base ratio} = \frac{\text{Payroll costs}}{\text{Value of production}}$$

Assuming that the historical base ratio is 0.20 and the employees' share is 75 percent, a production value (sales plus or minus inventory) of $1 million leads to an allowed labor cost of

$$\$1,000,000 \times 0.20 = \$200,000$$

If actual labor cost during the month was $160,000, the employee bonus pool would be 75 percent of the difference between allowed and actual cost:

$$(\$200,000 - \$160,000) \times 0.75 = \$30,000$$

A portion of the bonus is usually withheld to cover any deficit months, and the accumulated leftovers are paid as a year-end jackpot.

The *Rucker* plan operates similarly through a suggestion system and Rucker committees to improve labor-management communications. The bonus calculation is based on a historical relationship between labor cost and value added. For example, if the Rucker standard ratio is 0.60 and

$$\text{Net sales} - \text{Purchases} = \$1,000,000 - \$400,000$$
$$= \$600,000$$

then the allowable payroll is $600,000 × 0.60 = $360,000. Any month that the actual labor cost is less than 60 percent of the production value, a bonus is earned. The formula encourages employees to save on materials and supplies because they share the gains.

Mitchell Fein is the architect of *Improshare*—Improving Productivity through Sharing. The plan compares the number of work-hours needed to produce a certain quantity of units in the current period with the number of work-hours needed to produce the same quantity of units during a base period. Both direct and indirect work-hours are included to allow both production and support workers to share the gains achieved together. For example, assume that 100,000 work-hours were consumed in producing 10,000 units in the base period. If it took only 95,000 hours to produce the same 10,000 units in the current period, the productivity gain is 5,000 hours. This gain is split 50-50 between the company and all the workers in the plant. When the gain is facilitated by capital investment, the sharing proportion is changed to reflect the new equipment's contribution, perhaps 80-20 in favor of the company.

SHARING STRATEGIES

Sharing plans are just one of many ways to motivate employees, and motivation is only one of many paths to higher productivity, but sharing is fundamental to employee involvement and this involvement is critical in any productivity improvement effort. Some form of sharing will fit firms large or small whether they are in manufacturing or service industries, and adaptations can be made to apply sharing in the government sector. But sharing is not a panacea. It can zero out or even backfire. It indisputably needs management's commitment and dedication of sufficient resources to make it work.

The U.S. General Accounting Office conducted a study of productivity-sharing plans that included the following considerations:[14]

- Productivity sharing and quality of work-life programs will probably increase because of
    - ☐ Accelerating recognition that employees do have an effect on productivity
    - ☐ The decline in the number of jobs where individual incentives are applicable due to advances in technology and automation
    - ☐ The availability of better and more flexible gain-sharing measurement systems
    - ☐ Growing recognition that gain sharing can be applied in service industries

- Do not consider sharing plans
  - ☐ As a substitute for sound, progressive management, but rather as a means of sharing a portion of management prerogatives with those who are an integral part of the production process—the employees
  - ☐ Unless the firm is in a position to market additional production that can result from implementation of a plan
  - ☐ If implementation is aimed at thwarting unionization
  - ☐ As a substitute for competitive wages and benefits
  - ☐ Without a commitment to monitor the implemented plan continually

The study closes with the observation that "productivity sharing plans may not work in all firms. Yet, we found that when properly implemented and administered, productivity sharing plans can effectively contribute to improved productivity."[15]

PRODUCTIVITY BY OBJECTIVES:
Organization and Implementation

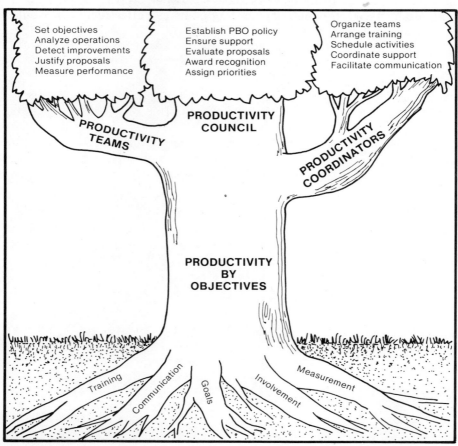

Set objectives
Analyze operations
Detect improvements
Justify proposals
Measure performance

Establish PBO policy
Ensure support
Evaluate proposals
Award recognition
Assign priorities

Organize teams
Arrange training
Schedule activities
Coordinate support
Facilitate communication

PRODUCTIVITY TEAMS

PRODUCTIVITY COUNCIL

PRODUCTIVITY COORDINATORS

PRODUCTIVITY BY OBJECTIVES

Training

Communication

Goals

Involvement

Measurement

Productivity by Objectives is a holistic approach to overcome the obstacles that inhibit productivity. It accommodates many of the subjects already discussed in a practical and proven process. In this and the following two chapters, we present detailed plans for organizing and implementing *PBO.*

The underlying thrust of PBO is aptly captured by its title—to improve productivity by systematically involving everyone in a comprehensive drive to achieve selected objectives. Key features of the approach are displayed in the symbolic PBO tree. As diagramed, the roots represent sound management principles, which support and nourish the program. The trunk of the tree is the PBO conduit in which respected productivity practices are integrated with operational functions. The limbs indicate organizational units of PBO, and each unit's responsibilities are suggested in the foliage.

PLANTING THE SEED

"Mighty oaks from little acorns grow" only when viable seeds are bedded in fertile soil. So too will productivity flourish only when sound practices are embraced in a receptive environment. The first phase of propagation is to select suitable seeds (practices) and prepare the soil (environment) for their germination.

EXHIBIT 42   *HERITAGE OF PBO*

The fecundity of PBO is derived from its genes. Its heritage can be traced to the following:

- *Work simplification* concepts were promoted five decades ago and still influence cost-conscious management. "Work Simp" was designed to encourage employee creativity. Cost-reduction ideas were sought at the operating level where improvements belong, not from cuts by a management hatchet. Training provided the impetus for improving and the analytical tools to do it. PBO follows the work simplification strategy for tapping the supervisor-worker interface for ideas and providing means to convert them into productivity boosters.

- *Teamwork* is the cornerstone of progressive processes, just as it is for all social endeavors. The old Hawthorne studies at Western Electric revealed how a team's unity of purpose improved its performance. Today, as explored in the preceding chapter, group-participation programs exist in many forms throughout the world, ranging from rigidly structured "product" teams to loose involvement groups. They share the critical goal, as does PBO, of creating a feeling of belonging that engenders cooperation and more open communication.

- *Goal setting and feedback on goal achievements* are key features of Management by Objectives. Besides borrowing from the respected MBO name, the same features are stressed in PBO, differing mainly in their applications to whole teams, rather than to individuals, and to all levels of an organization. The emphasis on results serves as a catalyst for change, and the feedback directs changes toward productive missions.

- *Integration of product quality, productivity, and quality of work life* concern has emerged in the past decade as a mutually beneficial approach to institute management commitment and employee involvement. PBO is structurally similar to quality circles but relies on broader training and systematic feedback to solicit more intensive involvement. Its up-front focus on productivity and management participation gives PBO more staying power to overcome the waywardness and lethargy that has hurt many circles.

- *Productivity measurement* is gaining stature as the prime criterion for judging the worth of workplace innovations. Although critics of technicism may distrust numerical ratings, they offer no alternative to recognizing numbers as the language of productivity assessment. Through reliance on the Objectives Matrix to distinguish goals and to record progress in achieving them, PBO has a built-in mechanism for directing activities and recognizing achievements. In effect, productivity measurement is the glue that binds training, creativity, goal setting, communications, and involvement properties into a coordinated undertaking—PBO.

A Way of Thinking

The characteristics claimed for PBO should sound familiar. Not only are they drawn from trusted managerial doctrines and popular tenets but they are also congruent with the basic beliefs of most managers. *PBO is simply a collection of proven tactics polished to serve current needs and woven into a synergistic synthesis.*

Calls for management's commitment routinely preface the introduction of any new program.[1] Full understanding and appreciation by managers of the factors present in employee involvement are especially critical because half-hearted participation inevitably collapses, usually leaving scars. By its very nature, participation cannot be delegated. Leaders have to lead by example.

Complete comprehension of what is involved in PBO is indispensable before implementation, since it is likely to recast management practices. PBO is not a workable strategy for managers who find authority sharing traumatic and employee contacts uncomfortable. Therefore it is not for everyone, nor is it needed in every crisply run, productive organization. PBO is most effective where its approach aligns closely with the way management is already thinking but has not yet converted the thoughts into deeds, although it can be the vehicle that transports management style from X to Y or Z.

A Way of Doing

A detailed prospectus for implementing PBO is laid out in the following pages. Few organizations will want to adopt the procedures intact, preferring instead to mold them to fit their own circumstances or to select pieces that complement existing practices. That is only natural. While implementing PBO in companies of various sizes and differing cultures, we have never seen identical plans adopted. The flexibility of PBO is one of its best attributes.

The ensuing outline for implementing PBO evolved from our long association with conventional production-oriented programs in diverse settings—improving work designs in large and small companies, organizing nursing teams to control hospital costs, introducing MBO-Type planning systems in public agencies, working with union-management groups in the automotive industry, and designing many cost-improvement programs. More recently, the generic totality of PBO was developed to serve clients of the Oregon Productivity Center. As a result of all this seasoning, PBO has progressed from a logical theory that tied together the more successful features of proven managerial techniques to a coordinated set of activities that do indeed enhance productivity. PBO principles have been successfully instituted in organizations large and small, private and public. It is a workable solution to the productivity puzzle.

THE SHADOW
ORGANIZATION

Every organization has a shadow counterpart to its published table of organization. Neatly boxed hierarchical displays allocate titles and responsibilities but do not accurately portray the flow of information and directions. Communication channels are implied, but the ubiquitous grapevine of information dissemination is ignored. These unofficial linkages do not detract from the formal organizational structure. They support it. PBO is shaped by a similar shadow organization that complements the standard structure.

The main components of a PBO structure are shown in Exhibit 43. A team-oriented program always superimposes a network of personnel clusters on the existing organizational structure. To some extent, a PBO network formalizes the legendary company grapevine by opening new vertical conduits to carry messages upward from the operating level and

EXHIBIT 4.3   *TYPICAL PBO COMPONENTS SUPERIMPOSED ON THE EXISTING ORGANI-
ZATIONAL STRUCTURE*

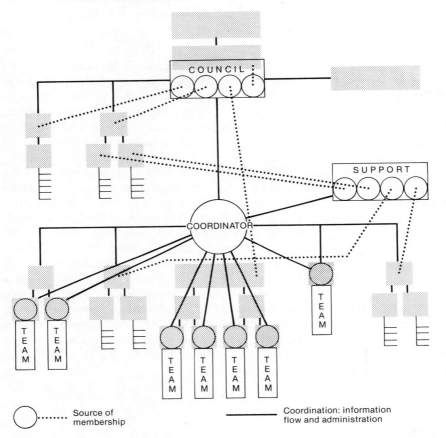

by giving identity to work groups that encourage horizontal information exchanges. The extent of the interchange and fostered familyness depends on the design.

Preplanning for PBO results in the creation of a *Productivity Council.* Membership on the council comprises high-level managers representing each major line and staff unit that has teams or provides support for teams. The council, or a kindred form of steering committee, acts with the approval of top executives to commit resources to get the process under way and to ensure its continuity. In the planning phase, the council acts as a catalyst, providing credibility. It determines direction for the PBO effort, format of participation, and mechanics of operation. As activities develop, the council confers visibility. Then it oversees implementation of productivity improvements.

Most organizations assign direct supervision of PBO to a

productivity coordinator. Depending on the size of the organization and extent of the program, the coordinator may be full or part time. The coordinator typically reports to the council and interfaces with the teams and support groups, being assisted if necessary by *facilitators* who directly minister to team needs.

Support groups are on call to help teams with advice on any projects they undertake. For example, a team leader may inform the coordinator, or a facilitator may recognize, that the team is concerned with a problem that involves, say, the purchasing department or engineering. Someone from that department would then be asked to attend the next team meeting to answer questions or provide guidance. Staff experts may also be called upon to assist in team training.

Teams of employees are the basic building blocks of PBO. They are usually composed of people who work in contiguous areas, do similar work, and share mutual concerns about production, whether it be producing a product or a service. The leader of the group could be elected but is usually appointed, most commonly from the supervisory ranks.

Interactions between the organizational components described above are the gist of PBO. In a smoothly functioning program, morale-building comradery envelops each unit and contagiously spreads to other parts of the organization. Successes of one unit buoy related units. Advances in productivity and quality of work life receive joint emphasis and the results are shared by all.

EXHIBIT 44   *COMMITMENT TO COMMIT*

A participation process such as PBO conventionally springs from top management's decision that a major stroke is necessary to fuel productivity. Occasionally the impetus comes from below. A middle-level manager may take the initiative to start a pilot program in one department, or a group of workers may request a trial exercise to improve conditions that bother them. When participation is on an experimental basis, upper management should obviously keep close tabs on developments, using the trial to learn how involvement groups impact their customary operating procedures.

Before embarking on an agency- or plant-wide PBO process, top managers should be comfortable with the following commitments and be prepared to actively participate:

- Recognize that involvement efforts may not provide the quick payback that is expected of facility investments—to minimize risk, managers should expect to become personally involved.
- Have at least a three-year plan in mind—anticipate that closely watched pilot teams will foster more teams to accommodate all who desire to participate.

- Provide an adequate budget—realize that low expenditures for physical goods do not mean that PBO is essentially free; the time allowed for employee meetings and the time spent by supporting staff personnel can amount to a significant expense.
- Deliver the message forcefully that "productivity is this organization's fundamental objective and we are prepared to do whatever is necessary to improve it"—make it equally clear that "improved quality of work life is crucial to continuing productivity improvement."
- Establish the general authority-responsibility framework in which PBO will operate—regularly review policies and objectives to keep the program on track and to be able to adapt it to emerging opportunities.
- Repeatedly vocalize support and visibly show enthusiasm for successes—attend management presentations by teams, award recognition, and listen to employee suggestions from all levels.

THE PRODUCTIVITY COUNCIL

Some top-level managers should sit on the Productivity Council. In a small organization consisting of, say, fifty or fewer employees, the residing executive usually heads the council. In larger organizations, the council often operates as a special executive task force, reporting directly to the top person in the plant or agency. Since the PBO process is so dependent upon upper management support, key executives who are not on the council should be included in the initial planning phase and take part in the introductory kickoff program.

An ideal council is broad based, forward thinking, and forceful. It possesses clout and authority to assign responsibilities, formulate productivity objectives, monitor performance, and reward excellence. Its size may range from five to twelve, large enough to represent anticipated activity areas without becoming unwieldy; eight is an average size for an organization consisting of two hundred to five hundred employees. Typical membership and duties include the following:

Plant, production, or operations manager—chairs meetings and provides leadership; represents the council at official functions

Controller—assesses financial requirements and implications of the various PBO projects

Human resources director—guides training and personnel development; represents industrial relations

Engineering manager—coordinates technical resources; often the industrial engineering manager

Quality assurance manager—maintains emphasis on quality enhancement

Marketing or service manager—relates operations to sales and service requirements

Union official—represents organized labor, if applicable; in some cases, two union representatives may be preferable[2]

Productivity coordinator—acts as liaison between the PBO units and the council

Other possible council members are managers of maintenance, office operations, data processing, purchasing, product development, industrial engineering, security, safety, or labor relations.

In a small organization, membership on the council might be composed of the company president, accountant, administrative assistant, sales manager, operations manager, and union steward or work-force representative.

Regardless of size, the council is itself an involvement team, one that directs, trouble-shoots, adjusts, and oversees the entire PBO process. It meets regularly—once a week for the first six months, and perhaps biweekly or monthly thereafter. And members should enjoy the experience as do other involvement teams. They have the satisfaction of directing an abundantly worthwhile operation from ringside seats, close enough to the participants to inhale their enthusiasm and be warmed by their pride of accomplishment.

COUNCIL CALENDAR

"Productivity awareness" is the theme of the first council meeting. A rallying gambit is to agree on a definition of *productivity* as it applies to the organization. Consensus that "making tomorrow better than today" is a good start, but physical and attitudinal issues have to be addressed. Objectives to build company loyalty and improve quality lead to somewhat different activities than objectives to ease labor unrest and reduce waste. Only those issues most critical to operations should be considered initially, and even those should be set in context with the overall productivity mission.

The following topics are unavoidable in discussing a productivity mission and the council's role in it:

Characteristics of a productive organization—What are they and how can they be influenced?

Strategic planning—What resources are available and how can they best be utilized?

Measurement—What are the advantages of monitoring productivity and how can it be done?

Involvement—What can the organization and its employees gain from greater participation and what form should it take?

If council members are uneasy with these topics, some tutoring will help. If a library of productivity literature has been accumulated, it should be required reading. Short courses and conferences on productivity can provide a good overview if they are attended selectively.[3] Hiring consultants to make in-house presentations saves travel time. Whatever the source, the intent of council training is to increase general awareness of productivity possibilities in order to avoid short-sighted solutions to parochial problems.

Once the council has reached consensus on the organization's basic productivity course, design of the PBO process commences. Subjects to consider over the first two months are listed below. The list is only a skeleton. Each council will add meat to the bones to customize PBO in its own image.

POLICY AND PROCEDURE CONSIDERATIONS (about two months' worth)

- Review employee involvement options
    - ☐ Quality circles
    - ☐ Management teams
    - ☐ Safety committees
    - ☐ Productivity sharing
    - ☐ Other options discussed in Chapter 8
- Establish productivity objectives
    - ☐ Quantity
    - ☐ Safety
    - ☐ Waste
    - ☐ Technology
    - ☐ Quality
    - ☐ Energy
    - ☐ Distribution
    - ☐ Downtime
- Establish quality of work-life objectives
    - ☐ Attitude
    - ☐ Morale
    - ☐ Cooperation
    - ☐ Involvement
    - ☐ Participation in decisions
    - ☐ Control over own time
    - ☐ Grievance reduction
    - ☐ Less Absenteeism
    - ☐ Lower turnover
    - ☐ Environmental factors
    - ☐ Workplace conditions
    - ☐ A better tomorrow
- Adopt a policy for union participation
    - ☐ Membership on the council
    - ☐ Assistance in planning the PBO process
    - ☐ Role in coordination and team activities
    - ☐ Joint objective setting
- Consider outside expertise to facilitate the process
    - ☐ Offers different perspective and unbiased opinion
    - ☐ Brings experience from comparable situations

- ☐ Shows commitment of the organization to success
- ☐ Provides additional training capabilities
- • Identify sources for awareness, measurement, and skill training
- ✓ Send productivity coordinator and council members to meetings
  - ☐ Professional societies
  - ☐ Productivity centers
  - ☐ Trade conventions
  - ☐ Consultants
  - ☐ Short courses
  - ☐ University courses
  - ☐ Staff presentations
- ✓ Initiate design of a measurement system
  - ☐ Review literature
  - ☐ Contact experts
  - ☐ Involve technical staff
  - ☐ See Chapter 11
- ✓ Determine method and scope of training
  - ☐ Explore local sources
  - ☐ Develop own capabilities
  - ☐ Consider "canned" materials
  - ☐ See Chapter 10
- • Identify means for upgrading in-house knowledge and awareness
  - ☐ Company newsletter
  - ☐ Subscription newsletters
  - ☐ Productivity flyers
  - ☐ Personal communications
  - ☐ Special on-site programs
  - ☐ Bulletin board displays
- • Choose a slogan and logo (see Exhibit 45)

EXHIBIT 45   *A DASH OF PEPPER*

Slang has been called worker poetry. Slogans have been called lots of things, but they do add sparkle to the workplace and attract attention if well conceived. A clever symbol or a poignant statement puts a personal stamp on a PBO drive. Two of the better logos and slogans we have seen are

People Action Links

developed at Electro Scientific Industries in Portland, Oregon, for its PAL Teams, and

Developing Our Ideas Together

the motto for PBO at Mail-Well Envelope Company in Milwaukie, Oregon, which also appears on bumper stickers that proclaim "DO IT at Work."

A Productivity Council exerts its creativity to hatch a motto. The search usually starts with acronyms, uncovering such dreadful combinations as "Save Our Business." A more fruitful approach is to look for an action verb and connect it to a phrase that intones cooperation or involvement; this avoids such dull names as Company X Circles, Partners in Progress, and Teams for Productivity. A thesaurus offers plenty of clues: *mobilize, achieve, improve, solve, innovate, go,* and *commit* are action words for *gangs, partners, crews, troops, clusters, knots,* and *teams.*

After an electrifying epithet has been concocted, a complementary logo can be devised by in-house artists, possibly through a contest. The artwork can then emblazon notebooks, training modules, banners, newsletters, and any other PBO-related materials.

Having addressed all the listed policy and procedure considerations over a stretch of about five meetings, the council should be prepared to start detailed planning of employee involvement activities. The break between strategic and tactical planning is a good point for a gathering of top managers with the council; representatives from corporate headquarters can be invited when PBO is being applied individually by a plant or division, rather than in accordance with a corporate-wide procedure. At such a meeting, the council describes its deliberations and reports progress in the form of a two- to three-year general plan. Even when most of the top managers are already serving on the council, a milestone meeting is worth scheduling to summarize and record events and accords from previous meetings, as well as to review established policies, before toiling with the specifics of implementation.

Approximately two more months of meetings are sufficient for the council to resolve start-up issues. Input may be requested from principal participants, such as supervisors and certain middle-level managers of support functions and line operations in which involvement teams will be introduced. Much of the contact work and data collection can be delegated to the newly appointed productivity coordinator. Suggested activities for the council follow:

ACTIVITIES AND RESOURCE COMMITMENTS (months 3 and 4)

- Outline a tentative schedule of the main events expected during the first PBO year. Assign names and dates to activities.
- Prepare a PBO budget for the scheduled activities. Account for planning time, meeting times, training expenses, consultants, publications, and so forth. The sum will be substantial, although most of it is attributable to employee hours spent on PBO activities rather than cash outlays. This budgetary commitment is proof of management's sincere belief in the value of the PBO process and should be recognized accordingly.

- Evaluate the impact of the involvement process on other company programs. For example, a cost reduction or quality improvement program will almost automatically be engulfed by the activities of involvement teams in that portion of the organization where PBO is implemented. That is, cost and quality control are natural objectives of PBO teams. Other management programs may be similarly complemented or superseded by corresponding features integral to PBO; possible overlap may occur in performance appraisal, suggestion systems, safety programs, management-by-objectives processes, incentive awards, work measurement, methods studies, and so forth. Areas of duplication that can be avoided, and on-going programs that will be bolstered by PBO, should be examined closely because the benefits so obtained are notable offsets against the budgeted costs of PBO. For instance, existing cash-rewarded suggestion programs can be phased out.
- Determine who will facilitate team operations. Facilitation involves attending team meetings, developing team cohesiveness, making contacts suggested by teams, conducting or arranging training, and watching over all the little but important details that promote PBO functions. We recommend part-time "facilitation" by several managers as *team advisers*. The productivity coordinator, as the title suggests, assists the part-time advisers by coordinating schedules, arranging training, and providing support materials. In a small organization, the productivity coordinator may also be the only adviser, serving the two or three teams that constitute the total PBO network.
- Define team boundaries. It is important to establish, early and firmly, the limits of legitimate concerns. Teams are typically prohibited from engaging in
  - ☐ Wage and benefit considerations
  - ☐ Grievance procedure topics: discipline, seniority, rights, overtime policies, labor contracts, etc.
  - ☐ Hiring and firing policies
  - ☐ Character defamation and interpersonal conflicts
  - ☐ Problems over which the group has no control, often the activities of another team
- Identify the departmental areas in which the first teams will operate. Recognize that success breeds success, pilot teams should be initiated in areas where a cooperative attitude already exists and leaders are likely to endorse the principles of involvement.
- Select the pilot team leaders. Usually the immediate supervisor of the team members is best qualified for the leadership position, although some organizations opt for an appointed or elected worker-leader. By appointing a supervisor, the existing order is not twisted and nominal communication lines are strengthened. Natural leaders, perhaps prospective supervisors, may emerge as teams mature, allowing the experienced supervisors to start new teams in their work areas.
- Choose "spinoff" team leaders to observe the pilot team meetings in anticipation of starting their own teams in the first expansion phase. Both pilot team leaders and spinoff team leaders should attend leader-training sessions held before the first PBO team meeting.
- Decide team-meeting schedules. Weekly, one-hour meetings on company time are the norm, but unusual conditions may necessitate biweekly meetings during off hours. Specific days and hours for meetings are governed

by the nature of operations, shift requirements, and availability of support personnel.

- Arrange for an adequate meeting place. A small room conveniently located near the work area is preferable to an auditorium or cafeteria. The room should be equipped for visual aids used in training and masked from distraction.
- Assign a small task force to design a measurement system. If the Objectives Matrix (see Chapter 11) is used, the productivity improvement criteria should represent the responsibilities of the pilot teams, because the measurement system is expected to provide feedback to the teams about their accomplishments and to track spillover cost savings from the PBO process. The productivity coordinator should head the task force and call on inside or outside consultants to help if needed.
- Determine the types and timing of team recognition. Consider the following occasions:
  - ☐ Team presentations to the Productivity Council on anniversary dates—every four or six months. Teams prepare a resumé of their activities, complete with charts and demonstrations. All team members attend. They get the satisfaction of knowing that someone cares about their progress and of expressing their views to a level of management above their normal contacts. A sensitive response from the council is a modest but effective form of recognition.
  - ☐ Completion of a series of training lessons given during regular team meetings over several months, or shorter, more intense sessions given for such specific purposes as the introduction of new technology and train-the-trainer course for team leaders and advisers. A respectable-looking diploma is a minimum award.
  - ☐ A sustained record of superior performance as justified by scores from the Objectives Matrix. Deserving teams, *not* individual members, can be rewarded by noncash awards such as a free lunch at an honor table in the cafeteria, dinner at a local restaurant, and gifts. A brag-banner for display in the work area or the team name placed on a PBO honor scroll may also be appreciated.
  - ☐ Submission of a major productivity-improvement plan or cost-reduction proposal developed and justified by a team. While modest improvements are expected as spontaneous outgrowths of PBO, teams occasionally come up with a blockbuster. A spectacular improvement deserves special recognition. The council should contemplate its response.
- Start a monthly PBO bulletin or reserve space in the organization's newsletter for a monthly PBO report. Arouse interest in involvement teams before the first ones are started and keep everyone informed of what is happening. Surprise is the antithesis of involvement.

THE PRODUCTIVITY
COORDINATOR

A *productivity coordinator* by any other name is still a productivity coordinator—a very important person in the PBO process. The coordinator is the hub of all PBO activities. As a member of the Productivity Council, the coordinator is the action agent, preparing the agenda and data for council meetings, attending to organizational details during the introductory phase, and arranging resources for sustained participation. Desirable attributes and capabilities to fulfill the manifold duties of this position include the following:

☐ *Experienced*—knows the organization, people, and operations—a respected veteran of administrative or production engagements

☐ *Diplomatic*—is able to interact cooly with individuals at all levels—can be tactful or forceful as the situation demands

☐ *Enthusiastic*—has personal motivation to make programs succeed and imparts that enthusiasm to colleagues—a self-starter

☐ *Humanistic*—is concerned with employees' expectations and aware of the need to improve the quality of their work life—a competent communicator and a great listener

☐ *Adventurous*—is willing to forge and promote new ideas, even if they are not immediately popular—an inquisitive speculator who is anxious to experiment and provoke productivity.

☐ *Organized*—is versatile enough to administer several commitments at once without losing track of the details—a disciplined operator who gets things done on time

☐ *Education oriented*—believes in the value of personal development and skill training—a capable instructor

☐ *Number conscious*—endorses performance measurement to track progress and is comfortable with objective/cost-accounting concepts—a realist

Much depends on the selection of a qualified coordinator. A pure administrative-type selectee could easily handle physical arrangements and documentation but would probably not spark excitement. Conversely, an energetic, inspiring person might overlook details and push too hard too fast. The role of the coordinator as set by the council thus rests, to some extent, on the coordinator's qualifications, reinforcing the desirability of finding a highly skilled person, even if it means a temporary sacrifice in services formally assigned to the appointed coordinator.

In some situations, co-coordinators may be feasible. Advantages of splitting the position include wider contacts, more experience, and less trouble in obtaining relief from other duties. For example, dual coordinators from engineering and personnel positions would complement each other in their operations- and people-oriented outlooks. The danger of duality is that directions originate from two sources, possibly causing confusion and dilution of effort.

While the Productivity Council is deliberating on PBO policies and procedures, the coordinator is researching and disseminating productivity-improvement ideas and materials, collecting data requested by the council, and, in general, facilitating the measurement and involvement preparations. In addition to maintaining the momentum of the PBO process, the coordinator will be occupied with the following activities during the third and fourth months of the implementation phase:

- Keeping selected individuals informed of the council's plans and encouraging them to "volunteer" to advise or lead team activities.
- Answering questions from managers and union or employee representatives who are not directly involved in the initial implementation activities.
- Meeting with first-line supervisors who have volunteered to become team leaders in order to get their input about prospective team participants and contacting support personnel to obtain their input.
- Making arrangements to accommodate team meetings. Reserve suitable meeting rooms and acquire needed instructional equipment and supplies: flip charts, slide or overhead projectors, duplicating materials, movie or TV equipment, notebooks for team members, etc.
- Determining training needs for advisers and team leaders. Make provisions for the training, drawing from internal sources or on outside assistance to have it completed before the first team meetings.
- Investigating types of training best suited for team members. Prepare a proposal for the council, laying out a time schedule and subjects to be covered.
- Designing and organizing the introductory program. A carefully orchestrated kickoff affair is the official PBO debut.

EXHIBIT 46   *PRODUCTIVITY PREMIERE*

The PBO premiere is a critical event. It is an introduction that signals more than just a new program; it is a declaration that the organization is headed along a new path that involves everyone and will affect everyone's operations. The program's purpose is to explain the PBO process, confirm management's commitment to it, and arouse enthusiasm for greater employee participation.

Depending on the organization's size, and the council's perception of what is best, the kickoff program can be attended by everyone in the organization or just those managers and support staff personnel who will be directly involved in the pilot implementation. When PBO concepts differ strikingly from current operating philosophy, a two-day seminar for management may be prudent; all managers from first-line supervisors on up must appreciate what is taking place and be convinced of its value. When PBO is essentially an extension of the current managerial style, a shorter program should enlist the necessary support.

A half-day program is sufficient when management is already united behind PBO and other employees are likely to be receptive to it. Considerable information about the productivity push will have been provided prior to the formal premiere and the union, if present, will have agreed to cooperate. An agenda we have found effective is outlined below. The meeting is typically held on a Saturday morning at a location near, but not in, the plant and takes place about three weeks before the pilot teams are scheduled to begin.

7:45 A.M.   *Preliminaries*
Coffee and rolls are available
—An agenda and a description of PBO are distributed.

8:10 A.M.	*Introduction of Participants by the Productivity Coordinator* —Top executive confirms the organization's commitment and explains how both the firm and the employees will benefit. —Union representative confirms cooperation and relates expectations of employees from a successful implementation. —Head of the Productivity Council explains PBO concepts, briefly discusses the main operational features, and announces the name-logo created for the program.
8:40 A.M.	*Overview of the Productivity Puzzle* —Speaker explains national productivity issues and the importance of greater productivity for everyone's welfare.
9:15 A.M.	*Discussion Break*
9:30 A.M.	*How Productivity Can Be Improved* —Speaker describes what different organizations are doing to improve their productivity and how PBO incorporates most of the more successful efforts; a film is a helpful complement.
10:20 A.M.	*Question/Answer Session and Discussion Break*
10:40 A.M.	*Productivity Measurement* —Speaker stresses the value of performance measurement and explains the Objectives Matrix System, or if measurement is to be introduced later, the focus switches to training.

11:00 A.M.	*Employee Involvement*
	—Productivity Council members and the coordinator discuss the PBO process and implementation plans:
	    Policy considerations and operating procedures
	    Organizational support structure
	    Training emphasis and expectations
	    Management presentation and employee recognition
	    Pilot team phase and future expansion

12:00 NOON	*Lunch and Discussion*
1:15 P.M.	*Summary Remarks by Productivity Coordinator* —Souvenirs bearing the productivity logo are distributed.
1:30 P.M.	*Adjourn*

SUSTAINING THE MOMENTUM

With the kickoff fete completed, most of the groundwork has been covered. Erection of the PBO structure begins. For the next few weeks, the productivity coordinator meets with the team leaders and advisers, conducts or arranges training in facilitation, and puts the finishing touches on preparations for the start-up of team meetings. The council, meanwhile, strengthens the communication mechanisms and makes adjustments in response to suggestions obtained at the introductory program(s).

The council continues to meet regularly after the PBO process becomes operational. In fact, its participation in the process grows as activities expand. As part of PBO maintenance, the council will

- Oversee the formation of additional teams.
- Deal with new problems and opportunities as they arise.
- Review new training modules as the training program matures.
- Assure special assistance as requested by teams.
- Determine criteria weights for objectives matrices in the establishment of the productivity measurement system (see Chapter 11).
- Monitor productivity performance and provide recognition where deserved.
- Participate in the team presentations. Critique them and award special recognition for outstanding successes. Distribute praise profusely.
- Continually evaluate progress. Maintain records and account for costs and benefits. Assess the effectiveness of PBO teams and task forces.

The productivity coordinator becomes busier too. As the resident expert on productivity training, measurement, and improvement, the coordinator is at the center of all PBO activities. Assistance may be needed as activities increase. In order to avoid creation of a "productivity kingdom," additional part-time coordinators can be phased in. The ongoing duties for coordinators of an active PBO process include the following:

- Attending team meetings as a silent observer, but evaluating the quality of training and participants' response.
- Ascertaining that records are made of each meeting and that managers are apprised of the teams' concerns and suggestions that pertain to their operations.
- Assisting new leaders and advisers in the conduct of team activities and in acquiring leadership-training skills
- Arranging for material needs of teams, information from functional support groups when requested, and outside expertise as needed
- Organizing management presentations and productivity measurement
- Editing a PBO newsletter or contributing PBO news releases.
- Preparing regular status reports for the council and upper management
- Acting as the chief productivity promoter, representing the organization in contacts about PBO from other organizations, including unions, and, in general, assuaging doubts that arise from changes spurred by PBO.

Both the Productivity Council and the coordinator should be thinking ahead—way ahead. Consequences of new technology that might affect team operations should be watched, as well as economic conditions that could influence operations. Productivity-oriented publications should be monitored, and better ideas should then be incorporated into the PBO process. A gradual decline in enthusiasm should be anticipated and plans laid to counteract this natural erosion; consideration could be given to

- A *PBO picnic* in which teams are honored
- A *PBO day* in which teams engage in friendly competition
- *PBO exchanges* in which teams visit teams in other organizations or attend a convention of teams from different divisions within the same large organization
- *PBO boosters* in which outside speakers entertain team gatherings
- *PBO contests* in which teams earn PBO trading stamps for certain types of activities
- *PBO special projects* in which selected teams are encouraged to undertake such out-of-the-ordinary projects as a customer survey, a community service sponsored by the company, the design of a company display for a civic affair, or the development of a tape show

PBO possibilities are boundless.

PBO: Involvement and Training

10

The team leader looked at her watch and at the seven workers from her assembly section seated in the small meeting room. She checked her flip charts and overhead transparencies. Everything was in order. At 3:30 sharp, the last member of her team entered the room, accompanied by the team adviser—the general foreman and her boss.

"Let's get rolling," she said. "We've got some sticky decisions to make and only an hour to do so." She turned to John, the late arrival, and asked, "Did you check with purchasing to get the cost estimates?"

John grinned and replied, "Yes and no. I checked, but I didn't get them. They said it wasn't a standard order and would probably have to be fabbed internally." He turned to the general foreman, "Who should I see now?"

"If you decide to go ahead with the current design, I'll set you up with someone in the model shop. Catch me later."

The leader continued to call on team members, getting reports of their work on the project since last week's meeting. She looked pleased. "We've come a long way since that first creativity kick. All of those lessons we fussed with seem to have paid off. Here's the latest prototype that Molly and Ruth ginned up."

She held a glovelike tool holder. Four finger sheaths were held in place by a wristband. A pocket in each sheath contained small tools and spare materials used in assembling circuit boards. It was designed to be a convenient carrier for easily misplaced items.

Each team watched a demonstration and discussed alternatives. Pros and cons were listed on the flip chart. Refinements were agreed upon. Near the end of the hour, the team leader summarized and got a consensus on what should be accomplished by the next meeting to stay on their self-imposed timetable—a completed proposal for presentation to the Productivity Council by the end of the month.

"Does anyone have anything to add?" asked the leader.

The general foreman, who had said little during the meeting, stood up. "Bob tells me our department's productivity index went from 420 to 435 this month. A big part of that is attributed to this team's quality push during the past quarter. I think we're doing great!" Several members smiled their agreement.

The group adjourned but kept right on talking about their index and pet projects as they walked back to their workplaces.

Not all team meetings go as smoothly as the one depicted above, but the cumulative effect of such gatherings profoundly influences an organization's culture—the relationship of the work force to its management, work environment, and productivity. If the Productivity Council can be likened to the brain of the PBO entity in which management commitment is the heart and the coordinator is the backbone, then team leaders are the nerves and team members are the muscle. Since muscles get stronger the more they are exercised, the whole PBO process is designed to stimulate team activity. Team talents fully surface only when they are honed by training and revealed by opportunities to contribute. This is the rationale for team training and employee involvement.

IMMERSION
IN INVOLVEMENT

The concept of involvement is intuitively appealing. Even hardliners who believe in rigid controls and strict discipline insist that their approach instills pride and a feeling of belonging, though it may be owed to the exhilaration of surviving harsh treatment. That is how the U.S. Marines build esprit de corps. A softer line recognizes that humans are communal and that they seek relationships at work similar to those found in recreation. Sponsored involvement groups simply assist the formation of better work relationships and attempt to point the resulting affiliations toward activities that favor work and workers alike.

The complexity of human relations precludes one formula for involvement for all situations. Several participation strategies were presented in Chapter 8, implying by their diversity that a guaranteed winner has yet to be discovered. PBO carries no guarantee. Its proven parts can be used like an erector set to build a structure suitable to the occasion. The four fundamental building blocks are described in Exhibit 47. Each organization can add its own appendages and ornaments, but productivity growth will probably suffer if involvement is built on less substantial bases.

EXHIBIT 47   *PBO FUNDAMENTALS*

Employees quickly realize the difference between a superficial scheme that boasts participation but is actually organized folksiness and a meaningful involvement plan. They know why management wants to get them involved, and they are usually willing to embrace management's goals if they can see where they too will be rewarded. This realization and the following four fundamental features of PBO distinguish it from most contemporary participation programs.

1. PBO Emphasis   Team efforts are primarily aimed at productivity improvement. The satisfaction of working together to accomplish something worthwhile is in itself a form of job enrichment. Other improvements to work life evolve because they support advances in productivity.

This effect-to-cause reasoning runs counter to programs that seek work-life improvements first and hope that productivity improvements will naturally ensue. Putting productivity ahead just concedes that work is supposed to produce results. When employees realize that they have a share of productivity—job security, wages, working conditions, etc.—they are less hesitant about becoming involved.

2. PBO Measurement   Team accomplishments are monitored with respect to team objectives. The productivity emphasis is clearly established by quantitative goals in the Objectives Matrix, which stresses the importance of improving all influential aspects of performance, not just quality or quantity of output.

Feedback on performance resulting from measurement shows employees what their involvement has produced. It can be a source of pride and undeniable proof of their contribution. When there is no benchmark by which to judge the worth of an involvement program, both management and workers may question its impact, wondering if it is worth continuing, thereby discouraging wholehearted participation. Knowledge of weaknesses stimulates corrections. Acknowledged success invites more success.

3. PBO Training Team skills are developed to improve individual skills and group cohesiveness. Every team member learns how to be a more effective problem solver. Such education goes beyond narrow technique-oriented lessons to become a regimen for personal improvement.

Training also forges a bond of shared experiences among team members and provides continuity to team meetings. Many involvement programs blossom at inception only to wither away as meetings become formalistic and repetitive. Training sessions can go on endlessly without serious redundancy, opening new possibilities for team actions and enlivening the routing.

4. PBO Management Team operations are supported by management participation. Team members become better acquainted with members of management, and vice versa. Awareness of each other's contributions builds cohesion and trust.

An involvement program that includes only the human resources staff and workers misses a big opportunity. Traditional participation programs often exist just at the interface of hourly and exempt workers, with upper levels of management just observing. Both managers and workers lose by this arrangement. Managers are exceptionally well qualified to instruct, guide team operations, and expedite projects when special resources are required. Workers win from this attention. Equivalently, managers win from exposure to work-force thinking; they get direct knowledge of workplace annoyances, ideas for improvement, and stimulation from sharing expectations. It is another win-win situation.

TEAM LEADERS AND ADVISERS

First-line supervisors are the recommended team leaders, at least during the initial training phase. They are assisted by managers from levels immediately above who act as team advisors or facilitators. One adviser may serve two or three teams and may present training sessions on their favorite subjects to several teams. A partial list of responsibilities for leaders and advisers follows:

Team Leader Duties

- Schedule team meetings and collaborate with the productivity coordinator in making facility arrangements and in fitting team activities to the overall PBO plan.
- Prepare a rough agenda for each meeting and avoid deviations from the planned format unless the group gets excited about a worthwhile subject. Eliminate distracting conditions. Start and end meetings on time.
- Ensure that all team members feel welcome and actively participate in the meetings. Do not let one member or a small clique dominate.
- Encourage open and thorough discussions, but avoid subjects that are off limits (grievances, wages, etc.). Create a nonthreatening and harmonious mood.
- Help define problems and formulate projects, but do not solve problems or bulldoze a project. Let the entire team have the challenges and opportunities.
- Be responsible for records of team meetings. Assist in the construction of the Team Objectives Matrix, when applicable, and help monitor team performance.
- Coordinate with the team adviser in team training and in securing support for the team. Consider every meeting a learning experience for everyone. Be prepared to share the experience with oncoming team leaders.
- Be enthusiastic. Recruit new members. Promote the PBO process. Let your enthusiasm be contagious.

Team Adviser Duties

- Attend as many team meetings as possible. Listen for the subtle messages as well as the obvious.
- Assist the team leader on request and provide advice as necessary, but do not overshadow the leader.
- Arrange technical support and resources for team activities and projects. Follow up on completed efforts.
- Provide input to the Productivity Council and coordinator. Assess team progress. Monitor team records.
- Become a competent instructor. Attend management training. Prepare thoroughly for presentations. Develop additional training modules and improve existing training materials. Make the training fun as well as educational.
- Search for ways to improve the PBO process. Read current productivity periodicals, attend professional meetings, and talk to people in other companies about their productivity activities. Invite outside speakers for team meetings, and be alert to other ways to enliven meetings.
- Convince nonparticipating managers that the involvement movement is not a threat to their authority and that they have more to gain from joining the movement than abstaining. Assure team members that management is indeed joining with them.

Train The Trainer

Most team leaders and advisers benefit from instruction to prepare them for their PBO duties. Three blocks of instruction are applicable:

1. *PBO Orientation*
    - Awareness of productivity issues and goals of PBO process
    - Mechanics of the organization's version of PBO (structure, resources, administration, performance measurements, individual functions, etc.)
2. *PBO Team Operations*
    - Team formation and group dynamics
    - Leadership, learning, and presentation techniques
3. *PBO Skill Training*
    - Creativity, operations analysis, and problem-solving techniques
    - Quality assurance and statistical methods
    - Work and workplace design, and proposal-cost justification
    - Personal development skills

The first two blocks are most important for team leaders, although prior exposure to skill training prepares them to prepare team members for the skill instruction. The productivity coordinator and team advisers should have all three blocks with special attention to skill training because they will be presenting the training.

Who trains the trainers depends on access to educational resources. Large companies employ education experts who can travel to individual plants to conduct training. Lacking the luxury of a corporate training staff, smaller companies or government agencies may send employees to courses provided by universities, consultants, professional societies, and productivity centers. Depending on proximity, budget, and number of participants, the whole troop of leaders and advisers can attend off-site courses, selected individuals can attend and then train their colleagues, or an educational agency can present on-site courses.

It is logical to have the coordinator and one or two other managers attend a facilitator short course while the program is still being planned. Such courses last from a day to a week and are specifically designed for coordinators-advisers-leaders of team-oriented involvement programs. Since they are usually taught by people who have implemented quality circles or similar programs, later problems may be avoided by adhering to the suggested tips and precautions. If the presented material is deemed sufficient, and those who attended have enough confidence, they can conduct subsequent in-house classes. Most facilitator-training courses provide profuse handouts, outlines, and other training aids. A better approach is to have a qualified instructor give the training on-site in two or three segments spread over six months. The three instructional blocks described previously are reasonable sessions. For a medium-size organization, on-site sessions are likely to be less costly per person; a good-size enrollment can be obtained by including managers who are not directly involved in the pilot phase but will probably participate later. In fact, brushup sessions on facilitator skills and operations improvement techniques would be useful to any manager. Additional advantages of on-site instruction are (1) curricula customized to fit the organization's specific needs, such as an emphasis on office operations improvement for a service organization instead of the customary attention to manufacturing quality, and (2) subjects delivered in easily digested segments timed to the PBO schedule instead of a single inclusive course attended whenever one was available.

Philosophy and Practicality

The ideal concept of having teams trained exclusively by instructors from management may not be practical. The concept is ideal because managers and workers become better acquainted, considerations peculiar to the organization are brought out, and managers identify themselves with the PBO process. It may be impractical, however, if managers feel inadequate to instruct or are reluctant to participate. "Train the Trainer" training is intended to relieve these reservations.

With first-level supervisors leading the teams, and higher levels responsible for support and training, the involvement process grows vertically as well as horizontally. When a dozen worker teams are functioning, a leader-adviser team is a natural complement. A management team of this nature would have different objectives and training subjects, of course, but the format and performance criteria would generally be the same as worker teams. An organizaion has truly embraced participative management when involvement teams inhabit the upper tiers of the hierarchy.

EXHIBIT 48   *MANAGEMENT TEAMS*

An automatic assumption that management teams will abet the involvement process is risky.

The theory of enhanced emloyee involvement rests on the redistribution of power. Privileges of self-management earned by employees are extracted from management authority. This transfer of power could be curtailed by the development of management teams that undertake solutions to the same problems as employee teams, and probably solve them faster because managers are closer to resource triggers. But the solution may destroy employee motivation to seek improvements, especially if the problems were first identified by employee teams. Creation of management teams also installs a new medium of information exchange that may choke off some communication between teams and upper levels of the organization.

Practical considerations must recognize that managers are busy and may resent formation of a meeting series that they perceive as being another bureaucratic burden on their work schedule. If meetings are established, results may not meet expectations due to politics of individuals trying to impress their colleagues and protect their turf. Management teams typically do not develop trust and openness as readily as worker teams, and conflicting time commitments often disrupt the continuity of team operations.

Nevertheless, management teams may be exactly what an organization needs to spur change, and they may hasten rather than retard the power-sharing process. The reservations described previously can be strengths if overcome carefully. Management teams can solve problems outside the province of employee teams. Familiarity with the team process may help managers to appreciate team activities and accomplishments, possibly improving vertical communications. Managers may also appreciate opportunities to interact with their peers in other departments to share expertise and solve common problems, especially in organizations that previously restricted managers to their functional areas.

Format, participation mode, and objectives for management teams can be arranged to serve different purposes and to conform to the prevailing style of management. There are four options:

1. *Information exchange sessions* supplement normal staff meetings to provide informal discussion of factors that affect the organization but are not of "brush-fire" problem nature that have to be dealt with immediately. Topics are brought out that interest individual managers but, owing to time constraints, have not been explored satisfactorily. A very competent discussion leader is required to develop a worthwhile agenda and keep discussions on track.

2. *Continuing education* features skill-development techniques and management-improvement methods applicable to the organization. Participants may present technical subjects within their expertise to instruct or inform. Current managerial lore can be reviewed. Instruction by outside experts can be provided. The intent is to upgrade personal skills and reveal existing talents in the organization that can be more fully utilized.

3. *Task force* focuses on one major problem at a time that affects most of the participants. The team becomes an elite trouble-shooting squad. Projects may be given to the team, but preferably they are self-determined.

4. *PBO update and review* complements the employee involvement structure by keeping everyone informed of developments, coordinating activities, and uncovering ways to promote interest and accomplishment. Team membership is conventionally composed of employee team leaders, advisers, and support staff, although management teams from areas without employee teams may organize to foster participation with subordinates. Members who are working with employee teams report their

team's activities and plans in order to

- Coordinate team activities to avoid duplication of effort and over-reliance on the same support resources
- Discuss team projects and provide guidance to increase cooperation
- Compare experiences that may reduce surprises and improve leadership capabilities
- Gain a spirit of unity

A management team may engage more than one of the options described. A natural combination is PBO review and continuing education, with the task force mission of making management participation a reality. Suggestions to encourage participation include the following:

- Organize meetings with an advance agenda.
- Set a schedule and send reminders if the meetings are not weekly; one-hour, biweekly meetings are a popular pattern.
- Create a clublike atmosphere rather than the conventional businesslike meeting; peer grouping encourages more openness.
- Have an enthusiastic and very talented facilitator; a member of the productivity council is a logical leader. The productivity coordinator can assist with arrangements

If leaders do indeed lead by example, management teams should be the prototype for employee teams.

TEAM OPERATIONS

In common with most quality circle and some quality of work-life programs, the PBO process shares the following features:

- Teams are formed from natural work groupings.
- Membership averages about eight but may vary from four to twelve.
- Teams meet one hour per week at a predetermined, regularly scheduled time
- Meeting time is paid for by the company.
- Membership is voluntary.
- Training is provided.
- Quality of output is stressed.
- Quality of work-life improvement is vital.
- Long-term commitment is essential.

Beyond the above ingredients, PBO departs from the classical mold by the four fundamentals described in Exhibit 47: undisguised emphasis on productivity, defined performance measurement, comprehensive skill training, and intensive management participation. Teams should be made aware of these features from the beginning.

The First Team Meeting

A new team does not yet know that it is a team. Individuals are hesitant to commit themselves and are unsure of what they are becoming involved in, especially when the organization has experimented and failed with other participative programs. They have some familiarity with the involvement process, or they would not have volunteered to join, but a clear explanation of their role and the organization's commitment is the first order of business. Subjects to discuss include the following:

1. **Purpose of PBO:** improve productivity and quality of work life
2. **Why productivity is important:** jobs, inflation, pride, etc.
3. **Organizational commitment:** statement of goals and long-term plans
4. **How the PBO process operates:** description of the PBO structure and administration, who is involved, expectations, limits, etc.
5. **Team opportunities:** a chance to be heard, develop individual skills, promote beneficial changes, and work together
6. **Individual responsibilities:** participate, come to meetings regularly and on time, bring ideas and share them, do not ridicule team members but feel free to criticize concepts, be open-minded and avoid disruptive behavior
7. **Importance of cooperation:** demonstration of the power of collective abilities and enthusiasm (see training schedule)

The upbeat theme of the first meeting should be to expect a lot from becoming involved. High expectations can be a self-fulfilling prophecy.

Subsequent Meetings

The only consistent observation about team development is its inconsistency. Some teams hit the starting line in full stride, eager to act and impatient with training sessions that appear to interfere. Other teams are lethargic and are held together initially only by the training and slowly pick up momentum as members become comfortable with each other and the PBO process. The surge of enthusiasm that propels teams near the culmination of a project is often followed by a period of stagnation. Productive teams may be broken up by promotion and transfers. Unproductive teams may suddenly blossom after overcoming a seemingly insignificant conflict among their members. PBO organizers need not be dismayed at the unevenness. It is inherent and manageable.

Continuity of team functions is sustained for at least the first half year by the core training regimen. During this period a team gains coherence and its own personality. Since members can leave anytime after an initial orientation period, disruptive influences tend to decline with prolonged operation. But longevity is not a very good measure of success. The leader of a sluggish team has to instill enthusiasm, not by goading, but by convincing members that they have the resources to help themselves and fellow workers.

EXHIBIT 49   *TEAM ANECDOTES*

Surprising developments are sure to happen as teams gather and forge their own identity. The following observed examples are instructive:

- All the employees in one department volunteered to join the pilot teams being formed. The twenty-four employees were split about evenly between an older clique who had been in the department for over a dozen years and a younger group of recent hirees. Since only three teams were planned for the phase-in trial and they were to be installed in different departments, just one team could be drawn from the volunteers. The team leader was tempted to invite the younger, more enthusiastic members because the older group still expressed cynicism about a participation program that had infamously folded a few years ago. Instead, a proportionately representative group was selected to combine youthful enthusiasm with seasoned insight. Not only did the mixed team jell into a vigorous unit that cleverly engaged projects but its fervor spread to nonmembers in the department, smoothly paving the way for expansion of the team movement.
- A hastily organized collection of circles in a large corporation quickly sank their teeth into a common project: They wanted a dental plan. Although fringe benefits should have been forbidden territory, the surprising aspect was the simultaneous demand for dental aid by nearly all the teams. Collusion was suspected. Correction was quick.
- A movie about productivity in Japan was shown during the second team meeting in a new involvement program at an aluminum plant. One team member with an aching back was fascinated by the group exercises of the Japanese. He reasoned that such limbering up before work might reduce back ailments that also bothered many of his co-workers. Within a month, the company agreed to buy floor mats for an experiment. The team designed a series of exercises and made arrangements for participation. Not enough evidence has been collected as yet, but it appears that the popular exercises are contributing to fitness.
- Teams decided to use the old suggestion boxes in their work area as a mail pouch for PBO activities. In one of the boxes they found suggestions submitted as long as two and a half years ago. The latest was dated just two months ago.
- To accommodate shift rotation in three-shift, seven-day operations and to tackle interdepartmental troubles, teams were organized to deal exclusively with a single problem. Problems were identified by management or other teams. Training and team structure were essentially conventional with the exception of continuity; teams were disbanded after each problem was solved or nothing more could be

> done. Special problems can be handled in a standard PBO process by inviting temporary members into the team while a solution is being sought.
>
> - Teams sometimes develop such close bonds that employees on temporary layoffs ask to continue to attend meetings and people on vacation have come back to take part in management presentations. Advisers have sent telegrams to their teams while they were away on assignment. Such participation suggests that the team structure appeals to social instincts and apparently satisfies a desire to belong.

TEAM TRAINNG
AND DEVELOPMENT

The importance of team training to an employee involvement process cannot be overemphasized. We have repeatedly alluded to its role in ensuring continuity. It provides team members with an obvious reason for attending meetings. It is tangible evidence of the organization's commitment. Not only can it be enjoyable to participants, both students and instructors, but it fosters an attitude conducive to improvement and imparts the skills needed to make changes to the people who affect and are affected by change.

According to Theory

Educational experts distinguish between training and development. *Training* is characterized as short-term and job specific, while *development* is long-term and oriented toward generalized organizational requirements. Since productivity improvement is to be both an immediate and a continuing objective, both training and development are incorporated into the PBO process.

Three strategies typify the way organizations view training and development. The *jungle theory* holds that individuals learn and develop by competing with their peers; it is survival of the fittest. According to *educational theory*, necessary skills can be taught in formal training programs apart from the organization; an individual acquires skills and then adapts them to fit the organization context. The third and most realistic is the *agriculture theory*, which suggests that educational programs be combined with jobs so structured that incumbents can apply their learning while carrying out assigned tasks. To these theories might be added the *synergistic theory*, which recognizes that the supportive property of team training and development may produce greater total effect than enhancing individual skill and talent. The PBO process is based on agriculture and synergistic theories.

While the subject of learning is exceptionally complicated, a few principles are of special relevance to productivity education. The following list associates key principles with PBO training and development:

- Individuals should want to learn—team membership is voluntary.
- Teaching should be geared to the learner's motives—training subjects are job specific, personally beneficial, and productivity oriented.
- Learners should be reinforced positively and negatively to shape their emerging behavior—team membership exerts peer pressure against negative actions, and positive recognition is awarded for superior performance by the team.
- Learners should be given feedback in the form of knowledge of results from the education process—scores registered by the Objectives Matrix measurement of productivity show all team members the collective effect of their training.
- Learners should have an opportunity to practice what is taught—training and development subjects are carefully selected to conform to organizational opportunities.

All the theories and principles of training and development programs are effective only if the organization is openly receptive to the changed behavior elicited by the programs. If management interdicts the activated behavior of teams, it nullifies the educational gains and extinguishes the ardor aroused by attitudinal changes. Instruction should raise expectations for both quality of work life and productivity, but the exact forms cannot be fully anticipated. Individual and team directions can take some strange twists, not always aligned with management's presumptions. Team leaders, advisers, and council members must be flexible to keep from undermining the whole PBO process by hasty reactions that could destroy team confidence and aspirations. As implied by the *agriculture theory*, management can plant the seeds of education and nourish growth, but it cannot control the climate during maturation; yet it must be prepared to harvest the crop.

According to Practice

Many education principles are accounted for in PBO training and development. However, the final form depends on the objectives, capabilities, and resources of the applying organization. The suggested training subjects can be altered to overcome specific weaknesses, and the schedule can be modified to fit organizational milestones. Every organization we have worked with has put its own stamp on the process.

In the PBO approach, training and development involve two phases. The first is a core of subjects that are individually useful to anyone in the work force but are most exploitable in team-oriented activities. Subject matter is first delivered via handouts distributed one week prior to a training session. They serve the dual purpose of assisting the instructor through organization of the topics to be covered and summarizing the key points for later reference by the participants.

Each instruction module contains an introduction, detailed examples, and a short review quiz. Handouts are printed on notebook-size paper for inclusion in a binder given to each team member. The narration is light and conversational in an open layout that allows room for note taking. Cartoons, brainteasers, and splashes of humor are included to make the training as enjoyable as it is educational.

Beyond the core subjects are extensions that present more-specialized instruction. Extensions can, and should, extend indefinitely. In addition to numerous skill-enhancing techniques, there is an almost inexhaustible supply of personal development subjects. Continuing education not only improves the quality of the work force but adds zest to the involvement process, reinforcing the trust in the organization's commitment and revivifying the routine of team meetings.

Training aids and assistance are available from many sources. Quality-circle consultants advertise facilitator training and training materials—videotapes, slide/audio presentations, and manuals. Some universities and community colleges have extension services that can help prepare or deliver selected educational packages. Visual aids and reference materials can be obtained from professional societies and associations, such as the American Institute of Industrial Engineers and the International Association of Quality Circles. A few business associations also offer applicable training services. Large firms may utilize their human resources department to handle all the training requirements. Small firms can draw on their managers' personal libraries to find plenty of material from which training modules can be molded if they wish to do it all themselves.

The challenge in training and development is not in finding subjects or canned materials but in making the selected subjects appealing and the presentations engrossing, even entertaining.

TEAM-MEETING CALENDAR

Because there is no indisputable list of preferred training subjects, there is no uniformly accepted training agenda. A suggested meeting calendar of training and team activities follows. We have found that this sequence quickly motivates the teams to cooperatively pursue productivity improvements yet spreads out the training to maintain team momentum.

Week 1: Introduction

The first gathering, as previously described, is an orientation and motivation session. About thirty minutes are spent introducing the mechanics and concepts of PBO. This may be followed by a short film or slide show that describes the twin drives toward improvements in productivity and quality of work life. A concluding exercise that begins the team-building process is to highlight the wealth of experience possessed by team members. Each person is asked to relate his or her work experience since high-school days. The various jobs held are recorded on a flip chart or chalkboard along with a cumulative tally of years spent working. One hundred to two hundred years of work experience is commonly recorded. The total is an impressive representation of team potential, and the familiarity gained by the recitation contributes to comradery.

Week 2: Creativity and Brainstorming

The first formal training session is a breezy presentation of techniques to expand creativity. The creative process is explained: irritation, investigation, incubation, inspiration, and inspection. A general interest discussion follows: What is creativity? Who is creative, when, why, and how? Tips for creativity are described: statement of problems to gain unique solutions, symbolism, checklists, trigger words, and so forth. Finally, the old reliable brainstorming approach is demonstrated. Rules of brainstorming are laid out: be bizarre, do not criticize, contribute any ideas, look for quantity rather than quality, and keep things informal. Enthusiasm is generated by brainstorming such examples as unusual uses for an inner tube, paper clip, or panty hose. This lively exchange of ideas brings the group together in a pleasurable venture.

Week 3: Ideas and Solutions

The meeting begins with a recap of creativity and continues to explore the entire problem-solving process. Using ideas from a brainstorming exercise conducted during the previous session, means to prioritize ideas are presented. Each team member is given ten votes to cast in the selection of the most-promising ways to solve the problem; the ten votes can be allocated to a single idea or distributed among several. The concept of Pareto analysis is thus introduced. From an explanation of the value of concentrating on the critical factors of a problem, successive steps are examined for implementing a solution. These steps are then shown to be the training subjects that will be covered during the next few months. The discussion is actually a preview of what to expect in future team meetings.

Weeks 4 and 5: Team Meetings

For two weeks, the team is essentially on its own. Members get to know each other better. The process is facilitated by the team leader, who suggests ways to apply creativity and prioritizing techniques to work situations. A brainstorming session typically uncovers at least twenty "problems." These problems are often stated in the form of solutions. For instance, commonly named "problems" are calls for better communications, cleaner work areas, less downtime, readier access to tools, and so forth. By evaluating each problem-solution in turn, and determining its relative importance, the team usually narrows the list to three or four prime candidates for future consideration. This examination keeps the focus on productivity and shows the team how it can contribute.

Week 6: Teamwork

Since the team was formed about a month and a half ago, members have become aware of the value of pooled knowledge and judgment, and they have probably noticed that their discussions tend to wander or become dominated by a few individuals. They are ready for teamwork training. The field of *group dynamics* is populated by many techniques designed to make small groups operate more effectively. A popular technique is to present a case study in which the group draws on the experiences of its members to understand what is involved in the case and then searches for a solution to the described conditions. The team then discusses how it arrived at the solution, noting what it did well and what could be improved. As a result of a group-dynamics exercise, a team should attain a greater appreciation of its function and the roles of individual members. At the same time, minor irritations among team members tend to be resolved.

Week 7: Team Meeting

By this time, a feeling of "togetherness" should be evident to everyone. If the team has not already done so, it should adopt a name for itself. Selections vary from the commonplace to the exotic, often indicative of the personality of the group: Thunderbolts, The Wild Bunch, Supply Storm Troopers, Die-Hards, Yahoos, Party Girls, Mugwumps, and all kinds of acronyms and initials. An interesting conjecture is whether a name molds the personality of a team or is reflective of its makeup.

After the session on group dynamics, a team may be very sensitive to interaction among members. Stronger personalities may feel restrained, and quiet participants may feel pushed. The team leader should review the characteristics of effective group encounters and direct attention to the progress that has already been made.

Week 8: Problem Analysis

Systematic problem solving is a vital ingredient of team operations. It builds on the cliché that "well begun is half done" to show the importance of developing a clean problem statement, one that does not presuppose a solution. This statement is the boxed problem definition of a cause-and-effect diagram (see Exhibit 9). The construction of a C&E diagram is explained and demonstrated. Typical entries for the main ribs are suggested, such as the seven M's: money, management, manpower, materials, maintenance, methods, and machines.

Weeks 9 and 10: Team Meetings

Team members do not fully appreciate the importance of problem definition and the usefulness of C&E diagraming until they have applied the concepts. A full meeting can be spent on diagraming one of the high-priority problems identified in previous meetings. The team leader or a volunteer can develop a diagram on a chalkboard or flip chart in response to suggestions from the team. The resulting problem portrait should reveal how many different factors need to be considered in even a seemingly simple situation. An interesting supplementary exercise is to diagram the team's mission. Discussion of the diagram should reconfirm how productivity and quality of work life are related, and the role of teams in influencing improvements to both.

Week 11: Data Collection

Every significant problem requires an accumulation of information. Some of the needed knowledge is already available from experience with similar problems, but additional data and opinions are usually wanted. To systematize the acquisition, categories of data are differentiated: frequency, magnitude, and cost. Probable sources of data within the organization are identified; department and staff functions are described. Then the tools of data collection are presented: elements of work sampling, checklists, data sheets, time blocks, work diaries, and so forth. This is a particularly rewarding hour in that team members not only acquire practical tools but also gain insight into the organization's management process, learning what various departments do in support of the whole operation.

Weeks 12 and 13: Team Meetings

These sessions continue the exploration of the team's first project. A few small improvements may already have been suggested, but the team is probably closing in on the solution to a significant problem that it has identified. Some of the tools presented in the preceding week can probably be applied to a more-detailed investigation of the problem's circumstances. "Work parties" may be assigned to gather information with the aid of staff departments or advisers, who are brought in to assist the collection of data from ongoing operations. Special assignments are usually welcomed by team members, so long as they can see the value of the effort.

Week 14: Data Displays

Charting is used to consolidate data and facilitate analysis, develop changes to improve operations, and summarize data to clarify the presentation of proposed movements. Teams are exposed to a new vocabulary: raw, continuous, and discrete data, variables, frequency distributions, and so forth. The intent is not to develop statistical expertise, but to show what can be done with data to extract more meaning. Practical analysis methods such as scattergrams and line graphs are presented along with such presentation devices as bar charts, histograms, and pie charts. By constructing charts to exploit sample data, a team learns when and how to use graphs effectively. Most team members find the charting exercises fascinating, especially the demonstrations of deceptive statistical practices.

Weeks 15 and 16: Team Meetings

The data collected in previous sessions can be charted to exercise the newly acquired graphing skills and to further refine the team's project. The team leader should point out how the sequence of training subjects parallels the team's project development.

With more than three months of meeting experience, the group should have its operating procedures fairly well defined: whether smoking is allowed, attendance conditions, management participation, admittance of visitors, and so forth. About this time a team may become a bit impatient with the deliberate pace of activities and the group approach to managing its own affairs, even while team members appreciate the methodology of involvement. If so, it is advisable to review the elements of group dynamics and emphasize the accomplishments to date. Conversely, some teams tend to be overambitious, spreading their activities over too many projects and becoming frustrated by the perceived inertia of the organization. A review of the Pareto principle should convince them of the value of concentrating their resources on achievable goals. Centered between the hasty teams and the anxious teams are the majority of well-organized groups that exhibit steady progress and growing enthusiasm.

An informal meeting with the Productivity Council may be scheduled at about this time. The purpose is to give the council an idea of how well the team is developing and to give the development a boost by showing management's interest in the team's progress.

Week 17: Decision Analysis

No one can escape demands for decisions. Decision analysis highlights the characteristics of decision making that build confidence and introduces methodology to organize the process. Inputs to a decision table are discussed, and practice exercises show how the table is constructed and utilized. Three features make this exposure particularly attractive:

1. A decision table is a tool that individuals can use for personal decisions and therefore sparks more intense interest.
2. The table also provides a format for seeking consensus in group decisions and has demonstrable use in team activities.
3. The tabular procedure for decision making that relies on rating the importance of factors that influence a decision has the same properties as the Objectives Matrix for productivity measurement; acceptance of the decision table paves the way for appreciation of weighted performance measures.

Weeks 18 and 19: Team Meetings

Most of the basic tools for problem investigation and solutions have now been presented. They should have been applied to the team project and other team activities. Initial planning for the first formal management presentation should begin. If a team's project is nearing completion, it will be the main feature of the presentation. If it is not ready, the team can report on other activities and its sentiments about the PBO process.

Week 20: Economic Factors

Preparation of an economic justification for an investment proposal is an enlightening experience. It begins with an explanation of where the organization gets its money and how much it has to pay for the use. This explanation often clears away misgivings that employees may have had about why expenditures they previously suggested were not approved. The concepts of benefit-cost analysis and discounted cash flow are described, and a basic economic-factors work sheet is provided for sample calculations. The work sheet includes the standard cost categories in a step-by-step procedure that yields a payback number by which a proposal can be rated. The correct interpretation of economic considerations is stressed. After working sample problems, team members should feel confident about their ability to prepare an economic justification for their project and to consider the time value of money in their personal finances.

Weeks 20 and 21: Team Meetings

As often happens after a training session, team members may wish to delve deeper into economic analysis. They quickly realize that the economic impact of their project will decide its acceptance and that cost-saving figures are not easily determined. These figures will be needed for the management presentation if a project is ready for submission. Effort during these meetings is directed toward completing at least one substantial productivity-improvement proposal.

Week 22: Presentation Preparation

For five months, team members have been on the receiving end of presentations. They now face the task of making one. The purpose of the meeting with managers is explained, and suggestions are offered for its enactment. A checklist is provided to tick off arrangement details: name cards, reminder notices, agenda, handouts, and so forth. Construction and use of visual aids is discussed. A tentative agenda is developed that insures everyone's participation.

Weeks 23 and 24: Team Meetings
and the Management Presentation

Meetings immediately prior to a management presentation are typically very busy. Last-minute refinements are made on the team's project proposal if one is to be forwarded. If not, a progress report usually replaces a formal proposal. Teams may wish to comment on the PBO process and other productivity-QWL suggestions. A rehearsal is advisable, complete with visual aids and any special effects the team has concocted. Team leaders must impart the value and seriousness of the presentation without downgrading the excitement and congeniality of the occasion.

The presentation can be scheduled whenever attendance is convenient; it usually replaces one regular team meeting. Every four to six months, teams meet with the Productivity Council to recount their experiences and/or to make proposals. For a number of reasons, these management presentations are an integral part of the involvement process:

- Team members and leaders alike take pride in their accomplishments. The presentation meeting is a milestone toward which a team can plan its activities and upper managers can review progress, bestowing special recognition for superior performances.
- Better communications are sought by both workers and managers. Presentations and the associated feedback on results are ideal exchanges because they are not precipitated by negative events and therefore foster positive interaction.
- The spirit of togetherness generated in team meetings can spill over to encompass management during the presentations. This is the elusive company pride that all organizations seek. Joint meetings, backed by the involvement of supporting units, create opportunities to build trust among all the participants.

Week 25: Team Development

The concepts of group dynamics are revisited to refine team workings further. There is typically a minor letdown after the first major management presentation. This affords an appropriate occasion to review the team's internal operations and explore new ways to improve them. Conventional team-building constructs are examined: group-centered versus traditional leadership styles, task/maintenance/building functions, dealing with conflict, attributes of a mature group, and listening skills. When a team is functioning exceptionally well and introspection might disturb the workings, the entire training session could be devoted to barriers that inhibit effective listening and actions to overcome them.

Week 26: Team Meeting

This meeting is an occasion to recapture the zest of the start-up phase. Perhaps certain training topics should be reviewed for new recruits who have joined the team since the earlier sessions, as a result of transfers and shift assignments. Possibilities for joint activities with other teams could be explored.

Observers invariably note how each team assumes a unique personality. Some are aggressive and intense, while others are more carefree or reserved. We have noticed that all-women teams tend to be highly attentive, very participative, and strongly attuned to getting things done. They are quick to assume ownership of their team, they develop a catchy name, and share group activities with co-workers and family, and they are more likely to conduct team activities on their own time. All-male teams are more inclined to be businesslike and reserved, and slower to embrace the team approach, but they are very systematic in problem solving. Both groups can be effective. A combination of men and women also gets the job done and seems to have more fun doing it.

Week 27: Implementation

Overcoming resistance to change is the theme of this training session. The message is not directed *at* team members but *for* their use in dealing with other groups. The importance of an implementation plan is emphasized: *who* will do *what* by *when*. Concepts of project scheduling are broached through a demonstration of the critical path method (CPM) and the logic upon which a networking is based. The need for coordination becomes very apparent.

Weeks 28 and 29: Team Meetings

When training time is subtracted from the team-meeting schedule, only about sixteen hours have been devoted to "business" during the first seven months. During this period, however, many little irritations have been eliminated, several minor problems have been solved, and one or two major cost-reduction or other productivity-improvement projects have typically been completed. When it is time to tackle a new project, teams usually opt for a supplemental brainstorming session rather than simply choosing another project from the original problem list. When an old problem is resurrected, it is examined in a more deliberate fashion than the team was capable of doing before being exposed to the full training regimen. For instance, newly acquired skills in network scheduling can be applied to lay out a timetable of activities and individual responsibilities. By now, an attentive team has developed into a contingent of analysts capable of detecting and correcting, or suggesting corrections for, all sorts of operating deficiencies in their work area.

Week 30: Productivity

This session is a celebration to commemorate completion of core training and to inaugurate the continuing drive to boost productivity. Each member receives a certificate that proclaims completion of the training: "Essentials of Productivity Improvement." The certificates should be treated as diplomas, be awarded with according esteem, and bear appropriate signatures, including that of the head of the Productivity Council. The remainder of the meeting is an update of what the rest of the organization is doing to promote productivity and a reaffirmation, possibly augmented by a film or an outside speaker, of the necessity to work together to solve the productivity puzzle.

EXHIBIT 50   *ALTERNATIVE IMPLEMENTATION*

In some instances where outside or in-house resources are available to facilitate and train teams during the early stages of PBO, a different implementation scheme can be used to institutionalize the process. In the accompanying schedule, a few informal orientation sessions for coordinators, facilitator/advisers, and team leaders would be held prior to week one. During this phase they would be apprised of their roles and of what is to come, in order to make them comfortable with the changes ahead. Formal training of these same individuals, team members, and other interested managers would be conducted as the PBO process develops. In this way, learning is complemented by past, present, and future experience, and concepts and techniques can more readily be assimilated.

Additionally, many organizations have a strong need for a quality emphasis at the team level. Such a focus is incorporated into this alternative schedule as well.

Alternative PBO Team Implementation Schedule

WEEK	ACTION	
1	INTRO—ORIENTATION—IDEAS AND SOLUTIONS	
2	CREATIVITY AND BRAINSTORMING	
3	Team Meeting	Listening
4	Team Meeting	Communications
5	PROBLEM ANALYSIS	Group Leadership
		—Trait
6	Team Meeting	—Functional
7	Team Meeting	—Contingency
8	DATA COLLECTION	Group Dynamics
9	Team Meeting (Facilitator/Adviser and	—Stages of Development
10	Team Meeting Team-Leader Training)	—Correct Leader Styles
		—Mature Groups
11	GRAPHS	—Group Functions
		—Personal Needs
12	Team Meeting	Training Modules
13	Team Meeting (First Spinoff Team)	—Development
		—Presentation
14	QUALITY—VALUE ORIENTATION	—Revision
15	Team Meeting	—Review First 6 Lessons
16	Team Meeting (Council Presentations)	
17	ECONOMIC FACTORS	
		Attitude and Behavior Change
18	Team Meeting	Group Dynamics
19	Team Meeting	—Structure and Function
20	MANAGEMENT PRESENTATIONS	—Conflict Resolution
		—Evaluations
21	Team Meeting (Facilitator/Adviser and	—Closure
22	Team Meeting Team-Leader Training)	Experiential Learning
		Training Modules
23	TEAM WORKINGS	—Use of Media
24	Team Meeting	—Development of Extensions
25	Team Meeting (Second Spinoff Team)	—Review Second 6 Lessons
26	QUALITY—STATISTICS FOR BEGINNERS	
27	Team Meeting	
28	Team Meeting	
29	DECISION MAKING	
30	Team Meeting	
31	Team Meeting	
32	QUALITY—SAMPLING PROCEDURES, CHARTING, AND MONITORING	
33	Team Meeting (Council Presentations)	
34	Team Meeting	
35	IMPLEMENTATION	
36	Team Meeting	
37	Team Meeting (Third Spinoff Team)	
38	PRODUCTIVITY—GRADUATION	

TRAINING EXTENSIONS

Beyond the core training are multitudinous extensions that can further develop skills within the work force to carry on the educational mission of PBO. Training gives credibility and continuity to the productivity-improvement effort. The means for delivery is already established, and most important, the learning process has become directly linked to the involvement process. A difficult-to-reconstruct opportunity is forfeited when training ceases after completing the core instruction.

Likely topics for more extensive or intensive training include the following:

- *Flow Process Charting*—A powerful and popular tool by which operations can easily be analyzed. It is pictorial and simple to apply. Most teams put it to use immediately.
- *Time Management*—Usually associated with executive training but readily adaptable to workers' activities. It helps employees allocate their time efficiently and is therefore a popular subject.
- *Workplace Layout*—Principles of material handling and office or plant design. It suggests ways to improve the flow of work and comfort in the workplace.
- *Quality Control*—Possibly a three-part presentation dealing with basic statistical measures, inspection techniques, and quality control charts. In quality-conscious operations, this topic has a high priority and may be inserted in the core sequence. QC creates greater awareness of quality and explains why certain quality assurance practices have to be followed.
- *Work Sampling*—Data about equipment utilization and the frequency of operational activities are conveniently collected by easily applied statistical-sampling techniques.
- *Work Methods*—Often given after flow process charting to assist the search for better methods of performing operations that stall the flow of work. Each operation is questioned as to whether it can be eliminated, combined with another operation, or done easier through improved motions or better control.
- *Cost Accounting Practices*—Knowledge about how the organization determines the cost of its operations can assist the collection of data for economic justification of proposals.
- *Human Factors Design*—Consideration of environmental conditions that affect human performance: illumination, temperature, ventilation, noise, and physiological factors.
- *Safety*—Most organizations have a safety program already established, but it can be reinforced through team training. Emphasis is given to the safety considerations most applicable to the team's activities.
- *Job Satisfaction*—Relationships that can be developed and possible changes in work routines that can make a job more interesting. Worker motivation and responsibilities are examined with respect to more significant and rewarding assignments.
- *Leadership*—How to develop and exercise leadership talents in different

situations. After examining the characteristics of various leadership styles, minicases are discussed to help individuals identify their own attributes and weaknesses.

- More-advanced training can be provided in most of the subjects introduced in the core course: communications and listening, problem investigation by cause-and-effect diagrams, problem solving with graphs, more complete economic analyses, project scheduling and resource allocation using critical path networks, and so forth.

- Specialized training may be requested by teams in such topics as blueprint reading, use of hand-held calculators, basic computer operations or programming, how to carry out certain operations or operate machines, and explanation of company policies. One team studied the art of fly-tying, but this was a reward to the fishing enthusiasts on a team that had completed a spectacular project.

Although the development of so many training packages may at first seem overwhelming, there are people in most organizations capable of handling every subject. Their participation gets them involved in the PBO process. They get the enjoyment of sharing their expertise and concurrently obtain feedback about how other employees perceive the subject. Meanwhile team members gain familiarity with new skills and an appreciation of why things are done as they are. It is that win-win proposition once again.

PBO:
Communications
and Measurement

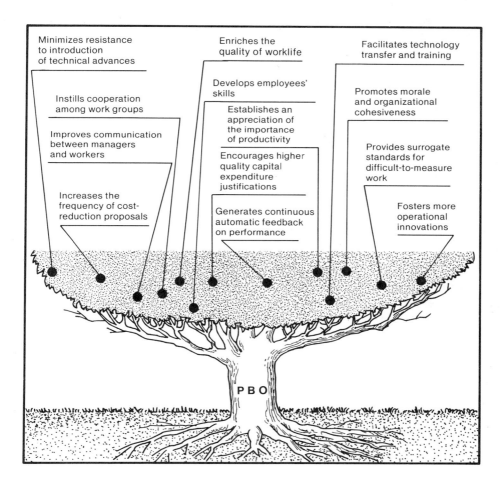

Minimizes resistance
to introduction
of technical advances

Enriches the
quality of worklife

Facilitates technology
transfer and training

Instills cooperation
among work groups

Develops employees'
skills

Promotes morale
and organizational
cohesiveness

Improves communication
between managers
and workers

Establishes an
appreciation of
the importance
of productivity

Increases the
frequency of cost-
reduction proposals

Encourages higher
quality capital
expenditure
justifications

Provides surrogate
standards for
difficult-to-measure
work

Generates continuous
automatic feedback
on performance

Fosters more
operational
innovations

PBO

Not all the fruit from the PBO tree on page 215 can be harvested in every PBO application, but the benefits are realistic expectations. Most of them are outgrowths of effectual communication and measurement practices.

COMMUNICATION

A recurrent theme in all discussions of management is communications. Reams of advice are offered on everything from the use of body language to the arrangement of office furniture for improving communications. When we realize that managers spend nearly 80 percent of their time communicating, the emphasis devoted to communication seems warranted.

The whole process of participation—involving employees with each other and their work—is founded on information exchange. More people are plugged into the communication network, and more frequent encounters between workers and managers tend to increase the speed and abundance of transmitted messages. Most conventional communication practices and devices serve a team-oriented organization, but some intensify cooperation better than others.

What They See Is What You Get

Visual communications are seldom employed to their full potential. Memos, letters, and notices are standard fare, of course, and are accordingly taken for granted. To attract attention for team activities, special effort is needed. Clever posters, unique flyers, colorful displays, and the like, are ways to draw attention, but these too are a challenge because a "new" display is new only once. Variety obtained from variations in regular information outlets is therefore the surest way to maintain attention. Avenues found effective in disseminating productivity messages include the following.

Bulletin Boards. Every organization has one, or several, bulletin boards, but most are sorely neglected. They are often placed in out-of-the-way locations, or next to time clocks where rushing workers seldom notice them. They are clogged with trivia—equal employment disclaimers, canned safety or quality proclamations, and offers to sell everything from eggs to erotic services. And many are updated sporadically, if at all.

On the other hand, a strategically located and policed bulletin board can be a well-read message center. The lunchroom or break area is a natural place for this information medium. Workers with ten or fifteen minutes of relaxation time twice a day have ample opportunity to observe the latest communiqués. Such updates may include notices of new positions, personnel changes, ideas being considered, requests for advice, recognition for performance achievements, and any other information that serves to enlighten workers on the workings of their organization. Productivity messages can also be displayed.

The productivity coordinator should be responsible for the postings on productivity. Contents should be changed regularly. Besides the many productivity-oriented articles that can be clipped from newspapers and magazines, internal sources can be tapped for contributions. Possible bulletin-board features include the following:

- Cartoon Corner—Space is reserved for posting productivity cartoons or quips. Cartoons could be obtained from a contest between teams.
- Series of Posters—Qantas Airlines developed a sequence of posters dealing with factors of productivity improvement. A cartoon character represented each factor and requested workers to jot their ideas on the poster to remedy the represented factor.
- Directed Doodling—A theme sheet is posted with an invitation to inscribe opinions. The theme is set by a display. For example, a skeleton floor plan would solicit ideas for changes in the work area, or a "problem-of-the-week" could be depicted by a photo of an accident for which corrective advice is sought.
- Brag Rag—A section can be set aside for teams to boast about an accomplishment or to issue a challenge to other teams. The productivity coordinator may use the space to give recognition to unusual team activities.
- Trigger Words—Creative ideas are stimulated by posting trigger phrases: Save water by ____, Better housekeeping starts with ____, Reduce damage to boxes by ____, etc.
- Weekly Features—A framed section where a photo, certificate, or similar form of bestowed recognition can honor the worker of the week, best suggestion, community service, etc.
- Progress Charts—Graphs of productivity performance updated daily can be particularly informative: BTUs per ton produced, errors per thousand units of output, etc. Such charts can be eye-catchers.
- Newsletters—Another valuable communication device that many organizations overlook is a *regular* newsletter. A modest monthly publication is not too difficult to put together, at least after it has been done a few times, and the benefits derived far outweigh the effort of preparation and distribution. A newspaper format with headlines, justified columns, articles, and photos is nice, but even one or two pages of informal reporting fosters togetherness. More ambitious organizations issue two or three publications. One is typically a monthly edition on general company happenings, another is a bimonthly report on what involvement teams are doing, and a third is an occasional update or special edition about new products, customers, quality concerns, productivity directions, etc. Newsletters can receive more attention when mailed to employees' homes rather than distributed at work; family members are informed of what their spouse and "their" organization are doing.
- More Messages—Marshall McLuhan once claimed, "The medium is the message." In support of productivity, the medium is the *massage,* coaxing and encouraging results. Auxiliary media include

☐Letters of encouragement sent to the home on special productivity stationery.
☐Brochures to kick off a new program or explain new procedures.
☐Short messages on time cards.
☐Bumper stickers that preach productivity.
☐Banners that publicize the name given to the PBO process, possibly with
streamers that represent each team.
☐Unusual displays to publicize short-term productivity ideas. Companies
have lofted large balloons to carry productivity slogans, erected entryway
facades to proclaim a productivity push, and cornered off areas in which
prizes are exhibited for a successful productivity-improvement program.
The intent of such exhibitions is to attract attention. They quickly become
ineffective if overused.
☐Distinctive clothing, such as T-shirts and hats emblazoned with team
names or slogans, is popular

What Is Said Is Not Always
What Is Heard

Spoken communications are more personal than most visual messages and are consequently more subject to misinterpretation. Written
documents can be carefully composed and edited to ensure that the desired effect is achieved. They are read and reread at the receiver's convenience. Most spoken messages rely on impromptu composition and are
often delivered in haste or under pressure. However, it is usually through
conversation that the threatened are reassured, the skeptics are convinced, the cynics are won over, and the productivity gospel is spread.

Training in verbal communication is essential. It should focus on
listening. Knowing what to say is largely a function of simply knowing
the subject. Making sure that what is said is received intact, however, requires special attention to whomever is being addressed; and receiving
verbal inputs with exactitude likewise requires special hearing attentive-
ness. Listening skills to facilitate team communications are discussed in
Exhibit 51.

EXHIBIT 51 $VERBAL\ PRODUCTIVITY = \dfrac{Listening}{Speaking}$

About twenty-three hundred years ago, Zeno of Citium is reported to
have said, "The reason why we have two ears and only one mouth is that
we may listen the more and talk the less." In team relations a pure listener
who refuses to say anything is seldom a source of inspiration; neither is a
steady talker who douses everyone's enthusiasm with heedless verbiage.
The ideal team member alternately absorbs and expresses ideas.

Active Listening—People posing problems usually have personal information or unusual insights about their own dilemmas which are valuable clues
to solutions. With active listening, sensitive responses can separate

thoughts from feelings to extract a solution by rephrasing and clarifying points as they are brought up.

TEAM MEMBER: (During the first team meeting)	This team stuff's a bunch of crap! We've tried it before. If the company would just give us the money they're blowing on this program, we'd *all* be more productive.
FACILITATOR:	Sounds like you're frustrated and wondering if management is going to abandon this program somewhere down the road too.

Explorative Listening—Once embarked on a conversation, detective work often reveals subtle aspects of a problem that can further define it.

TEAM MEMBER:	I'm not frustrated, I just think that management doesn't really give a damn about us. They're just out to get us to work harder.
FACILITATOR:	Would you mind working harder if you really enjoyed doing it?

Passive Listening—Being attentive, but knowing when to stop talking and start listening, is almost a lost art, yet it is often the best technique.

TEAM MEMBER:	What makes you think I'm enjoying this? (pause) And how is this stuff going to make me enjoy my job more? (pause) Are you going to pump dance music into our area or something?
FACILITATOR:	Maybe . . .

Persuasive Listening—Careful listening discloses the clues that can subsequently be used to influence an outcome that is more likely to be mutually satisfying. Knowing what the other person wants is the first step in persuasion. Sincerity is the next step.

TEAM MEMBER:	No way! I asked management once before; I even turned in a suggestion to have music piped in. They didn't even give the idea a second thought.
FACILITATOR:	That's what these meetings are for—to give every idea a second chance, and a third and a fourth if necessary. We'll take ideas like piped-in music and discuss them. If this team thinks music can improve operations or working conditions, it will make a presentation to the Productivity Council to try to get approval for it. If we can prove it's worthwhile, we'll get it. (pause) But you're going to have to help, and so is everyone else in here.

Supportive Listening—Once the conversation is moving toward compatible objectives, a concluding response that refers to the other speaker's concerns will affirm that his or her message has indeed been heard. The summation is also an opportunity to switch the direction of the conversation.

> TEAM MEMBER: I'll believe it when I see it.
>
> FACILITATOR: You'll see it. In fact, you'll all be seeing a lot of changes around here if you give this process a good, honest try. Don't get frustrated. These meetings will soon have you making many of the decisions that affect your activities and the company's future. Kathy (the manager) and I are here to make sure you get all the help you need. How about it?

The communication concepts in Exhibit 51 barely suggest what can be done to foster open exchanges within team meetings. Skillful team leaders and facilitators can work wonders in pulling a team together and keeping it there. A few individuals naturally possess the talent to weld a group into a smoothly functioning team, but most people benefit from training to have their communication skills improved. For this reason, the development of communication abilities is prominently featured in team-leader and facilitator training courses.

Intrateam communication techniques differ from those applicable to manager→worker, worker→manager, and manager→manager interchanges. Training should prepare employees for each situation. Applying active listening on a furious, red-faced boss by saying, "I see that my actions have angered you," might be like pouring gasoline on an inferno. Equally bad are parable recitations when a direct approach is needed, needling when sensitivity is required, and information overloading when a succinct summary will suffice. The following considerations should guide every oral communicator:

- Prepare for important oral messages as you do for written notices or memos. Determine what is to be said, how to say it, and what reaction is wanted from the listener.
- Anticipate delicate issues. Think through an oral exchange to avoid stumbling over your own words.
- Clarify difficult or complex issues. Have in mind a logical order of presentation to be able to state an issue clearly and confidently.
- Forestall negative responses by anticipating what might disturb a listener and by being prepared to either explain what is causing distress or offer an alternative approach.
- Close the exchange with a summary that states or reemphasizes expected future actions. Know when to stop.

ASSESSING PRODUCTIVITY

Measurement is a subset in the subject of communications. The language of measurement is numbers, and numbers provide the preciseness necessary for exacting information exchanges, written and oral. A statement that utilizes a number to compare current productivity with the previous period, say "2 percent better," may be accurate but the claim is still not completely clean. Only after the methods of measurement and calculation have been revealed is the communication complete.

Measurement methods were examined in Chapter 4 where the *Objectives Matrix* was introduced. Applications of the matrix to team-oriented management are explored in this section.

The Objectives Matrix is a surrogate measure of productivity. That is, it does not measure just the actual output of goods or services per unit of input but instead measures the characteristics of performance that are known to affect the productivity of the group being measured. Goods or services produced are then just one characteristic of total performance. Other criteria complement the conventional ratio of output quantity divided by labor-hours. When scores from all the criteria are collected into a single number according to a weighting process, the resulting figure is a comprehensive productivity index for group performance.

A surrogate system is particularly useful for assessing productivity under the following conditions, which are difficult to handle with conventional ratios.

1. *Output is not physically measurable.* Most white-collar or knowledge workers do not produce readily identifiable end products that can be tallied to account for labor input. Many blue-collar workers are engaged in activities that add value to a product, but the increments of value added are too small or vary too much over time to measure accurately. In both of these cases, measurement of surrogates can establish a reference level of performance in several categories from which successive indicators reveal the rate of change from one time period to the next. This aggregate performance index substitutes for a measurement of physical production quantity; it is an output surrogate.

2. *Engineered standards are not available.* Every well-run organization employs some sort of standards to determine its cost of operations and to control its production of products or services. Many standards are crude, especially in small companies and service agencies that do not have qualified personnel to establish them. Surrogate productivity measures are not adequate for product pricing but are relatively easy to implement and can be very effective for production management.

The commonly held perception that an engineered standard is a ceiling on output, rather than a norm, tends to restrain productivity gains. This obstacle is overcome in the Objectives Matrix by establishing a ladder of expectations for each characteristic of performance for a team, rather than the physical output of each jobholder. *The two concepts differ radically.* Individual standards are a declaration of the minimum acceptable level of performance. Measures of team performance objectives are benchmarks to encourage improvement through group cooperation.

3. *Broad output/input measures do not disclose which activities most need improvement to boost productivity.* A conventional productivity ratio for a firm, a plant, or even one department is an overall measure of resource utilization that at best only suggests where improvements are needed and who should make them. By measuring several performance factors for groups of employees, the relative contributions of the groups are observable and specific factors that need improvement are easily discerned. Moreover, the composite indexes from all the groups can be combined to provide a firm, plant, or department index that serves essentially the same purpose as a conventional productivity index—measurement of the periodic percentage change in the efficiency of resource utilization.

OBJECTIVES MATRIX FORMAT

Procedures for setting up an Objectives Matrix and conducting calculations for a team productivity index were described on pages 85–92. A format to accommodate the procedures and calculations is shown in Exhibit 52. The body of the sample matrix is filled out to represent the production activities of a specific group, and actual performance during the period is shown by the entries directly above the matrix body. Stepwise development of the matrix cell values and productivity computations are indicated by ten circled numbers in the exhibit and are described below.

(1) Major criteria of the group's activities that impact productivity are identified, and appropriate ratios are defined to measure each characteristic. These are entered in the slanted boxes as shown.

(2) The current level of performance in each criterion is measured to establish the range of values that correspond to a score of 3 across the indicated row.

(3) A top score of 10 is associated with the highest performance level a team can realistically expect to attain. These goals are the group's *productivity objectives* and are entered in the top row of the matrix.

(4) The bottom row of the matrix indicates unsatisfactory performance levels for which the score is zero.

(5) Entries in the body of the matrix above row 3 are steps of accomplishment that represent targets for productivity improvement. Below level 3 are levels of decline. When each column has been completed, that criterion is profiled by a range of values for every productivity score from 0 to 10. Input from the group represented by the matrix is needed to obtain agreeable scoring profiles for the productivity criteria.

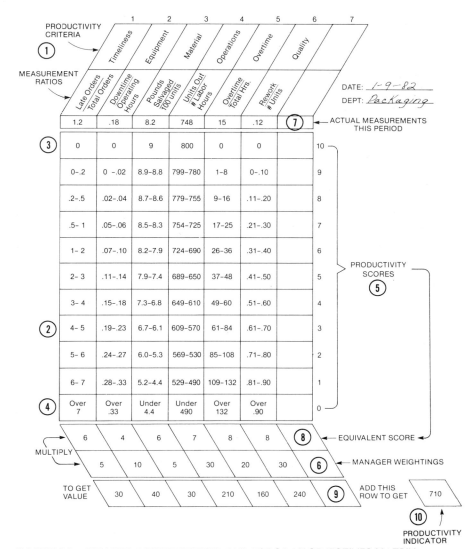

EXHIBIT 52   *FORMAT, CONSTRUCTION, AND USE OF AN OBJECTIVES MATRIX*

(6) Managers determine the weighting for each criterion with respect to organizational objectives. The sum of these weights equals 100, with larger proportions distributed to the criteria of greater importance. In Exhibit 52, quality and operations are given the largest weights, 30 for each.

(7) Once the criteria have been defined, performance ranges have been assigned for each scoring level, and relative importance weights have been allocated, the matrix can be used without modification for periodic productivity evaluations. The row immediately above the body of the matrix is where actual performance measures for all criteria ratios are inserted during the review.

(8) Point scores associated with the period's performance measures are en-

tered in the row immediately below the body of the matrix. These are easily identified by circling the range in each criterion's column that contains the measured value. Thus 1.2 late orders per total orders during the period, as indicated for the "timeliness" criterion, falls in the range of 1–2 late orders, which is circled, and converts to a score of 6.

(9) Weighted values shown in the bottom line are calculated by multiplying the point score by the respective management weighting. For the timeliness criterion, the weighted value is $6 \times 5 = 30$.

(10) The productivity indicator for the period is the sum of all the weighted criteria values. That is, the period's total performance score is the sum of all the numbers in the bottom row.

A productivity indicator has meaning only when it is compared with scores obtained in other periods; groups cannot be compared on the basis of their scores because the criteria probably differ and operating conditions certainly vary. Total weighted scores can be treated as a performance index and charted to assess progress over time, or a productivity index can be calculated to relate performance from one period to the next:

$$\text{Productivity Index} = \frac{V_2 - V_1}{V_1} (100\%)$$

where

$V_2 =$ weighted score this period

$V_1 =$ weighted score previous period

If the total weighted performance score in the period prior to the one measured in Exhibit 52 was 694, the percentage change in productivity would be

$$\text{Productivity Index} = \frac{710 - 694}{694} (100\%)$$
$$= 2.3\%$$

That is, a productivity gain of 2.3 percent has been recorded during the period measured.

MATRIX CONSTRUCTION EXAMPLE

There are many ways to construct an Objectives Matrix. In a team environment, members of a team can identify the characteristics of their performance that contribute most significantly to the group's productivity and, in conjunction with PBO team advisers, establish performance ranges for each point level for all of the selected criteria. Where a team structure does not exist or is just forming, supervisors can take the lead in establishing matrix measurement for a crew, contiguous group, or department. They should still seek input from the group being measured, but they draw mainly on their familiarity with the production process to define objectives and set performance scores. The following case example illustrates the development of an Objectives Matrix for a production unit.

Under the guidance of a productivity coordinator, a task force of first-line supervisors was empowered to establish measures for a produc-

EXHIBIT 53   *IMPLEMENTATION OF AN OBJECTIVES MATRIX*

"A" HOUSINGS / LABOR HOURS	"B" HOUSINGS / LABOR HOURS	HOUSINGS REJECTED / HOUSINGS PRODUCED (%)	LATE DELIVERIES / TOTAL DELIVERIES (%)	OVERTIME HOURS / STRAIGHT TIME HOURS (%)	DAYS ABSENT / DAYS SCHEDULED (%)	DOWNTIME HOURS / SCHEDULED HOURS (%)	Productivity Criteria
3.35	4.4	6.3	4.0	17	2.75	7.25	Performance
4.3	5.5	0	0	0	0	0	. . 10
4.1	5.3	1	1	3	.5	2	. . .9
3.9	5.1	2	2	6	1	4	. . .8
3.7	4.9	3	3	9	1.5	6	. . .7
3.5	4.7	4	(4)	12	2	(8)	. . .6
(3.3)	4.5	5	5	15	2.5	10	. . .5
3.1	(4.3)	6	6	(18)	(3)	12	. . .4
2.9	4.1	(7)	7	21	3.5	14	. . .3
2.7	3.9	8	8	24	4	16	. . .2
2.5	3.7	9	9	27	4.5	18	. . .1
<2.5	<3.7	>9	>9	>27	>4.5	>18	. . .0
5	4	3	6	4	4	6	Score
23	17	30	4	10	6	10	Weight
115	68	90	24	40	24	60	Value

Scores

Score

Index 421

OBJECTIVES MATRIX

tion department, one that averaged twelve workers, produced several versions of two basic bell housings, and used nine pieces of equipment to machine the parts. Being supervisors and totally familiar with the production process, they easily recognized the key productivity criteria for the department and defined ratios to measure them:

1. Number of "A" housings produced/Total labor-hours
2. Number of "B" housings produced/Total labor-hours
3. Number of "A" rejects/Number of "A" housings produced
4. Number of "B" rejects/Number of "B" housings produced
5. Machine downtime hours/Machine-hours scheduled
6. Number of changeovers/Total number of housings produced
7. Late deliveries to stock/Total deliveries to stock
8. Days absent/Total man-days available
9. Overtime hours/Straight-time hours

After reviewing the list with the affected employees, it was decided to eliminate either number 6 or number 7, since they both reflected the same result, and to combine numbers 3 and 4 together in the matrix, although separate records would be kept for both. These seven criteria are the matrix headings in Exhibit 53.

Setting Objectives

Data were obtained for the past six months, and since nothing unusual had occurred during the period, performances were averaged to establish the level for a score of 3. Objectives were then established for each criterion. Looking many months down the road, a 40 percent increase in output per hour was set as a quantity target. Perfection was deemed to be a reasonable goal for quality, downtime, overtime, attendance, and deliveries. Objectives were set accordingly, as shown in the matrix.

Scaling the matrix was the next step. This was done linearly. That is, the numerical distance from one step to the next was the same over the entire range of each criterion. This is not a rigid requirement, but the straight-line relationship guarantees that early gains will be rewarded with good-sized percentage increases, while movements in the upper region of each column will be more challenging. A score of zero was given to the worst feasible performance levels in all criteria.

Next to establishing objectives, weighting is the most crucial input to matrix development; it defines the production mission. Relative importance is usually determined by the Productivity Council or a similar body composed of middle-level managers. Through weights, workers and supervisors are informed of the precise emphasis management attaches to each performance factor. No longer is *everything* weighted 100 percent, with quality being all-important one day, schedules the next, and output shortly thereafter. In the example, quantity is weighted 40 percent (23 + 17), quality 30, machine downtime and overtime 10 each, attendance 6, and deliveries 4. They total 100 percent.

Computing and Interpreting the Index

Although daily accounts were kept by the organization for most of the department's productivity criteria, it was decided to compute the matrix weekly to introduce the concept. Later, depending on circumstances, the index computations might revert to once a month or quarterly.

In Exhibit 53 an index of 421 has been calculated for one of the later periods. This was done by measuring actual performance in each criterion and relating it to a score in the matrix. A measured ratio must meet or exceed the number associated with each score before that score can be claimed. Scores were then multiplied by the respective weights, and the resulting seven weighted values were summed. For instance, 1,005 "A" housings were produced during the period using 300 labor-hours; 1,005/300 = 3.35 housings per labor-hour. This corresponds to a score of 5 for that criterion. The number 5 was then multiplied by 23 to obtain the weighted value of 115. The number of "B" housings per hour was 4.4, with a score of 4 and a weighted value of 68. And 6.3 percent rejects corresponds to a score of 3, and so on across the chart.

The productivity index resulting from each period over which performance is measured is readily comparable with indexes from previous periods. Since the purpose of measuring is to provide feedback to employees and to encourage improvement, the result of each assessment should be reported promptly and explained when appropriate. Each member of the group could be given a completed matrix, or one could be posted in the work area. A chart of successive index ratings is revealing evidence of progress. As shown in Exhibit 54, index totals for twelve months are plotted on a graph, and a regression line has been inserted to indicate the rate of productivity increase. The group represented by the graph improved its productivity at an average rate of about four points per period to achieve an annual productivity gain of 16 percent.

Growth of the productivity index does not mean equal improvement in all the measured criteria. Employees may concentrate more on one criterion than another, usually in response to the weights assigned by management. For instance, an increase in quality might require a slowdown in output quantity to allow more meticulous inspections, or it might necessitate an increase in machine downtime to fine-tune adjustments. A decrease in overtime could affect output per hour, while an increase might impact attendance. Such trade-offs are accounted for by

EXHIBIT 54   *PRODUCTIVITY PROGRESS CHART*

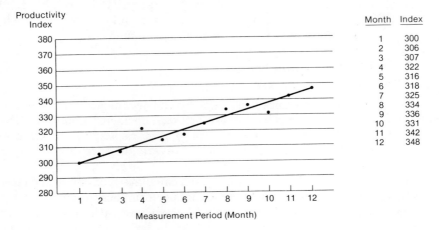

Measurement Period (Month)

Month	Index
1	300
2	306
3	307
4	322
5	316
6	318
7	325
8	334
9	336
10	331
11	342
12	348

the scaling steps and weights, which reinforce the need for care in constructing the initial matrix. Management stands to lose credibility if scales and weights have to be juggled as a result of undesirable relationships revealed by experience, and confidence in the whole measurement concept suffers accordingly.

Following are tips and considerations for the scaling and weighting process:

- A memo can be distributed to supervisors in the initial phase of matrix measurement implementation requesting input to the process. Answers to four questions should assist a task force or team in constructing the matrix:
  1. What are the duties and responsibilities of the group (or department)?
  2. What factors affect the efficiency of operations?
  3. What criteria indicate the effectiveness of operations?
  4. What information, fed back regularly, would assist supervision and contribute to improved productivity?
  In some cases, an informal discussion of the four questions is more productive than a written response, especially when a team assumes a significant role in the design of its Objectives Matrix.
- Care should be given to criteria in which greater output is normally beneficial, although its value can occasionally be distorted. For example, an increase in the number of reports published, or the number of lines programmed, may actually reduce productivity if the reports are not needed or the computer programs are unnecessarily long.
- A few criteria must be judged subjectively. Rating consistency is improved by written statements that describe performance   characteristics associated with point level (see page 230).
- The 10-point objective should be realistically obtainable within a set period, say two or three years, yet it should be a mighty hurdle. For some criteria, a 100 percent improvement is reasonable, while for others, a 25

percent gain may be the best that can be expected. Since it is the employees in the work area who must be motivated by the objectives, their understanding and agreement with each criterion scale is vital.

Instead of equal increments for each step as demonstrated in the simple matrices, steps 3 to 10 can be increased by a fixed percentage. Multiplying each successive step by 1.06 yields a 10-point level that is a 50 percent higher level than the 3-point base level. A multiplier of 1.11 doubles performance between levels 3 and 10.

Introduction of new equipment into the production process can distort a group's rating profile. A major capital investment may completely change the original method of operation and staffing requirements, necessitating a whole new Objectives Matrix. A minor change may just involve one or two aspects of an operation and can be accommodated by adjustments to the performance ratings of affected criteria.

Any change in the measurement scale should be discussed with the affected employees. Not only will they be more likely to embrace the adjusted rating profile but their insight into the workings of the organization will also improve. For example, acceptance of new technology is hastened by sharing production gains. If a machine is expected to increase output by, say, twenty units per hour, part of that gain should be allotted to the operators because the increased output will be maintained only through their cooperation. Maybe the rating steps should be raised only ten or fifteen units in recognition of the role operators are supposed to fill in meeting the new output expectation and perhaps finding ways to boost output even higher.

MORE OBJECTIVES MATRIX APPLICATIONS

Much of the advice offered by management experts is reflected in the principles that underlie the Objectives Matrix. Time-management proponents stress the importance of identifying goals, assigning priorities to them, constructing "to-do" lists, and carefully noting progress. An Objectives Matrix accommodates each of the directives. MBO specialists suggest repeated cycles of the following three phases:

1. Supervisor and subordinate discuss goals for the subordinate that support the organization's objectives.
2. Mutually acceptable and reasonably attainable goals are agreed upon and recorded.
3. In subsequent meetings, the subordinate's performance is evaluated in terms of the recorded goals and the results obtained during the appraisal period.

The Objectives Matrix is used in the same way except that it is usually applied to a group rather than an individual.

Objectives Matrix for Appraisal of Individuals

The application of an Objectives Matrix to appraisal of an individual's performance is logical and easily accomplished. By associating achievement levels with the 0–10 scale, suggesting emphasis through weights, and providing periodic, one-numbered feedback, the evaluation of individuals becomes more objective and systematic. Matrices can be customized to represent unique positions in the organization.

Performance criteria are drawn from the major duties and responsibilities of a position. Since the purpose is less to measure productivity directly than to guide development and judge capability, criteria are keyed to effectiveness and inferential evaluations of performance. Individualized knowledge-worker jobs are nicely handled in this way.

The sample criteria that follow can be adapted to the duties of a particular position. For each position the question is posed, How well does the jobholder . . .

>. . . know the job?
>. . . develop subordinates?
>. . . handle labor relations?
>. . . communicate?
>. . . lead by example?
>. . . operate within budget limitations?
>. . . establish priorities?
>. . . handle pressure?
>. . . follow through?
>. . . maintain quantity-to-quality balance?

Next, levels of skill are keyed to the 0–10 scale. Since most of the criteria rely on subjective assessment, a description is needed for the performance expectation at each point level. The following general statements can be adapted to specific criteria:

10   Outstanding in every way. The employee has mastered the criterion and actively pursues creative paths to establish increasingly higher standards of performance for the category.

8   Exceptional in most activities. The employee has mastered the criterion and consistently meets or exceeds expectations.

6   Good to excellent. The employee has learned the functional criterion and has acquired the necessary skills to perform effectively. Needs very little guidance.

4   Average. The employee performs adequately in this criterion. Needs occasional guidance. Is still learning and desirous of doing so.

2   Below average. The employee performs at novice level. Much needs to be learned. Requires frequent advice and guidance.

0   Unacceptable. The employee performs counter to the objectives of the criterion. Needs regular redirection or "counseling." Is on the verge of being discharged with respect to this criterion.

The criteria are weighted to better define the requirements of the position and precisely link organizational goals with the position descriptions. An inexperienced new-hire is expected to receive an index of about 200 initially, and to work up to summary value of 800 within a reasonable time. Indexes over 800 would only be attributable to a select few truly innovative and outstanding individuals.

Objectives Matrix
for Productivity Sharing

Tying wage increases to improvements in profits or productivity has been proposed for decades to bolster organizational vitality. And indeed many "gain-sharing" plans have contributed to higher motivation, stronger loyalty, and continuing gains in effectiveness and efficiency. In some Japanese companies, "bonuses" based on performance are substantial, at times approaching six months' equivalent wages per year, and these "incentives" are considered to be a major factor in Japanese productivity successes.

Closer to home, a 1981 General Accounting Office study reported that "Many [American] firms achieved significant savings from their productivity sharing plans, and the majority of firms expressed satisfaction with them." Effective sharing plans must possess a believable system of measurement that accurately accounts for and relates gains or declines in performance to hard dollars. Moreover, logic dictates that unless the criteria used to determine the wage increases or bonuses are controllable by those striving to receive them, interest will lag, and the program will be viewed more as a ploy than as a genuine desire to share.

The Objectives Matrix is well suited to equating performance and financial gains and can even be negotiated into a wage settlement at contract time—or can be unilaterally implemented in nonunion environments. In either case, more exactitude is required than is exercised in establishing team or department measures.

Criteria are identified for the work force as a whole, including such factors as safety, waste, indirect materials, quality, output per hour, timely deliveries, attendance, and other influences on productive performance. Since criteria must be equated to relatively firm dollar figures, foresight and cost-accounting input are necessary to relate key factors to each other correctly. For example, an improvement in quality should result in some cost savings. How much? Should the potential increase in reliability be considered? How about marketability? These are not easy questions to answer. In effect, it is necessary to place a dollar value on the "quality" of output. Safety, timeliness, and attendance are other areas that are difficult to monetarize.

Once the criteria have been determined, two matrices must be constructed:

1. A standard matrix that contains criteria, objectives, and performance scaling much like a departmental Objectives Matrix.
2. A dollar matrix that equates improvements from one level to another in the standard matrix to actual cash flow for the organization.

The body of the first matrix is filled with unit values, and the second with cash values. Exhibit 55 shows a matrix where, for simplicity, the two have been combined. The shaded columns are the dollar values associated with productivity gains in the unit columns.

EXHIBIT 55   *KEEPING SCORE WITH DOLLARS—AND SHARING THEM*

An overly simplified productivity-sharing plan is shown by the combined point and dollar scales in the Objectives Matrix. Only three criteria are included. A company with several products and cost centers would have to construct separate matrices for each operational entity, combining them as appropriate for a unified system. An Objectives Matrix with just five criteria has been accepted by the union at one plant where wage increases are directly proportional to increases in the point-scaled productivity index.

Objective criteria selected for productivity sharing are output quantity, safety, and scrap, as shown in the slanted headings of the matrix. The associated dollar returns from improvements are determined from labor, safety, and material savings. Expected monetary values for each performance score are shown in the shaded columns and are calculated as follows:

- Assume that current output per labor-hour is 2.0 units and twenty workers contribute to this output. At a $10 average hourly wage, including fringes, the labor cost per unit is $5 ($10/2). Increasing productivity to 2.1 units per labor-hour yields a $19,200 annual cost savings, assuming a production rate of 320 units per day, and 250 working days per year.

(Total units)×(Savings per unit)= Total savings at 2.1 units per hour
[(320 × 250) × ($5.00 − $10/2.1)]= $19,200

Other labor savings in the column are computed in the same fashion.
- Safety savings are related to lower insurance rates, reduced accident-related lost-time payments, less personnel shuffling, and the intrinsic value of a safe work environment.
- Scrap savings, in this example, are solely tied to reduced raw material costs. Associated savings in production labor (scrap units need to be made twice) are accounted for in the output/hour category, as are potential reductions in quality assurance labor time.

OUTPUT/LABOR HOUR	LABOR COST SAVINGS	SAFETY SEVERITY + 5× SAFETY FREQUENCY	SAFETY SAVINGS	SCRAP UNITS/TOTAL UNITS × 100	MATERIAL SAVINGS		Productivity Criteria
2.0		445		7			Performance
2.7	$104,000	0	$63,000	0	$19,600		..10
2.6	92,000	50	54,000	1	16,800		...9
2.5	80,000	100	45,000	2	14,000		...8
2.4	66,400	175	36,000	3	11,200		...7
2.3	52,000	250	27,000	4	8,400		...6
2.2	36,000	325	18,000	5	5,600		...5
2.1	19,200	400	9,000	6	2,800		...4
2.0	-0-	475	-0-	7	-0-		...3
1.9	-20,800	500	-3,000	8	-2,800		...2
1.8	-44,800	525	-6,000	9	-5,600		...1
<1.8		>525		>9			...0
3		3		3			Score
58		32		10			Weight
174		96		30			Value

Scores

INDEX 300

OBJECTIVES MATRIX

Raw material cost is $4.00 per unit. Salvage value of scrap, including handling, is $0.50. The current 7 percent scrap material cost is thus:

(Total scrap units) × (Cost per unit) = Total cost at a 7% scrap rate
$$[(0.07 \times 320 \times 250) \times (\$4.00 - \$0.50)] = \$19,600$$

Each percentage of scrap reduction reduces this cost by .01 × 320 × 250 × $3.50 = $2,800. Each step up the material savings column from the 3-point level is increased accordingly.

Once the two matrices have been constructed, weighting is accomplished by distributing 100 percent according to the potential savings in each category. Using output quantity, for example, working across the row of savings associated with a score of 7, reveals a weighting of

$$\frac{\text{Criterion } \$}{\text{Total } \$} \times 100 = \text{Weight}$$

$$\frac{\$66,400}{\$66,400 + \$36,000 + \$11,200} \times 100 = 58$$

The other columns are weighted commensurately; the numerator changes in each computation. Weighting in this fashion means that if the index moves from 300 to 700, regardless of which criterion contributes to such movement, the dollars associated with the changes in performance will be representative of actual savings.

The only exercise left is to determine the amount to be shared when improvement occurs. Fifty percent to employees and 50 percent to the company is close to average for sharing plans.

RECOGNITION FOR ACCOMPLISHMENTS

Organizations that use PBO rarely offer cash rewards to teams and never to individuals within teams. Problems occur when PBO is installed and an existing suggestion system is still operational. If PBO teams are excluded from suggestion rewards, an atmosphere of secrecy may arise as teams attempt to keep their ideas from being purloined by other employees. When teams do participate, the distribution of cash awards within the teams sometimes leads to dissension among members who feel that not everyone contributed equally. We therefore recommend that suggestion awards be phased out as PBO is phased in.

Cash awards are generally discouraged from team-oriented organizations because the teams participate in management functions. Once a week, or more, a team engages in managerial activities that affect the team members' jobs and working conditions. Since managers do not normally receive extra compensation for their productivity-improvement or cost-reduction ideas, a team should not routinely expect extra cash for its "managerial" activities.

Teams nonetheless deserve recognition beyond a simple "thank you" for their accomplishments. Modest but tangible awards not only emphasize an organization's appreciation but also nurture other positive aspects of employee involvement such as cooperation, commitment, and communications. Forms of recognition should be devised that appeal to everyone, reward each team member, and, so far as possible, promote team cohesiveness and enthusiasm for continued productivity improvement. Possible awards for special achievements include the following:

- Sack lunches provided at presentations made to the Productivity Council.
- A table reserved for a week in the company cafeteria with free refreshments given at breaks.
- Dinner with immediate managers at a nice restaurant. Spouses or dates may be included.
- Weekend at a resort for the same group.
- Field trip to visit a vendor, a customer, or another organization, from which job knowledge is enlarged.
- Attendance at an off-site seminar. A team may vote to send just one or two members, expecting a report when they return.
- Presentation by a vendor or an expert in a certain subject to assist team effort.
- Presentation of a general-interest talk or movie on such subjects as fishing, gardening, cooking, exercising, and dieting.
- Team presentations to internal organizational groups such as other teams, sales personnel, or headquarters staff. Presentations may also be made to visiting VIPs, professional society meetings, or teams in other companies.
- Graduation fetes where training diplomas are awarded. Pictures can be taken and mementos distributed.
- Formal letters of appreciation, copies of which become part of the employee's permanent record.
- Team-of-the-month recognition: banner in the work area, reserved parking in a prime location, features in the company newsletter or on bulletin boards, etc.
- Clothing emblazoned with team logos or names: baseball hats, T-shirts, patches, jackets, etc. At one company, baseball hats given out early in a program later became prized status symbols.
- Trinkets may seem tacky, but with slogans or logos affixed, they are tangible reminders of appreciation. Possibilities include key chains, headbands, belt buckles, pins, mugs, pens, pencils, towels, golf balls, candy boxes, statuettes, posters, plaques, books, stationery, bumper stickers, framed mottoes, necklaces, calendars, etc.
- More substantial awards may be made for very special accomplishments. Vacation trips and even cash awards are sometimes suitable. A few companies have allowed teams to bank the equivalent value of several small awards to accumulate a larger fund which can be spent at the discretion of team members.

Recognition awards are to PBO as a dessert is to a dinner. Awards are a treat but not vital to nourishment; involvement through the PBO process is what sustains motivation and raises productivity.

FOOTNOTES

Chapter 1

[1]Results published in *Workers' Attitudes toward Productivity*, U.S. Chamber of Commerce, 1980, p. 6.

[2]See Charles G. Burck, "What Happens When Workers Manage Themselves," *Fortune*, July 27, 1981, p. 65.

[3]Gerald C. Meyers at the AIIE Annual Conference, Detroit, May 1981.

[4]Darrell Huff (New York: W. W. Norton, 1954).

Chapter 2

[1]According to the U.S. Bureau of Labor Statistics, as calculated on the basis of output per hour per *production* worker, not *all* employees.

[2]*Population* is defined as all persons in the nation, and *employment* includes both civilian and armed forces employees.

[3]Introduced in M. S. Inoue and J. L. Riggs, "Describe Your System With Cause and Effect Diagrams," *Industrial Engineering*, April 1971.

[4]How much capital investment contributes to productivity growth varies with the assumptions made. It is usually calculated as the percentage change in the capital/labor ratio with differences due to the way capital, labor, and output are measured. Edward F. Denison, in *Accounting for Slower Productivity Growth* (Brookings Institute, 1979), estimates that increases in the amount of capital per worker contributed about one-third of a percentage point to the annual growth in natural income during 1948–78. In contrast, J. R. Norsworthy, Michael J. Harper, and Kent Kunz, in *The Slowdown in Productivity Growth: Analysis on Contributing Factors* (Brookings Papers on Economic Activity, 1979), calculated that net capital investment per man-hour accounted for two-thirds of a percentage point of the annual growth in output/man-hour during the same period. To put the latter percentage in perspective (0.67 percent), capital investment may be responsible for one-fourth of the total productivity advance.

[5]Data from the U.S. Department of Commerce, Bureau of Economic Analysis.

[6]Cited in *The Productivity Problem: Alternatives for Action* (Report to Congress by the U.S. Congressional Budget Office, 1981).

[7]The Occupational Safety and Health Administration conducts more than fifty thousand safety inspections yearly, representing 40 million workers in 3 million workplaces. Job-related illnesses dropped from 10.4 per one hundred full-time workers in 1974 to 9.1 in 1975 but slowly climbed again to 9.5 by 1979. Still, any decrease is a step toward greater labor productivity.

[8]See Robert W. Crandall, "Regulation and Productivity Growth," *The Decline in Productivity Growth* (Federal Resesrve Bank of Boston, 1980).

[9]Cited in "Business Gets a Safety Break from OSHA," © *U.S. News & World Report*, October 5, 1981.

[10]Ibid.

[11]A modest-sized poll by the House of Representatives Task Force on Industrial Innovation and Productivity (March 1981) found that 53 percent of the companies believed R&D is *very important* to company performance and 32 percent say it is *somewhat important.* The main impediments cited for innovation were tax policies, federal regulations, and inflation.

[12]*Basic* research represents original investigation for the advancement of scientific knowledge, although it may have commercial application. *Applied* research is directed by commercial objectives toward new discovery of new knowledge. *Development* translates research findings or other general scientific knowledge into products or processes.

[13]From *Science Indicators 1978* (Report of the National Science Board, National Science Foundation, 1979), p. 6.

[14]See Roger Rinner and Miriam Alexander, *The Role of High Technology in Economic Growth* (Cambridge, Mass.: Data Resources, Inc., 1977).

[15]Annual average growth of the work force is projected by the U.S. Department of Labor to be 1.7 percent until 1985 and 1.1 percent from then to 1990.

[16]Denison, *Accounting for Slower Productivity Growth*, p. 94.

[17]See Ivar Berg, *The Great Training Robbery* (Boston: Beacon Press, 1971).

[18]Government actions implicitly alter the industrial structure by way of military contracts, price supports for agriculture, tax benefits for housing, health-care programs, and other investments for social objectives, but explicit interventions of the Chrysler and Lockheed nature are rare.

Chapter 3

[1]Reported in *Time*, March 30, 1981, p. 58.

[2]Interview in Portland, Oregon, December 1981.

[3]According to Hiroshi Okamura, chief economist of the Japan Securities Research Institute, *JMA Newsletter*, February 1, 1979.

[4]The report titled "The Vision of MITI Policies in the 1980's" was developed through the combined efforts of ministry officials, consumer groups, industrialists, labor union leaders, and professors.

[5]William Chapman, *"Where Small Is a Virtue,"* *Washington Post*, November 24, 1981.

[6]C. Northcote Parkinson, *Parkinson's Law* (Boston: Houghton-Mifflin, 1957).

[7]This generally unnoticed report was endorsed unanimously by twenty House and Senate, Democratic and Republican, committee members. It is an apple-pie collage of rehashed ruminations, notable only as a "reminder" that the productivity banner is still aloft, limp but visible. Nine recommendations of a general economic nature consisted of the following:

Incentives to increase investment supported by measures to increase savings
Lower interest rates
Economic growth, reduced inflation, and full employment
Taxes that encourage productivity improvement in the private sector
Investments in public and private infrastructure
Reduction of paperwork economic regulations, and cost-ineffective social regulations
Long-run planning by business to make products more competitive
Cooperation between labor and management
Improved productivity within the federal government

[8]Vice-President Rockefeller also served as chairman of the center's board of directors. Membership of the board comprised twenty-two top-level leaders from business, labor, and government.

[9]According to the 1980 Annual Report of the Asian Productivity Organization (APO, Tokyo, Japan, 1981), there are twelve member nations, each having a productivity center or equivalent institute. Countries not bounded by the Pacific are India, Nepal, Pakistan, and Sri Lanka. APO expenditures in 1980 amounted to about $4.7 million.

[10]Reported by Robert Reinhold in "Engineers See Untimely Erosion of Schools," *New York Times*, December 25, 1980.

[11]Arguments against specialized technical education and vocational training are lucidly presented by James O'Toole in *Making America Work* (New York: Continuum, 1981), pp. 168–83.

[12]Neville R. Norman, *The Productivity Connection* (Fitzroy, Victoria: VCTA Publishing Pty Ltd., 1977).

[13]*The King and The Four Learned Men* was published by Krish Pennathur & Associates (19/4, India House, Demp's Corner, Bombay 400-036, India) in 1977. In conversations, one is continuously impressed with Dr. Pennathur's devotion to the productivity cause and his equalitarian beliefs that the prosperity of rich and poor countries alike depends on increasing productivity by convincing people that it can be done through dedication.

[14]Report of a panel chaired by Jim Riggs on "Ways to Increase the National Awareness of the Importance of Productivity" (*Proceedings of the Industry-University Conference on Productivity Improvement*, March 1978), pp. 12–22.

[15]The John Morrell and Company plant is located in Estherville, Iowa (population 7,550), and employs more than seven hundred people. Employees belong to Local 79 of the International Food and Commercial Workers Union.

[16]*Fortune*, June 1, 1981, p. 72, records a Japanese song translated for introduction into the Kyoto plant in San Diego:

As the sun rises brilliantly in the sky,
Revealing the size of the mountain, the market
Oh, this is our goal.
With the highest degree of mission in our heart we serve our industry,
Meeting the strictest degree of customer requirement.
We are the leader in this industry and our future path
Is ever so bright and satisfying.
©1981 Time Inc. All rights reserved.

[17]In 1981 unions won votes at the Sanyo E&E Corp. in San Diego and Sharp Manufacturing Co. of America in Memphis. The big test will be in 1983 when Nissan Motor Manufacturing Corp. USA comes on line as the largest U.S. investment ever made by a Japanese company. About three hundred Japanese-owned plants in the United States employ some 110,000 Americans.

[18]Examples of crises cited in "Starting a Labor-Management Committee in Your Organization: Some Pointers for Action," (National Center for Productivity and Quality of Working Life, Spring 1981,) p. 5, include loss of markets to competitors, declining profitability, excessive grievances or strikes, high absenteeism or turnover, increased work spoilage, and low productivity.

[19]Productivity in other industries was obviously affected by such retardants as energy costs and health environmental regulations. However, it must be admitted that productivity measurement in construction is less reliable than in most industries, so results deserve questioning.

[20]Described by Irwin Ross in "The New Work Spirit in St. Louis," *Fortune*, November 16, 1981, pp. 92–106.

Chapter 4

[1]Even personal feelings can be subjected to quantification, especially those associated with economic ventures. Sensitivity analysis assists decision making under conditions of risk. Utility theory helps explain how uncertainty affects decisions. The "standard gamble" technique can be employed to rate factors that do not possess a natural scale. These methods and others are described in James L. Riggs, *Engineering Economics, 2nd ed.* (New York: Mc-Graw Hill, 1982).

[2]Adapted from James L. Riggs, "Prospective Productivity Perspectives," *Management Services*, September 1978.

[3]Over sixty companies from *Fortune* magazine's list of largest corporations completed questionnaires, the results of which are reported by David J. Sumanth in "Productivity Indicators Used by Major U.S. Manufacturing Companies: The Results of a Survey," *Industrial Engineering*, May 1981, pp. 70–73.

[4]A complete 449-page discussion of U.S. measures of productivity, including theory and critiques, is given in *Measurement and Interpretation of Productivity* (National Academy of Sciences, Washington, D.C., 1979).

[5]Ibid., p. 21.

[6]The thrust of federal in-house productivity measurement is to increase the efficiency of government. From such productivity indicators as those in the following list, composite indexes are developed for functional areas; for example, Audit of Operations, Communications, Library Services, Medical Services, Postal Service, Records Management, etc.

ACTIVITY	OUTPUT INDICATORS
Dining facilities operations	Number of meals served
Flight training	Student-year trained
Background checks	Number of cases closed
Invoices and travel processing	Number of invoices and claims processed
Consumer complaints	Number of complaints processed
Patent application exams	Applications completed

Productivity ratios result from dividing the composite output by the unweighted employee years involved.

[7]*Measurement and Interpretation of Productivity*, p. 17.

[8]The multiplier is called the "capital-recovery factor." Tables of factor values are available for different asset lives and interest rates. The product of the first cost times the capital-recovery factor is the annual charge that repays the investment plus interest on the unrecovered balance. Tables and calculation procedures are included in such books as Riggs' *Engineering Economics*, 2nd ed. pp. 38–40, 644, 744–70.

[9]Between 1920 and 1970, the ratio of labor costs to electricity increased by a factor of 10. It is now reversing. Energy conservation has gone beyond operational savings to the consideration of plant locations with respect to transportation of inputs and outputs, product design, and work methods. These are genuine productivity factors.

[10]Two complementary indexes recommended by the American Productivity Center were reported by J. Hamlin in "Developments in Firm Level Productivity Measurement" (AIIE Proceedings, Spring Conference, 1979), pp. 194–99. The additional indexes contrast prices and costs in the different reporting periods to suggest the effects of economic change. Based on the same symbols defined previously,

$$\text{Price Recovery Index} = \frac{(\Sigma O_1 P_1)/(\Sigma O_1 P_0)}{(\Sigma I_1 C_1)/(\Sigma I_1 C_0)}$$

indicates to what extent the firm has been able to absorb increase in the costs of inputs by its pricing policy. The other index,

$$\text{Cost-Effectiveness Index} = \frac{(\Sigma O_1 P_1)/(\Sigma O_0 P_0)}{(\Sigma I_1 C_1)/(\Sigma I_0 C_0)}$$

is an unadjusted comparison of current output and input performance with that in the base period. The relationship between the basic Partial Productivity Index and the complementary measure is given by

$$\text{PPI} = \frac{\text{Cost-effectiveness Index}}{\text{Price Recovery Index}}$$

For the data given in the sample application of PPI,

$$\text{Price Recovery Index} = \frac{\$620,000/\$480,000}{\$275,500/\$250,000} = \frac{1.292}{1.102} = 1.172$$

and

$$\text{Cost-Effectiveness Index} = \frac{\$620,000/\$430,000}{\$275,500/\$228,000} = \frac{1.442}{1.208} = 1.194$$

from which the relationship to PPI is shown to be

$$\text{PPI} = \frac{1.194}{1.172} = 1.02, \text{ or } 2\% \text{ increase}$$

[11]Contrary to what Peter F. Drucker stated in "Managing the Knowledge Worker," *Wall Street Journal*, November 7, 1975: "We do not know how to measure either the productivity or the satisfaction of the knowledge worker," considerable progress has been made in that direction. The PBO matrix described in Chapters 4 and 11 has been so employed quite successfully.

[12]From *Interfirm Comparison: Signpost to Increased Profitability* (Australian Department of Productivity, Sydney, New South Wales), p. 1.

[13]From "Interfirm Comparison at Enoch Manufacturing," Oregon Productivity

Center's *PRIMER* publication, April 1981. It should be noted that both the Business Index and Management Ratio Report are available only to NSMPA members. Young also reported an application of the ratios in which he noted that Enoch's indirect labor expenses were inordinately high compared with those of similar companies. A concentrated effort cut indirect labor by eight hours per shift through combining and reallocating duties. Since Enoch was comfortably profitable at the time, the saving would probably have gone uncollected without the prod from interfirm comparison.

[14]Inference of illegal collusion is minimized by adhering to the following conditions: (1) there is valid reason for participation, (2) participation is voluntary, (3) only historical data are used, (4) data are held strictly confidential by the collecting agency, (5) data and analysis results are not disclosed or discussed between participants, (6) nonmembers of the nominal association of participants may buy into the program, and (7) results will be supplied to those who have a valid reason for seeing the information.

[15]A double-blind reporting system is used at the Oregon Productivity Center. Companies send data to their association headquarters in a sealed envelope which is coded and sent to the center. The association knows the company code but never sees the data. The center processes the data without knowing their source. Although confidentiality is ensured, retracing the route to correct errors prolongs the processing.

[16]A standardized rating form is commonly used for personnel performance ratings. Scales for rated traits typically run from 1 to 10 with explanations of the attributes expected at each interval. A rater is asked to assign a number or choose a proficiency level that describes the person being rated. An equivalent procedure can be used by a team to rate its own performance. The discussion that accompanies the rating process is likely to contribute to better performance in the future.

Chapter 5

[1]Seventy percent of the people surveyed worked in manufacturing and 95 percent had two or more years of college. They held positions in top management (21%), middle-level management (33%), staff (28%), and consulting, supervision, etc. (18%). Results were analyzed in J. L. Riggs, "Improved Productivity Needs Leadership—Yours!" *Industrial Engineering,* November 1978.

[2]From "Organizing for Higher Productivity: An Analysis of Japanese Systems and Practices" (Asian Productivity Organization, Tokyo, 1982), p. 49. It is an English translation of an article in the *Tsusan Journal,* April/May 1981 (Research Institute of International Trade and Industry, Tokyo).

[3]By comparison, about 50 percent of the top two hundred companies in France are family partnerships, as are approximately 30 percent of the top five hundred in the United States.

[4]The low regard accorded shareholders is exemplified by corporate employment of the *Sokaiya*—someone who holds a few shares and receives travel expenses to attend general shareholder meetings in order to expedite proceedings. The Sokaiya sits in the front row, cheering management pronouncements and jeering any opposing motions. By heckling and calling for "point of order," the Sokaiya contingent keeps a meeting moving along lines laid out by the management.

[5]Akio Morita, who built Sony Corporation into a $4 billion annual sales giant, criticizes the top-heavy salaries of U.S. executives. He says a chief executive's salary after taxes in Japan is only six or seven times that of a newly hired college graduate. In the United States, the ratio is occasionally as high as fifty to one and is usually double Japan's ratio. Mr. Morita reports that Japanese corporate salaries, including his own, rarely exceed $200,000 and are subjected to top-of-the-bracket tax rates of nearly 90 percent.

[6]A survey by Boyden Associates found that 31 percent of the managers in manufacturing wanted to switch out of it, while only 11 percent of the other managers wanted in. The disgruntled manufacturing executives cited "insufficient challenge" and "slow career path" as their disenchantment. Salary may also have been an influence because pay in manufacturing lagged well behind compensation in other functional areas.

[7]There is no steadfast rule for optimizing the ratio of supervisors to subordinates.

Spheres of control vary within and among organizations in response to the ability of leaders, complexity of tasks, importance of objectives, type of responsibilities, environmental conditions, and nature of the personnel.

[8]See Bruce A. Jacobs, "Does Westinghouse Have the Productivity Answer?" *Industry Week*, March 23, 1981, p. 96. Mr. Hudspeth also stated that Westinghouse conservatively estimates future productivity gains of 6.1 percent per year.

[9]Too much reliance on market surveys constricts product development to massaging existing designs. Stated consumers preferences do not always lead to sales, as witnessd by surveys that said people wanted gas guzzlers when they were actually buying compact cars. Even expert opinions are suspect. In 1945, experts estimated total worldwide sales for computers at ten units per year.

[10]Cross-fertilization between management teams flows from designating specialists in each team for specific productivity issues, such as technology transfer from outside sources, internal innovation, developments by competitors, future effects of inflation, and impact changes in the national economy. Delphi discussions can produce team position papers, and team specialists can meet with their counterparts to develop solutions for problems in their area of interest.

[11]As reported in the JMA newsletter of the Japanese Management Association, November 1, 1980.

Chapter 6

[1]The million-dollar computer of 1950 costs just twenty dollars today, and computing speed is one hundred thousand times faster. A whole roomful of computer gear from the past era is now contained on a "chip" smaller than a postage stamp.

[2]Fiber optics is part of the "phototronics revolution" based on light-wave technology. As applied to communications, a miniature laser beam converts voice signals from electrical impulses to light, blinking on and off 0.45 million times per second. The beam is aimed at the end of a glass strand. A bundle of two hundred strands, about the diameter of a cigar, can handle 67,200 simultaneous phone conversations. They can also carry video transmissions.

[3]Summary of a 1980 report prepared for U.S. congressional committees by the Technological Assessment Board, "U.S. Industrial Competitiveness," June 1981.

[4]In 1980, imports as a percentage of U.S. consumption of consumer electronic products ranged from 100 percent for videotape players/recorders and household radios to 18 percent of the color TVs.

[5]Compared with the 11,250 programmable robots operating in Japan in 1980, other nations had approximately the following number: West Germany, 5,850; United States, 3,225; Poland, 720; Sweden, 570; Norway, 200; and Britain, 185. East Germany plans to install 45,000 robots by 1986.

[6]Quoted by Ikehata Keijiun, "The Front Line of Robotization," translated from an article in *Ekonomisuto*, April 10, 1981, which appeared in *Japan Echo*, 7, No. 3 (1981), 116. Also included in the article was a discussion of the acceptance of robots by the Japanese work force. Three problems were mentioned: (1) workers replaced by robots may have trouble adapting to new jobs, (2) workers may be reluctant to work more night shifts to keep up with twenty-four-hour-per-day robots, and (3) monotonous labor increased in some cases by the need to repeatedly set up specific arrangements of materials for repetitive robot movements. A sobering quote concludes the article: "Because people associate robot-company employees with defiance of the gods and denial of humanity, the day may well come when these people will be ostracized from society because they work for such firms."

[7]Prices for robots, like prices of many electronic devices, have not escalated much. In 1965 a typical model sold for $25,000. In 1982 prices ranged from $7,500 to $150,000, depending on capabilities.

[8]A flexible manufacturing system replaces stand-alone tools by connecting integrated machine tool modules with a computerized delivery network; a master control

computer coordinates system production as a whole. Since FMS is most appropriate for mid-volume, mid-variety production, most machine tools use numerical control technology and travel between machinery modules is by automatic conveyance. Successful FMS increases a firm's ability to respond to unpredictable demands and reduces operating costs.

[9]*Group technology* is a subset of CAM that groups materials and parts into families on the basis of required production operations. About 75 percent of all parts made by U.S. manufacturing plants are produced in small batches. By appropriate coding and computer monitoring, parts flow smoothly through the system to give batch production many of the advantages of mass production. Group technology is adaptable to inventory management in service organizations as well as manufacturing.

[10]According to the Fall 1981 issue of *Skill*, the UAW international magazine for skilled trade members, amber and red lights have been installed over every work station in the nonunion Kawasaki plant in Lincoln, Nebraska. The red light goes on and musical chimes play a lullaby when a worker slows down, calling everyone's attention to that worker.

[11]Also reported was a 1977 study at Exxon that said 90 percent of all "captured" documents were handwritten, and that an average of nineteen copies were made of each original. Of these copies, eight were stored indefinitely "to increase the chances of getting a hit if we were to look for a particular document." Only about 5 percent of the stored information was ever retrieved.

Chapter 7

[1]The same thumb-and-finger analogy is handy for speeches about productivity. A thumbs-up sign says productivity is OK. The OK sign language is continued by touching, in turn, each finger to call attention to quality, quantity, safety, cooperation, or whatever chosen properties the fingers represent in "getting a grip on productivity." Dexterous speakers can elevate manual oratory to signal eloquence.

[2]The Deming prize was created in 1951 to reward innovation in quality control annually. It has become so famous in Japan that the ceremony is broadcast live on national TV. With a little imagination, it could be the prototype for an annual U.S. productivity prize, surely more constructively rewarding than an Emmy or an Oscar.

[3]Only 27 percent of the respondents to the ASQC survey felt that foreign products were of better quality than American products. Nearly 50 percent felt that in today's economy, making a quality product simply costs too much, and 73 percent felt that U.S. industry is more concerned with profit than with quality.

[4]Based on excerpts from a talk by Denis A. Ossola, director of operations at Matsushita Industrial Company, reported in *Manufacturing Productivity Frontiers,* May 1981, pp. 1–8. The article concludes with a statement by Richard Craft, president of MIC, that the closest thing to the secret of Japan's productivity success is a strong commitment to superior quality.

[5]In quality control jargon, product specifications are based on the *precision* sought by customers and the *accuracy* attainable by production facilities. *Precision* describes the refinement of the product, and *accuracy* pertains to conformance to design requirements. Given a process capable of desired precision and needed accuracy, unacceptable variations may, and usually do, occur. Blunt tools, misalignments caused by wear and tear on machinery, worker carelessness, and similar causes downgrade output from a process inherently capable of acceptable quality.

[6]At a Volkswagen plant, two rejected cars are parked each day in conspicuous places. Each car has its defects marked with scribbled comments about the cause: sloppy weld, dent, chipped, fuel line not clipped. Such defects can be traced to a particular shift and crew.

[7]An MRP system links the planned production schedule with the bill of materials needed to make a product and examines the manufacturing inventory to see which parts and raw materials have to be ordered. By considering when components of the end product are scheduled to be produced and the length of needed lead times for supply, replenishment

orders are triggered so that parts and materials arrive when they are required at work stations. This procedure minimizes the amount of work-in-process inventory but enlarges data-processing and coordination costs.

⁸There are several Kanban cards in addition to the basic withdrawal and production-ordering Kanbans: subcontract Kanbans to tell a supplier when and where to deliver specified products, emergency Kanbans to deal with the unexpected, and special Kanbans for job-order productions. Automatic machines are equipped with limit switches that conform to the as-needed procedure, sometimes known as "electric Kanban."

⁹Reported in Jeremy Main, "How to Battle Your Own Bureaucracy," *Fortune*, June 29, 1981, p. 54. The article also describes savings generated at Intel by flow chart analyses of procedures for hiring, paying bills, and other clerical functions. These work simplification activities are expected to result in productivity gains of 30 percent. Close monitoring guards against sacrificing quality to increase productivity.

¹⁰Several surveys of office workers have indicated that the following factors, listed roughly according to priority, affect performance: (1) noise distractors, (2) uncomfortable temperature, (3) constricted access to supplies, (4) lack of privacy, (5) inadequate lighting, (6) inability to adjust work surfaces, and (7) insufficient storage space.

Chapter 8

¹Ted Mills, "Quality of Work Life: A Clear and Present Danger" (Paper presented at the 1981 AIIE Conference and World Productivity Congress and published in the *Proceedings*), pp. 252–60.

²A related approach called "social-technical systems theory," developed at the Tavistock Institute in England, relates technology to social considerations. It proposes that different working relationships are necessary in industries using different technologies. Thus the preferred work structure in a steel mill would not be the best one for an electronics company.

³Japan was not included in the comparison of worker participation in industry because the Japanese social order narrows the demarcation between labor and management and masks specific forms of involvement.

⁴The International Association of Quality Circles was formed in 1977 and publishes a quarterly magazine, *Quality Circle*. The American Society for Quality Control has created a separate subsection to feature quality circles. The first International Quality Circle convention was held in 1978.

⁵Reported by Dr. Goodfellow in "Study of Quality Control Circle Programs," *Machine Fabricating News*, March-April 1981, pp. 3, 4, 17. In the study he found that the common element in all the successful implementations was strong supervisory training programs.

⁶Leighton F. Smith, a partner at Arthur Andersen & Co., quoted in *Industry Week*, February 8, 1982, p. 29 (reported by Bruce A. Jacobs). He goes on to compare starting quality circles to improve productivity with starting a meal with dessert.

⁷Rintaro Muramatsu, "Examples of Increasing Productivity and Product Quality through Satisfying the Workers' Desires and Developing the Workers' Motivation" (Paper presented at the 1981 World Productivity Congress).

⁸From "Japanese Management Not Magic, but Science," *Japan Times Weekly*, March 8, 1982. The article also pointed out that small groups simply apply industrial-engineering tools developed in the United States, but they are used by everyone in a factory, not just specialists as in the United States.

⁹From an interview by Steven Carter in the *Oregonian*, January 16, 1981. Freiesleben also noted that "unions in Germany tend to cooperate, as long as they get their share. There is less antagonism. There are worker representatives on plant supervisory boards."

¹⁰Pay levels based on mastery of more jobs can lead to a situation where all the employees want to spend all their time training for new jobs. An alternative plan is to base wages on breadth of skill *and* additional proficiency in an existing skill.

[11]Reported in *Fortune*, April 6, 1981, p. 16.

[12]Described in the booklet *Starting a Labor-Management Committee in Your Organization*, published by the National Center for Productivity and Quality of Working Life, Spring 1978, p. 18.

[13]Ibid., p. 54.

[14]The study, *Productivity Sharing Programs: Can They Contribute to Productivity Improvement?* (AFMD-8-22), was issued March 3, 1981. A free copy can be obtained from U.S. General Accounting Offices, Document Handling and Information Services Facility, P.O. Box 6015, Gaithersburg, Md. 20760.

[15]Ibid., p. 30.

Chapter 9

[1]Rather arbitrarily, we distinguish between a program and a process: A *program* has a distinct duration, whereas a *process* continues indefinitely. PBO is a process.

[2]If the organization is nonunion, one or two respected leaders from the work force might be on the council. When there is a union, it is advisable to have upper management broach PBO to the union, rather than going through the formal industrial relations process. This avoids contractual complications and distinguishes the properties of the PBO process.

[3]Many well-traveled management techniques have been relabeled to attract the productivity audience, and born-again productivity pundits are delivering old sermons under new titles. While such advice may be useful, it is probably not germane to current concerns. Unlike most lessons for self-improvement and handy ways to manage time, change, and stress, good productivity courses are usually disturbing. In place of the ebullience generated by personal enrichment lectures, productivity-improvement advice often challenges the customary way of doing things, leaving the listener uncomfortable and perhaps a bit confused by technical terms. Indeed, the degree of discomfort caused is a reasonable measure of the worth of productivity instructions.

INDEX

K

J

L

Q